C000158115

THE FOURTH BOOK OF
OCCULT PHILOSOPHY

Henry Cornelius Agrippa

Henry Cornelius Agrippa

his

FOURTH BOOK OF OCCULT PHILOSOPHY

Containing:

Of Magical Ceremonies – Henry Cornelius Agrippa

Heptameron: or, Magical Elements – Peter de Abano

Of the Nature of such Spirits – Georg Villinganus

Arbatel of Magick: Of the Magick of the Ancients

Of Geomancy – Henry Cornelius Agrippa

Of Astronomical Geomancy – Gerard Cremonensis

*Edited, with Introduction
and Commentary
by Stephen Skinner*

*Translated into English
by Robert Turner*

Ibis Press
An Imprint of Nicolas-Hays, Inc.
Berwick, Maine

First Latin edition published Marburg, 1554
First English edition published London, 1655
First facsimile edition Askin Publishers Ltd., 1978
First complete, modern type re-set edition published in 2005 by
Ibis Press, an imprint of
Nicolas-Hays, Inc., P. O. Box 1126
Berwick, ME 03901-1126 USA
www.nicolashays.com
Distributed to the trade by
Red Wheel/Weiser, LLC
P. O. Box 612, York Beach, ME 03910-0612
www.redwheelweiser.com

Library of Congress Cataloging-in-Publication Data
Agrippa von Nettesheim, Heinrich Cornelius, 1486?-1535.
    [De occulta philosophia. Book 4. English]
    The fourth book of occult philosophy / Henry Cornelius Agrippahis ;
edited with introduction and commentary by Stephen Skinner ; translated
into English by Robert Turner.
        p. cm.
    ISBN 0-89254-100-8 (alk. paper)
    1. Occultism--Early works to 1900. I. Skinner, Stephen II. Title.
    BF1600.A3713 2005
    130--dc22
                                                    2004028471

MV

Cover design by Daniel Brockman.
Typeset in Minion 10/12
Printed in the United States of America
12   11   10   09   08   07   06   05
8   7   6   5   4   3   2   1
The paper used in this publication meets the minimum requirements of the
American National Standard for Information Sciences—Permanence of Paper
for Printed Library Materials Z39.48–1992 (R1997).

CONTENTS

Introduction to the 2005 Edition..IX
Introduction to the 1978 Edition...XV

PART I. MAGIC

Title Page of the 1655 Edition..3
The Preface to the Unprejudiced Reader 5
Commendatory Verses for the First Edition................................11

1. OF OCCULT PHILOSOPHY, OR OF MAGICAL CEREMONIES:
   THE FOURTH BOOK—Henry Cornelius Agrippa 19
   HOW TO GENERATE THE NAMES OF SPIRITS 20
   GENERATING THE CHARACTERS
     AND IMAGES OF THE SPIRITS.. 24
       THE CHARACTERS OF GOOD SPIRITS.............................27
       THE CHARACTERS OF EVIL SPIRITS..............................28
   THE VISIBLE APPEARANCE OF SPIRITS 29
       THE SHAPES FAMILIAR TO THE SPIRITS OF SATURN 30
       THE FAMILIAR FORMS TO THE SPIRITS OF JUPITER 31
       THE FAMILIAR FORMS OF THE SPIRITS OF MARS 31
       SHAPES FAMILIAR TO THE SPIRITS OF THE SUN 32
       FAMILIAR SHAPES OF THE SPIRITS OF VENUS 32
       THE FAMILIAR FORMS OF THE SPIRITS OF MERCURY ...33
       THE FORMS FAMILIAR TO THE SPIRITS OF THE MOON .34
   MAKING PENTACLES AND SIGILS 34
   BINDING SPIRITS 39
   CONSECRATION OF RITUAL EQUIPMENT 39
   THE LIBER SPIRITUUM OR BOOK OF SPIRITS 44
   THE INVOCATION OF GOOD AND EVIL SPIRITS 46
   PREPARATION OF THE PLACE OF WORKING........................47
   THE HOLY TABLE AND LAMEN... 48
   ANOTHER RITE FOR CALLING FORTH SPIRITS................... 49
   ORACLES AND DREAMS...50
   CALLING FORTH SPIRITS TO A MAGIC CIRCLE 52

The License to Depart....................................54
Nature Spirits 55
Necromancy.................................56

2. Heptameron or, Magical Elements—Peter de Abano..........59
Introduction by the Translator 59
Of the Circle, and the composition thereof 60
Of the names of the hours,
    and the Angels ruling them......................61
        The Angels of the Spring 62
        The Angels of the Summer 62
        The Angels of the Autumn 63
        The Angels of the Winter 63
The Consecrations and Benedictions:
    and first of the Benediction of the Circle 64
The Benediction of perfumes 64
The Exorcisme of the fire upon
    which the perfumes are to be put...........................64
Of the Garment and Pentacle.....................64
An Oration to be said, when the
    Vesture is put on..................................65
Of the manner of working.......................66
An Exorcisme of the Spirits of the Air.....................67
A Prayer to God, to be said in the four
    parts of the world, in the Circle...........................70
Visions and Apparitions.................................72
Additional Considerations,
    Conjurations and Times 75
The figure of a Circle for the first
    hour of the Lords day, in Spring-time 75
Considerations of the Lords day 76
    Conjuration of the Lords day 77
Considerations of Munday 78
    Conjuration of Munday.................80
Considerations of Tuesday 80
    Conjuration of Tuesday.................82
Considerations of Wednesday ......:.................83
    Conjuration of Wednesday 84
Considerations of Thursday.................85
    Conjuration of Thursday 87
Considerations of Friday 88
    Conjuration of Friday.................89

CONSIDERATIONS OF SATURDAY.. 90
   CONJURATION OF SATURDAY 91
TABLES OF THE ANGELS OF THE HOURS,
ACCORDING TO THE COURSE OF THE DAYES 93

3. ISAGOGE: AN INTRODUCTORY DISCOURSE ON THE
   NATURE OF SUCH SPIRITS—Georg Pictorius Villinganus...........97

4. ARBATEL OF MAGICK: OF THE MAGICK OF THE ANCIENTS 135
THE FIRST SEPTENARY OF APHORISMS.............................. 139
THE SECOND SEPTENARY 141
THE THIRD SEPTENARY.. 145
THE FOURTH SEPTENARY 154
THE FIFTH SEPTENARY 160
THE SIXTH SEPTENARY 162
THE SEVENTH SEPTENARY 168

PART II. GEOMANCY

5. OF GEOMANCY—Henry Cornelius Agrippa............................ 177
INTRODUCTION.. 177
PLANETS AND THE GEOMANTIC FIGURES........................... 178
ZODIACAL SIGNS AND THE FIGURES 180
ASTROLOGICAL TRIPLICITIES AND THE FIGURES 181
THE COMMON TECHNIQUE FOR
   GENERATING OR PROJECTING THE FIGURES 182
TECHNIQUE FOR GENERATING AN
   ASTROLOGICAL GEOMANTIC FIGURE............................. 185
DETERMINING THE INDEX 187
THE SIGNIFICANCE OF THE HOUSES 188
THE 16 GEOMANTIC FIGURES... 189
   THE GREATER FORTUNE.. 189
   THE LESSER FORTUNE...190
   WAY 192
   PEOPLE 193
   GAIN...195
   JOY...196
   MAID 197
   LOSS...199
   CONJUNCTION 200
   WHITE 201
   CHILD...202

RED...203

PRISON 204

SORROW 205

DRAGON'S HEAD 206

DRAGON'S TAIL 207

JUDGEMENT 207

6. OF ASTRONOMICAL GEOMANCY—Gerard Cremonensis 209

QUESTIONS OF THE FIRST HOUSE.................................... 212

QUESTIONS OF THE SECOND HOUSE 214

QUESTIONS OF THE THIRD HOUSE 215

QUESTIONS OF THE FOURTH HOUSE.............................. 215

QUESTIONS OF THE FIFTH HOUSE 216

QUESTIONS OF THE SIXTH HOUSE 218

QUESTIONS OF THE SEVENTH HOUSE 220

QUESTIONS OF THE EIGHTH HOUSE 225

QUESTIONS OF THE NINTH HOUSE 225

QUESTIONS OF THE TENTH HOUSE.................................226

QUESTIONS OF THE ELEVENTH HOUSE 227

QUESTIONS OF THE TWELFTH HOUSE.............................. 227

Bibliography...228

About the Author & Editor..229

INTRODUCTION TO THE 2005 EDITION

At the time I produced the first facsimile edition of this book for publication in 1978, I had planned to also print the full *Three Books of Occult Philosophy* in facsimile form. This would certainly have been very useful to many students of magic at that time. My long-term plan was to produce editions of both books in modern English, with detailed footnotes and commentary. I am delighted that Donald Tyson has done this in his excellent edition of the *Three Books of Occult Philosophy*, published in a massive paperback by Llewellyn in 1993. This is truly a milestone in the publication of classical texts on Renaissance magic, and the modern occult scholar has much to thank him for. Joseph Peterson is another author who has rendered a great service to the study of magic by making many of the classics of grimoire and scholarly magic available outside the confines of a few depositories of rare books and even rarer manuscripts.

It therefore only remains to me to complete my original plan by issuing this modern re-set and annotated edition of the *Fourth Book of Occult Philosophy*. In the 1655 edition, the books appeared in the following rather haphazard order: *Of Geomancy*; *Of Occult Philosophy*; the *Heptameron*; the *Isagoge* of Georg Villinganus; *Of Astronomical Geomancy*; and the *Arbatel of Magick*. In this edition I have retained all of the six original books, but changed the order in which they appear; the magical texts are contained in Part I, and the geomancy texts are contained in Part II, so that the magical and geomantic texts are grouped together. Although individual constituent volumes of *The Fourth Book of Occult Philosophy* have been republished several times since 1978 by other publishers, this is the only complete re-set publication to contain all the constituent volumes.

Over the intervening years it has slowly been dawning on those interested in Western magic that the Golden Dawn (with its masonic trappings), Aleister Crowley's work (with its new age hedonism and thelemic beliefs) and Wicca (which has been synthesized from many different strands) although very valuable are not the be-all and end-all of magic. In some ways they are a change of direction, for magic was originally and primarily about invoking spirits, demons, angels, and other "spiritual creatures." To access the original techniques for doing this you have to go back to the 17th century and earlier. Agrippa's book *Magical Ceremonies*, printed here, gives many specific and practical hints on these techniques. Currently available printed copies of grimoires do not have all the hints necessary to perform successful evocation, but manuscript sources containing more detailed material are slowly becoming available.[1]

Heinrich Cornelius Agrippa (1486–1535) was the most influential writer on Renaissance magic. His *De Occulta Philosophia* appeared in manuscript between 1509 to 1510. These books were truly a *tour de force* as Agrippa was only 23 at the time. The books circulated widely in manuscript, and were eventually printed in 1533. Their influence upon John Dee, Francis Barrett, and many other magicians up to and including the founders of the Golden Dawn is immense.

The Fourth Book of Occult Philosophy has however had a bad press; by this I mean that many reviewers have slighted it as "spurious." This is to a large extent due to John Harrison's (the first English publisher) titling of the book. If he or Robert Turner had simply called it "A collection of texts on Magic and Geomancy, including Agrippa's book *Of Magical Ceremonies*," then nobody would have batted an eyelid. In fact, that is precisely what it is, and out of more than 200 pages in the first English edition, only 38 actually comprise Agrippa's *Of Magical Ceremonies*. From the Contents page you can see that there are actually six complete and separate books included in this work. Only the 1655 and 1978 editions have the full English text of these books, while other reprints have simply selected one or two texts from the full six.[3] Although only two of the books therein are by Agrippa, all of these books have had a strong influence on the Golden Dawn and other magicians in the English-speaking world.

I believe that of these six books, *Of Magical Ceremonies* and *Of Geomancy* are both by Agrippa. Some scholars, including Johann Weir (also spelled/known as "Weyer," Agrippa's English pupil) have doubted that the first is from Agrippa's pen. I am inclined to think,

---

[1] See for example Stephen Skinner and David Rankine, *The Practical Angel Magic of Dr. John Dee's Enochian Tables* (London: Golden Hoard, 2004) which contains the full and expanded invocations used by Dee and his 17th-century successors, transcribed from manuscripts which have never before been published.

[2] Later editions such as the 1985 Heptangle or the 2003 Trident editions only print two (Agrippa and de Abano) of the six original books.

from internal evidence, that it is. It appeared in Latin just thirty years after Agrippa's death. Weir denounced the work as spurious in his *Praestigiis Daemonum* in 1563. I think that the denial by Weir was simply sour grapes on his part from not having been involved in its publication, and because the collection also included a book by one of his greatest enemies. *Of Magical Ceremonies* quotes from and expands on themes from Agrippa's *Third Book of Occult Philosophy*, in a style typical of Agrippa, creating a more concise and practical synopsis of the techniques for summoning spirits than he was able to put in his main work.

Of the other books in this volume, the most significant is De Abano's *Heptameron*. It is an important grimoire, dating from 1513. It is called the "Heptameron"[3] because it deals with the angels of the seven days of the week. Its conjurations (in Latin) turn up later in editions of the *Goetia*, where they are rendered into English. Interestingly, some of the words of power point to Greek origins. Although the structure of invocations according to the day of the week is not followed in the *Goetia*, it is very interesting to see these same invocations and names of power being later used in the *Goetia*.

It has been suggested that the attribution to the famous physician Peter de Abano (1250–1316) may be spurious, as his accepted works betray no acquaintance with the occult sciences. Agrippa, however, refers to Peter de Abano in his *Third Book of Occult Philosophy* as being his source for the Theban alphabet of "Honorius of Thebes," the author of the *Sworn Book*. This suggests that the attribution is genuine. The *Heptameron* is part of the Solomon cycle of grimoires, and in fact has a lot in common with the Hebrew Key of Solomon (*Mafteah Shlomoh*).

The next most important book in this volume of magical texts is the *Isagoge* by Georg Villinganus. It is a collection of many references to the nature of spirits, from ecclesiastical and classical authors. The *Isagoge* is structured around a supposed conversation between the Greek twins Castor and Pollux, discussing the nature of daemons, devils, and spirits. Castor and Pollux were the offspring of Leda and Jupiter disguised as a swan. Leda gave birth to an egg, from which sprang these twins. Helen, so famous afterwards as the cause of the Trojan war, was their sister. The point here is that the twins are able to present opposite sides of an argument, enabling the author to make quite contradictory statements without difficulty. On one hand one twin can confidently assert that spirits can be successfully bound by

---

[3] From the Greek prefix, *hepta*, meaning "seven."

man, and can achieve quite miraculous effects for him, while on the other hand the other twin states that this is done "only by God's permission." Villinganus thereby protects himself from too much unwanted attention from the ecclesiastical authorities.

He explains that the first order of spirits "are nourished of the most pure element of Air . . . and they do inhabit the Coelestial Theatre." The second order "spread abroad from the bounds and border of the Moon." The third order of spirits "is of a divine deitie, which . . . Plato have [*sic*] called *Daemons*." This thinking is much closer to the spirits of Shakespeare's *Tempest* than to the then popular conception of devils.

The book makes it very clear that "devil" and "daemon" are two vastly different things, although confused in the King James version of the Bible by being translated with the same word. Among other things, Castor and Pollux also retell one of the most convincing ghost stories of antiquity. In it Anthenodorus, a philosopher, buys a house which has a reputation of being haunted. After ignoring the ghost for some time, he allows the ghost, which is an old man laden with chains, to lead him to a gateway. Instead of investigating himself, he prudently has the town magistrates arrange to dig around the gate, where they duly find the body of an old man, obviously the victim of foul play, buried and wrapped in chains. This may well be the origin of the belief that ghosts can be heard clanking their chains.

The last book of magic in this collection is the *Arbatel*. The *Arbatel de Magia Veterum*, to give it its full name, first appeared in Latin in Basel in 1575. It is mentioned by John Dee in his *Mysteriorum Libri*, and was obviously read by him and Edward Kelley. The *Arbatel* is a rather dry and pompous collection of aphorisms, written by an author who appears to have little direct experience of his subject. It does, however, contain some useful hints and a section on the Olympic spirits Aratron, Bethor, Phaleg, Och, Hagith, Ophiel and Phul (in Aphorisms 15 to 21), which were an important part of magical practice in this period.

Finally, the two remaining books are both geomancies, the first by Agrippa and the second by that famous translator of Arabic texts into Latin, Gerard of Cremona (ca. 1114–1187). Gerard (or Gerardus Cremonensis to give him his Latin name) was also famous for translating Ptolemy's *Almagest*, probably the most influential text on astrology ever. Nobody doubts that *Of Geomancy* is by Agrippa, and as such it is a classic of geomancy, but it has been translated in such an abridged manner that I have had to supply more expansions and elucidations for this text than any other in this volume.

Geomancy is a technique of divination which originated in the 9th century A.D. in the Arab world of North Africa. It is not in any way connected with the Chinese locational practice of feng shui (despite the same name sometimes being used for the latter). The most complete modern text on divinatory geomancy, which covers both the history and practice, is misleadingly titled *Terrestrial Astrology*.[5] Because of its binary nature, geomancy is a fascinating form of divination, and was, after astrology, the most important form of divination in 17th-century Europe.

After geomancy fell out of favor in the 18th century, the Golden Dawn and Aleister Crowley helped renew interest in it during the 20th century. It is therefore remarkable that very few people have actually attempted to go back to early texts on geomancy to flesh out the skeleton used by the Golden Dawn. So here is your chance to do just that. Gerard of Cremona's *Geomancy*, however, uses a completely different method to generate the figures than that which is more commonly described by Golden Dawn derived books, and will be of particular interest to readers interested in astrology.

The original spelling and grammar of the *Fourth Book* has been retained to preserve the character of the original. However, additional paragraph breaks have been silently inserted to improve readability, and to break up long blocks of text covering differing subjects. Some long sentences have also been split to help understanding, and where this happens the break is always marked by a "SB" (sentence break) footnote. I have introduced additional section headings, and these are marked with square brackets to show they are not part of the original text. I hope this work makes these important texts much more accessible to the reading public, as well as completing my original intentions of 1978.

Stephen Skinner
Johor Bahru, 2004

---

[5] Stephen Skinner, *Terrestrial Astrology: Divination by Geomancy* (London: Routledge Kegan Paul, 1980).

Introduction to the
1978 Edition

It is amazing how often it is said that *The Fourth Book of Occult Philosophy* is spurious. This is repeated by one "authority" after another, obviously without any reference to the text itself. For this volume is not so much a single book as a collection of six treatises on various aspects of practical magic and divination. A glance at the table of contents will confirm that only two treatises actually claim to be by Henry Cornelius Agrippa.

Agrippa (1486–1535) was in many ways a Renaissance man, being a writer, soldier, and physician. However, his main claim to an important place in the history of the thought of the period is as a magician, and this is by no means a belittlement of his other attainments for as Agrippa himself says:

> Some that are perverse . . . may take the name of Magick in the worse sense and, though scarce having seen the title, cry out that I teach forbidden Arts, sow the seed of Heresies, offend pious ears, and scandalize excellent wits; that I am a sorcerer, and superstitious and divellish, who indeed am a Magician: to whom I answer, that a Magician doth not, amongst learned men signify a sorcerer, or one that is superstitious or divellish; but a wise man, a priest, a prophet.

Turning to the contents of this volume let us examine each treatise in turn:

I. Of Geomancy—Henry Cornelius Agrippa

Probably it is this treatise that is mentioned by Agrippa in 1526 when he sent to Metz for his work on geomancy. Again Agrippa refers to a work on geomancy in his *De Incertitudine* (Cap 13), where after listing earlier geomancies by Haly, Gerard of Cremona, Bartholomew of Parma, and Tundinus, he says of his own geomantic treatise, "I too have written a geomancy quite different from the rest but no less

superstitious and fallacious or if you wish I will even say 'menda-
cious.'" Agrippa was nothing if not frank about his own work!

Geomancy was from the 12th to the 17th century one of the major
forms of divination in Europe, taking second place to astrology but
precedence over the tarot. The first part of this book is concerned
with the mechanics of geomantic divination, the second part with
their application in an astrological context, and the third, and by
far the bulkiest part, is concerned with the meanings of each of the
sixteen geomantic figures in each of the 12 Houses of heaven.

This text on geomancy is extremely interesting in that it provides much of the material for later derivative works on the subject.
Interestingly, it expands greatly Agrippa's remarks on the subject
in his *Three Books of Occult Philosophy*.

The actual practice of geomancy is set out in a rather com-
pressed form. For example, in the 1655 edition, the table on page
6 is not very clear, and the diagram on the following page suffers
severely from the deficiencies of the printer's art. In the modernized
text presented here, I have reconstructed these. Complete instructions for geomantic practice appear in my book, *The Oracle of
Geomancy* (New York: Warner Destiny, 1977). You will find a history
of the subject in my *Divinatory Geomancy* (London: RKP, 1980).

II. *Of Occult Philosophy, or Of Magical Ceremonies: The Fourth Book—* Henry Cornelius Agrippa

This treatise, which appeared in Latin about 30 years after Agrippa's
death, is effectively a self-contained grimoire or grammar of sorcery that draws upon the *Three Books of Occult Philosophy* for its
theoretical background.

Johannes Weir, who was for a while Agrippa's disciple and amanu-
ensis, declared in one of his voluminous works that this treatise was
not after the style of his master, but elsewhere admits that Agrippa
was so prolific that it was impossible to be sure exactly what among
posthumously published material was actually by him.

After an initial excursion into an astrological system for generating
the names of good and evil spirits, Agrippa goes on to discuss the
magnitudes of the stars and their symbols. A set of characters for both
good and evil spirits follows, according to their rank and dignity.

The familiar shapes of the spirits of the various planets are
delineated to identify a particular spirit with its planetary ruler.
Agrippa then explains how to make pentacles and what signs are to

be used in their preparation. The form of these pentacles is similar to some given in *The Key of Solomon,* where the picture is drawn representing a biblical or Apocalyptic theme and then surrounded with the appropriate verse and godname.

The work then touches upon the details of consecration of the various instruments necessary for the art of magic, the types of conjurations, unctions, suffumigations (perfumes), prayers, and benedictions to be used. There is special emphasis on the consecration of water, fire, oils, and perfumes. Details of the consecration of the circle, which is to be the *sanctum sanctorum* for the practice of magic and the use of the *Liber Spirituum,* or Book of Spirits, are explained. This book must be inscribed with the image and sigil of the spirit together with the oath that it must take when it is conjured.

Finally, Agrippa discloses the details of the actual invocation of spirits. He outlines the type of place in which the ceremony must take place, the preparation and condition of the magus, the names to be worn and the days and times in which the operation is permissible. Furthermore, Agrippa explains dream oracles and the tablets and talismans requisite for this art, so covering the various forms of invocation not requiring a circle, and dealing with nature spirits as well as the spirits of the grimoires.

III. *Heptameron: or, Magical Elements—* Peter de Abano

Peter of Abano (1250–1317) was one of the most influential men of learning of his time. Many of his writings on medicine, philosophy, and astronomy are extant, together with works on geomancy and magic often attributed to him, the latter possibly spurious. It is easier, however, to consider the *Heptameron or Magical Elements* and the *Geomantia* as by him: as he had quite a well paid practice as a physician and a place in society to keep up, it is conceivable that the above treatise remained in manuscript form until sometime after his death, especially as he was in some trouble with the Inquisition.

He studied medicine in Paris before returning to Padua to practice as a physician. Toward the end of his life he was actually accused by the Inquisition of practicing sorcery and was imprisoned. He was later acquitted but then re-arrested and died in prison in 1317 while awaiting trial.

Among the less salubrious works from his pen was a work on poisons, commissioned by the then incumbent pope, possibly Pope Honorius IV.

Of the books of magic attributed to Peter, the *Heptameron* is the best known, but Naudé states that two other books of his were banned after his death, the *Elucidarium Necromanticum* and *Liber Experimentorum Mirabilium de Annulis Secundum 28 Mansiones Lunae*, or "Book of marvelous experiments with rings according to the 28 mansions of the moon."

The *Heptameron*, which draws heavily on the *Picatrix*, a magical text by the Arab pseudo-Magriti, may have first appeared in Latin at Venice in 1496 before being bound with Agrippa in 1565. The *Heptameron* has well earned its reputation as a key work on practical magic and it follows in the tradition of Trithemius' *Steganographia* in as much as it catalogues the names of many angels and the times of their conjuration.

He commences his book on the magical elements by describing the composition of the circle, which is described as a certain fortress to defend the operator against the evil spirits. The names of the hours and the angels ruling them follow his succinct description of the circle, giving the names for each season, its beginning and end.

Next follow the consecrations and benedictions to be performed before the magical operation, the exorcism of the fire, the manufacture of the garments to be worn and the pantacle to be used as a lamen on the magician's breast. Orations similar to those in the *Key of Solomon* are given for the donning of robes before the ceremony.

In many ways, Abano's instructions for invocation are much more straightforward than most grimoires, the emphasis being on the careful recitation of the conjurations in Latin to the spirits of the elements. These conjurations are primarily qabalistic words of power, with the occasional word of Greek or Gnostic derivation cropping up every so often. After these, specific instructions are given for each day of the week, beginning with the circle to be used, the name of the angel for the day, his sigil, planet, and sign of the zodiac, together with his ministers and the names of power to be used at each quarter, which precede a specific conjuration suitable for the day in question. Peter also wrote a geomancy that is a classic in its field, neatly complementing the two studies of the subject included in this collection.

IV. *Isagoge . . . Of the Nature of Spirits*— Georg Pictorius Villinganus (ca. 1500–1569)

The fourth treatise is an introductory discourse on the nature of such spirits as occur in the sublunary sphere; their origin, names, offices, illusions, powers, prophecies, miracles; and how they may be expelled.

Pictorius began his career as a schoolmaster at Freiburg-im-Breisgau, where he acquired his M.D. and became professor of medicine, before taking the position of physician at the archducal court at Ensisheim in Alsace. His first publications (1530) were medical works, commentaries, scholia, collections, and tabulations of medieval authors such as Macer on herbs and Marbod on gems, or classical writers such as Hippocrates, Pliny, Aristotle, Galen, and Oppian. In 1563 Pictorius published the work here translated.

Much of Pictorius' writing is a summary of earlier writers, often unimaginative, but quite faithful to the originals and conscientiously acknowledged. As such, Pictorius' writings are valuable in accurately indicating the longevity and survival of the ideas on magic that he puts forth.

In the *Isagoge*, Pictorius cites Apuleius, Augustina, Iamblichus, Pliny, Saxo Grammaticus, Psellus (whom he calls a necromancer), Peter Lombard, Trithemius, and Marcus Cherrhonesus (whom he refers to as a "distinguished devotee of demons").

The Isagoge is set out as a conversation between the classical Greek twins Castor and Pollux. The argument attempts to prove that the word daemon "is not an horrible or odius name, but the name of one that doth administer, help or succor unto another, and whom Pliny calleth a god." This book is an important essay for the time because it seeks to differentiate between the evil spirits of Christian theology and Greek daemons, who were of three degrees, ranging from spirits of the air up to what Homer called gods. It was certainly important then, and of interest to practical magicians now, to distinguish the difference between these types of spirit. This book forms a bridge between the magical theory of Iamblicus of Chalcis and the grimoires such as Peter de Abano's *Heptameron*. Using the form of dialogue, Pictorius is able to set forth the objections of the Church and counter each one by referring to various authorities, including scripture, Peter of Lombard, Sappho, and Diocletian concerning the position of spirits in the world, and the form and nature of their bodies.

The doctrine that spirits are guardians of the treasures of the earth, gems and precious metals, as well as buried treasure, is examined in detail, for the discovery of buried treasure by the use of spirits was an all-absorbing pastime. In days before banks, the burial of treasure was quite a common occurrence and its discovery by accident or magic almost as common. Various acts of the devil and his ministers on Earth, together with accounts of apparitions and the occurrence of spirits naturally are then invoked with long anecdotes from Pliny.

In many ways, this book is an excellent summary of all of the diverse influences both Christian and pagan that came together during the late Middle Ages and early Renaissance to form the magical tradition of the West. It in fact is almost a bibliography of source books on magic and stories about demons, as well as being an insight into the attitude of the period toward magic.

Pictorius dwells at some length upon the different types of divination, all of which he attributes to the agency of the devil, and goes into detail about the different demons, distinguishing between northern and southern sublunar demons, *criminatores* and *exploratores*, and *tentatores* and *insidiatores* (who accompany each person as his or her evil genius). Pictorius' armory against spirits is very traditional and includes the name of Jesus, fire, the sword, contumelies, suffumigations, the bell, and even the shaking of keys and clash of arms!

Unfortunately, Pictorius took a very strong line against witches and would have them all put to death, not so much for their non-Christian or malefic activities, but for having carnal intercourse with spirits, which Pictorius thought were both fertile and potent!

Johannes Weir, Agrippa's pupil I mentioned earlier, spoke rather slightingly of Pictorius' "jejune writing . . . concerning sublunar matters." It may be that the publication of this work by Pictorius with the alleged *Fourth Book* by his master prompted Weir to deny the authenticity of the latter. Weir thought it was not by Agrippa because of the time that had passed between Agrippa's death and its publication, but for no other reason.

V. *Of Astronomical Geomancy—* Gerard Cremonensis (1114–1187)

Gerard of Cremona was perhaps one of the greatest translators of the twelfth century, having been responsible for translating into Latin the *Almagest* of Ptolemy (the most influential book on astrology of the age), works by Aristotle, Euclid, Galen, Avicenna, and many more. Working at Toledo, he is credited by his pupils with translating most of the Greek and Arabic texts available in the Middle Ages, a total of 71 different texts, some of immense size. Critics have suggested that our present text was translated by Gerard of Sabbionetta, a town near Cremona, but this seems unlikely.

The *Astronomical Geomancy* offers a different system of geomancy than that outlined by Agrippa in the first treatise in this volume. Although the points are generated in the same manner, the figures are immediately translated into their planetary or zodiacal equivalents and placed into a horoscope.

The bulk of the treatise is devoted to questions of the different astrological houses and their interpretation according to the geomantically generated planets and signs occupying that House.

VI. *Of Magick*—Arbatel

This small treatise on the magic of the ancients was issued at Basel in 1575 as Arbatel, *De Magia Veterum*. Despite the fact that the word "Arbatel" is also printed in Hebrew, it is obvious, by the liberal sprinkling of pious sentiments and biblical quotes, that the author was a Christian. Because of references in the 30th and 31st Aphorisms to obscure details of Italian history, the author may have been from that country, perhaps even a Neapolitan magistrate. The word "Arbatel," however, is probably not an assumed name, but that of a revelatory angel of one of the four quarters.

This book supposedly contains nine "tomes." The first "tome" containing 49 Aphorisms upon the general precepts of magic forms the introduction or *Isagoge*, and is the only part included in the 1575 edition or its present translation.

However the preface to the book claims eight more, of which none appear to be extant.

Although it is likely that the first "tome" was the only one actually written it more than once overlaps with what should have followed.

For example, the 16th Aphorism concerns itself with the 7 Olympic Spirits and their Provinces. (In the text the number of Provinces is put at 186 of which 32 are ruled by Bethor. This is probably a misprint for 196 and 42 respectively, for with the later arrangement each Olympic spirit rules 7 less Provinces than its predecessor). Each Olympic Spirit is said to govern an epoch of 490 years (of which the current governing spirit is Ophiel). Each is also attributed various planetary correspondences, a sigil, a list of powers, and an enumeration of the legions of spirits under their command.

It is interesting to note that a grimoire called *The Secret Grimoire of Turiel* by Marius Malchus, which was supposedly discovered in Las Palmas in 1927 as a Latin manuscript dated 1518, appears to be derived from this Aphorism with additional details drawn from other parts of this volume.

TRANSLATION

This translation is the first English translation of this collection of six treatises. A. E. Waite (who was only too happy to criticize the scholarship of other translators) gave Robert Turner's work the highest accolade when he wrote: "I shall depart from my usual custom of translating at first hand, and make use . . . of the version of Robert Turner, which is quite faithful and has, moreover, the pleasant flavour of antiquity."

The translation was published in 1655 just one year before his translation of Paracelsus' work *Of the Supreme Mysteries of Nature* which was published in 1975 as *The Archidoxes of Magic* (reprinted by Ibis Press in 2004).

Turner's contribution to the spread of magical knowledge in the vernacular of seventeenth century England is considerable as he made some of the best occult writings of the time more widely available.

Turner felt obliged to defend magic in terms of his own period, using biblical and classical quotations, and to point out the difference between *malefici* or *venefici* (the sorcerers or poisoners who relied for the most part on low cunning, fear and poison) and the committed student of "natural philosophy" for whom the gates of experimental science were just beginning to open. The latter took all of nature, including that which seemed beyond nature, or supernatural, as his territory: he could be equally interested in spirits or in the refractive and image-projecting properties of glass lenses (as was Dr. John Dee), and feel that both fields were equally within his area of study, or if you prefer, equally outside his range of scientific certainty: both were to him still miraculous.

Today, only spirits remain miraculous, the fabulous "burning glas" long since having been accommodated within the realms of the known. But opinion today is in a sense less open to experiment, less honest, and less open-minded than in the late Renaissance. For the idea of spirits is no longer open to dispute: it has simply been dumped on the scrap heap.

However, since the beginning of the last century an insidious phenomena has begun to grow up within magic itself, a phenomena roughly equivalent to Turner's seventeenth century attempts to make magic acceptable in the eyes of his religiously-minded contemporaries. In some ways this modern growth is an extension of the religiously orientated defense of magic, except that it is in fact a scientifically-orientated defense, as there has always been a compulsion by apologists to bend their argument into a contemporary mould.

Magic is basically the science and art of causing change to occur in conformity with Will, through spiritual creatures that have been evoked or invoked from either the microcosm (our own normally subconscious wellsprings of power) or the macrocosm (the universe). This definition also includes the "magical technologies" such as the various forms of divination that are necessary adjuncts. It is the loss of the latter half (macrocosmic part) of the definition, which has allowed modern apologists for magic to hint that the changes are all internal and psychological, aimed at improving the interior person and enabling him or her to transcend personal limitations and achieve enlightenment. The early stages of this phenomena can easily be explained away in terms of Jungian psychology—the pursuit of integration; the latter stages can be explained by invoking religious and mystical precedents, thereby avoiding the essence of magic as it was worked prior to the nineteenth century.

This is not to say that there is not a great deal of value in a Jungian or Reichian approach to magic, just that it leaves a proportion of magic unaccounted for.

One might say that magic has developed over the last couple of centuries, but how can a subject develop that narrows its focus so far as to throw out the bulk of its theory (for the belief in external entities was a central belief) without actually improving on its techniques?

It is for this reason that this book is being republished, to bring forward some of the best thought in the field, before it is smothered by a mass of "scientific" rationalization, just as oppressive in its own way as religious bias.

Stephen Skinner
London, 1978

PART I
MAGIC

Henry Cornelius Agrippa

HIS

Fourth BOOK

OF

Occult Philosophy.

Of GEOMANCY.

MAGICAL ELEMENTS of *Peter de Abano.*

ASTRONOMICAL GEOMANCY.

The NATURE of SPIRITS.

Arbatel of MAGICK.

Translated into English by *Robert Turner,*
Φιλομαθης.

LONDON,
Printed by *J. C.* for *John Harrison*, at the Lamb
at the East-end of *Pauls.* 1655.

THE PREFACE

To the Unprejudiced Reader.

 S the fall of man made himself and all other creatures subject to vanity; so, by reason thereof, the most noble and excellent Arts wherewith the Rational soul was indued, are by the rusty canker of Time brought unto Corruption. For Magick it self, which the ancients did so divinely contemplate, is scandalized with bearing the badg[e] of all diabolical sorceries; which Art (saith Mirandula[1]) *Pauci intelligunt, multi reprehendunt, & sicut canes ignotos semper allatrant:*[2] Few understand, many reprehend; and as dogges barke at those they know not: so do many condemn and hate the things they understand not. Many men there are, that abhor the very name and word *Magus*, because of *Simon Magus*,[3] who being indeed not *Magus*, but *Goes*,[4] that is, familiar with evil Spirits, usurped that Title.

But Magicke and Witchcraft are far differing Sciences; whereof *Pliny* being ignorant, scoffeth thereat: for *Nero* (saith *Pliny*[5]) who had the most excellent Magicians of the East sent him by *Tyridates*, king of *Armenia*, who held that kingdome by him, found the Art after long study and labour altogether ridiculous. Now Witchcraft and Sorcery, are workes done meerely by the devill, which with respect unto some covenant made with man, be acteth by men[6] his instruments, to accomplish his evil ends: of these, the histories of

---

[1] Giovanni Pico della Mirandola.

[2] The Latin is translated in the sentence following this.

[3] A famous first-century A.D. magician and miracle worker whose magic is well documented. He levitated in front of both the Emperor Nero and St. Peter and many other credible witnesses.

[4] *Goes* is derived from "Goetia" and implies one who deals with demons, as contrasted with a Theugist who invokes gods, or a Thaumaturgist who deals in miracles.

[5] Caius Plinius Secundus (23–79 A.D.). Margin note: Plin[y]. lib[er] 30. Nat. Hist[ory].

[6] Through men.

all ages, people and countries, as also the holy Scriptures, afford us sundry examples.

But *Magus* is a Persian word primitively,[7] whereby is exprest such a one as is altogether conversant in things divine; and as *Plato* affirmeth, the art of Magick is the art of worshipping God: and the Persians called their gods *Magous*[8] hence *Apollonius*[9] saith that *Magus* is either *a worshipper or the gods*, or *a god himself*[10] that is, that *Magus* is a name sometime of him that is a god by nature, & sometimes of him that is in the service of God: in which latter sense it is taken in *Matth[ew]* 2:1, 2. when the wise men came up to worship Jesus, and this is the first and highest kinde, which is called divine Magick; and these the Latines[11] did intitle *sapientes*, or wise men; for the feare and worship of God, is the beginning of knowledge.

These wise men the Greeks call *Philosophers*; and amongst the Egyptians they were termed *Priests*: the Hebrews termed them *Cabalistos*,[12] Prophets, Scribes and Pharisees; and amongst the Babylonians they were differenced[13] by the name of *Caldeans*; & by the Persians they were called *Magicians*: and one speaking of *Sosthenes*, one of the ancient Magicians, useth these words: *Et verum Deum merita majestate prosequitur, & angelos ministros Dei, sed veri ejus venerationi novit assistere; idem daemonas prodit terrenos, Vagos, humanitatis inimicos; Sosthenes* ascribeth the due Majesty to the true God, & acknowledgeth that his Angels are ministers and messengers which attend the worship of the true God; he also hath delivered, that there are devils earthly and wandering, and enemies to mankind.

So that the word *Magus* of it selfe imports a Contemplator of divine & heavenly Sciences; but under the name of *Magick*, are all unlawful Arts comprehended; as Necromancy and Witchcraft, and

---

[7] Originally.

[8] In Greek characters in the 1655 translation.

[9] Apollonius of Tyana was a first-century A.D. magician whose miracles were thought by some to compare with Christ's. His biography by Philostratus deserves much wider circulation.

[10] This phrase is originally in Greek, and is a quote from Apollonius of Tyana, *17th Epistle to Euphrates*: "The Persians call divine people 'magicians.' So a magician is either a worshipper of the gods or someone who is divine by nature. You, however, are not a magician but a godless man."

[11] Romans.

[12] Or Kabbalists.

[13] Distinguished.

such Arts which are effected by combination[14] with the devil, and whereof he is a party.

These Witches and Necromancers are also called *Malefici* or *venifici*; sorcerers or poisoners; of which name witches are rightly called,[15] who without the Art of Magicke do indeed use the helpe of the devill himself to do mischief; practising to mix the powder of dead bodies with other things by the help of the devill prepared; and as other times to make pictures of wax, clay; or otherwise (as it were *sacramentaliter*) to effect those things which the devil by other means bringeth to pass. Such were, and to this day partly, if not altogether, are the corruptions that have made odious the very name of Magick, having chiefly fought, as the manner of all impostures is, to counterfeit the highest and most noble part of it.

A second kind of Magick is Astrologie, which judgeth of the events of things to come, natural and humane, by the motions and influences of the stars upon these lower elements, by them observ'd & understood.

Philo Judaeus[16] affirmeth, that by this part of Magick or Astrologie, together with the motions of the Stars and other heavenly bodies, *Abraham* found out the knowledge of the true God while be lived in *Caldea, Qui Contemplatione Creaturarum, cognovit Creatorem*[17] (saith *Damascen*) who knew the Creator by the contemplation of the creature. *Josephus*[18] reporteth of *Abraham*, that he instructed the Egyptians in Arithmetick and Astronomy; who before *Abraham's* coming unto them, knew none of these Sciences.

Abraham sanctitate & sapientia omnium praestantissimus, primium Caldaeos; deinde Phoenices, demum Egyptios Sacerdotes, Astrologia & Divina docuerit.[19] *Abraham* the holiest and wisest of

---

[14] Agreement.

[15] Rather an unfair and sweeping statement. Turner is trying to plead that magic is a religious pursuit, while all its darker sides belong to witchcraft: he knew better than that, but was trying to defend himself from the inevitable criticism that descended upon him after the original publication of this book. At this time in the mid-seventeenth century, the anti-witch sentiment stirred up by King James was just beginning to die down.

[16] Early first century A.D. Jewish philosopher and Pythagorean who attempted to reconcile the philosophy of the Greeks with the Pentateuch, the five books attributed to Moses.

[17] Translated in the following sentence.

[18] A Jewish historian.

[19] Translated in the following sentence.

men, did first teach the C[h]aldeans, then the Phoenicians, lastly the Egyptian Priests, Astrologie and Divine knowledge.[20]

Without doubt, *Hermes Trismegistus*, that divine Magician and Philosopher, who (as some say) lived long before *Noah*, attained to much Divine knowledg[e] of the Creator through the studie of Magick and Astrologie; as his Writings, to this day extant among us, testifie.

The third kinde of Magick containeth the whole Philosophy of Nature; which bringeth to light the inmost vertues, and extracteth them out of Natures hidden bosome to humane use: *Virtutes in centro centri latentes*; Vertues bidden in the centre of the Centre, according to the Chymists: of this sort were *Albertus, Arnoldus de Villa nova, Raymond, Bacon*, and others, &c.[21]

The Magick these men profess'd, is thus defined. *Magia est connexio a viro sapiente agentium per naturam cum patientibus, sibi, congruenter respondentibus, ut inde opera prodeant, non sine eorum admiratione qui causam ignorant.*[22] Magick is the connexion of natural agents and patients, answerable each to other, wrought by a wise man; to the bringing forth of such effects as are wonderful to those that know not their causes.

In all these, *Zoroaster* was well learned, especially in the first and the highest: for in his Oracles he confesseth God to be the first and the highest; he believeth the Trinity, which be would not investigate by any natural knowledge; he speaketh of Angels, and of Paradise; approveth the immortality of the soul; teacheth Truth, Faith, Hope, and Love, discoursing of the abstinence and charity of the *Magi*.

Of this *Zoroaster*, *Eusebius* [says] in the Theologie of the Phoenicians, using *Zoroaster's* own words: *Haec ad verbum scribit* (saith *Eusebius*) *Deus primus, incorruptibilium, sempiternus,*

---

[20] Rather an exaggerated claim.

[21] Albertus Magnus (1206?–1280) wrote several works on natural magic; Arnoldus de Villa nova (1235?–1313) was a Spanish alchemist and astrologer; Raymond Lull (1235?–1315) wrote a number of philosophical and mystical works, and was the inventor of the idea that problems of philosphy could be solved by a series of interconnecting wheels inscribed with various abstract terms, a device that has come to be called a Lullian machine. Roger Bacon (1214?–1294?), an English philosopher, alchemist, and reputed conjuror of spirits, was held in such high esteem that he was requested by Pope Clement IV to compose three treatises on the sciences of the time. He was also thrown into jail by order of a later Pope.

[22] Translated in the following sentence.

ingenitus, expers partium, sibi ipsi simillimus, bonorum omnium auriga, munera non expectans, optimus, prudentissimus, pater juris, sine doctrina justitiam perdoctus, natura perfectus, sapiens, sacrae naturae unicus inventor, &. Thus saith *Zoroaster,* word for word: God the first, incorruptible, everlasting, unbegotten, without parts, most like himself, the guide of all good, expecting no reward, the best, the wisest the father of right, having learned justice without teaching, perfect, wise by nature, the onely inventor thereof.

So that a Magician is no other but *divinorum cultor & interpres,* a studious observer and expounder of divine things; and the Art it self is none other *quam Naturalis Philosophiae absoluta consummatio,* then the absolute perfection of Natural Philosophy. Nevertheless there is a mixture in all things, of good with evil, of falshood with truth, of corruption with purity. The good, the truth, the purity, in every kinde, may well be embraced: As in the ancient worshipping of God by Sacrifice, there was no man knowing God among the Elders, that did forbear to worship the God of all power, or condemn that kinde of Worship, because the devil was so adored in the Image of *Baal, Dagon, Astaroth, Chemosh, Jupiter, Apollo,* and the like.

Neither did the abuse of Astrologie terrifie *Abraham,* (if we believe the most ancient and religious Writers) from observing the motions and natures of the heavenly bodies. Neither can it dehort[23] wise and learned men in these days from attributing those vertues, influences, and inclinations, to the Stars and other Lights of heaven, which God hath given to those his glorious creatures.

I must expect some calumnies and obtrectations against this, from the malicious prejudiced man, and the lazie affecters of Ignorance, of whom this age swarms: but the voice and sound of the Snake and the Goose is all one. But our stomacks are not now so queazie[24] and tender, after so long time feeding upon solid Divinity, nor we so umbragious and startling, having been so long enlightned in Gods path, that we should relapse into that childish Age, in which *Aristotles* Metaphysicks, in a Councel in *France,* was forbid to be read.

But I incite the Reader to a charitable opinion hereof, with a Christian Protestation of an innocent purpose therein; and intreat the Reader to follow this advice of *Tabaeus, Qui litigant, sint ambo in conspectu tuo mali & rei* [that is, roughly translated, by arguing,

---

[23] Deter.
[24] Easily unsettled.

both parties will lose]. And if there be any scandal in this enter-
prise of mine, it is taken, not given. And this comfort I have in
that Axiome of *Trismegistus, Qui pius est, summe philosophatur.*[25]
And therefore I present it without disguise, and object it to all of
candor and indifferencie: and of Readers, of whom there be four
sorts, as one observes; Spunges, which extract all without distinguishing; Hour-glasses, which receive, and pour out as fast; Bags,
which retain onely the dregs of Spices, and let the Wine escape;
and Sieves, which retaine the best onely. Some there are of the last
sort, and to them I present this *Occult Philosophy*, knowing that
they may reap good thereby. And they who are severe against it,
they shall pardon this my opinion, that such their severity proceeds
from Selfguiltiness; and give me leave to apply that of *Ennodius*
that it is the nature Selfwickedness, to think that of others, which
themselves deserve. And it is all the comfort which the guilty have,
Not to find any innocent. But that amongst others this may find
some acceptation, is the desire of

R[obert] Turner.
London, ult[imo] Aug[ust] 1654.

---

[25] He who is devout is the greatest philosopher.

To his special friend Mr. R. Turner, on his judicious Translation of Corn[elius] Agrippa.

As one that just out of a Trance appears,
Amaz'd with stranger sights, whose secret fears
Are scarcely past, but doubtful whether he
May credit's eyes, remaineth steadfastly
Fix'd on those objects; just like him I stand,
Rapt in amazement to behold that can
By art come neer the gods, that far excel
The Angels that in those bright Spheres do dwell.
Behold *Agrippa* mounting th' lofty skies,
Talking with gods; and then anon be pries
Int' earths deep cabinet, as t' *Mercury,*
All kindes of Spirits willing subjects be,
And more than this his book supplies: but we
Blinde mortals, no wayes could be led to see
That light without a taper: than thou to us
Must be *Agrippa* and an *Oedipus.*
Agrippa once again appears, by thee
Pull'd out o' the' ashes of Antiquity.
Let squintey'd envie pine away, whilst thou
Wear'st crowns of Praise on thy deserving brow.

I.P.B. Cantabrigiæ.[1]

---

[1] Cambridge University.

To his ingenious friend Mr. Turner,
upon his Translation.

Thrice-noble Soul! renown'd Epitome
Of Learning and Occult Philosophie;
That unknown Geomancie dost impart,
With profound secrets of that abstruse Art!
T' expound Natural Magick is thy task;
Not hellborn Necromancie to unmask;
Exposing Mysteries to publick view,
That heretofore were known to very few.
Thou dost not keep thy Knowledge to thy self,
(As base covetous Misers do their pelf;
Whose numerous bags of rusteaten gold,
Profits none, till themselves were laid in mold)
But studious of Publicke good dost make
All of th' fruits of thy labours to partake.
   Therefore if some captious Critick blame
Thy Writings, surely then his judgment's lame.
Art hath no hater but an empty pate,
Which can far better carp, then imitate.
Nay *Zoilus* or *Momus* will not dare
Blame thy Translation, without compare
Excellent. So that if an hundred tongues
Dame Nature had bestow'd and brazen lungs;
Yet rightly to chuccinate[1] thy praises,
I should want strength, as well as polite phrases.
But if the gods will grant what I do crave,
Then *Enoch's* Translation shalt thou have.

W. P. S[t]. John's [College] Cambr[idge University].

---

[1] Sing.

To his friend the Author, on this his Translation.

What, not a *Sibyl* or *Cassandra* left?
What *Apollo* ceas'd? Has sharpfang'd Time bereft
Us of the Oracles? Is *Dodan's* grove
Cut down? Does ne'er a word proceed from *Jove*
Into the ears of mortals that inherit
Tiresias soul, or the great *Calcha's* spirit?
What is become o' th' *Augurs* that foretold
Nature's intents? Are th' *Magi* dead, that could
Tell what was done in every Sphere? Shall we
Not know what's done in the remot'st Country
Without great travel? Can't we below decry
The minde o' th' gods above? All's done by thee,
Agrippa; all their Arts lie couch'd in thee.
Th' Art that before in divers heads did lie,
Is now collect int' one Monopoly.
But all's in vain; we lack'd an *Oedipus*,
Who should interpret's meaning unto us:
This thou effect'st with such dexterity,
Adding perhaps what th' Author ne'er did see;
That we may say, Thou dost the Art renew:
To thee the greater half of th' praise is due.

J.B. Cantabrigiæ.[1]

---

[1] Cambridge.

To the Author, on his Translation of

Cornelius Agrippa.

Pallas of Learning th' art, if Goddess nam'd;
Which Prototype thy knowledge hath explain'd;
Which Nature also striving to combine,
Science and Learning, in this Form of thine,
To us not darkly, but doth clearly shew
Knowledge of Mysteries as the shrine in you.
By thy permission 'tis, we have access
Into Geomancy; which yet, unless
Thou hadst unmask'd, a mystery 't had lain,
A task too hard for mortals to explain.
Which since thou hast from the *Lethaean* floods
Preserv'd, we'll consecrate the Lawrel buds
To thee: (*Phoebus* dismissed) thine shall be
The Oracle, to which all men shall flee
In time of danger; thy predictions shall,
To whatsoever thou command'st, inthral
Our willing hearts; yea, thou shalt be
Sole Prophet, we obedient to thee.

J. R.

To the Author, on his Translation of
Cornelius Agrippa.

Doth *Phoebus* cease to answer t' our demands?
Or will he not accept at mortals hands
A sad Bidental? And is *Sibyls* cave
Inhabitable? Or may *Tiresias* have
No successor nor rival? How shall we
Then *Oedipus* to th' world direct? If he
Do Incest adde to Parricide, th' are dumb,
That could predict what things should surely come:
And they are silent that knew when t' apply
T' our body Politick Purge and Phlebotomy.
How will bold thieves our treasures rob, who shall
Loft goods regain, or by his Charms recal
The nocent? Th' Art is by thee repriv'd:
In thee the *Magi* seem to be reviv'd.
Phoebus is not brain-sick, *Joves* doves not dead,
Th' Oracles not ceas'd: Agrippa's bed
(Like the Arabian birds self builded nest,
Which first her Urn proves, then her quickening rest
Hath thee produc'd more then his equal sure,
Else had this Art as yet remain'd obscure,
A miracle to vulgars, well known to none,
Scarce read by deepest apprehension.
Then I'll conclude Since thou dost him explain,
That th' younger brother hath the better brain.

John Tomlinson,
of St. John's [College] in Cambridge.

To his good friend the Author, on his Translation of Occult Philosophy and Geomancie.

Most noble undertakings! as if Art
And Prudence should a bargain make, t' impart
Refulgent lustres: you send forth a ray
Which noblest Patrons never could display.
Well may *Diana* love you and inspire
Your noblest Genius with cœlestial fire,
Whose sparkling Fancie with more power can quell,
And sooner conquer, then a Magick Spell.
The Author thought not, (when he pen'd the Book)
To be surmounted by a higher look,
Or be o'ertopt b' a more triumphant strein,
Which should exalt his then-most pleasant vein.
But seeing that a later progeny
Hath snatch'd his honour from obscurity,
Both shall revive, and make Spectators know
The best deservers of the Lawrel bow.
Nature and Art here strive, the victory
To get: and though to yeeld he doth deny,
Th' hast got the start: though he triumph in praise,
Yet may his Ivie wait upon your Bays.

M. S.
Cantabrigiæ.

To the Author, on this his ingenious Translation of Cornelius Agrippa.

What is 't I view? *Agrippa* made to wear
An English habit?[1] Sure 'tis something rare.
Or are his Romane garments, by thy Wit,
Translated to an English garb so fit
T' illustrate him? for that thou hast, we see,
Enlightned his obscure Philosophie;
And that which did so intricate remain,
Thou hast expos'd to ev'ry vulgar brain.
If then thy beams through such dark works shine clear,
Now splendent will they in thine own appear!
Then go thou on, brave soul, to spread such rays
Of Learning through the world, may speak thy praise.
And fear no Criticks: for thou, by a Spell,
Canst force their tongues within their teeth to dwell.

Jo. Tabor,
of St. John's [College] in Cambridge.

---

[1] Clothing.

Of Occult Philosophy

or

Of Magical Ceremonies: The Fourth Book

Written by Henry Cornelius Agrippa.

IN OUR BOOKS of Occult Philosophy, we have not so compendiously, as copiously, declared the principles, grounds, and reasons of Magick it self, and after what maner the experiments thereof are to be chosen, elected, and compounded, to produce many wonderful effects; but because in those books they are treated of, rather Theorically, then Practically; and some also are not handled compleatly and fully, and others very figuratively, and as it were Enigmatically and obscure Riddles, as being those which we have attained unto with great study, diligence, and very curious searching and exploration, and are heretofore set forth in a more rude and unfashioned maner. Therefore in this book, which we have composed and made as it were a Complement and Key of our other books of Occult Philosophy, and of all Magical Operations, we will give unto thee the documents of holy and undefiled verity, and Inexpugnable and Unresistable Magical Discipline, and the most pleasant and delectable experiments of the sacred Deities. So that as by the reading of our other books of Occult Philosophy, thou maist earnestly cover the knowledge of these things; even so with reading this book, thou shalt truely triumph. Wherefore let silence hide these things within the secret closets of thy religious breast, and conceal them with constant Taciturnity.

[How to Generate the names of Spirits]

This therefore is to be known, That the names of the intelligent
presidents of every one of the Planets are constituted after this
maner:[1] that is to say, By collecting together the letters out of
the [astrological] figure of the world, from the rising [degree] of
the body of the Planet, according to the succession of the Signes
through the several degrees; and out of the several degrees, from
the aspects of the Planet himself, the calculation being made from
the degree of the ascendant. In the like maner are constituted the
names of the Princes of the evil spirits; they are taken under all
the Planets of the presidents in a retrograde order, the projection
being made contrary to the succession of the signes, from the
beginning of the seventh House.

Now the name of the supreme & highest intelligence, which
many do suppose to be the soul of the world, is collected out
of the four Cardinal points of the figure of the world, after the
maner already delivered [above]: & by the opposite and contrary
way, is known the name of the great *Dæmon*, or evil spirit, upon
the four cadent Angles. In the like maner shalt thou understand
[how to generate] the names of the great presidential spirits ruling in the Air, from the four Angles of the succedant Houses: so
that as to obtain the names of the good spirits, the calculation is
to be made according to the succession of the signes, beginning
from the degree of the ascendant; and to attain to the names of
the evil spirits, by working the contrary way.

You must also observe, that the names of the evil spirits are
extracted, as wel[l] from the names of the good spirits, as of the
evil: so not withstanding, that if we enter the table[2] with the name
of a good spirit of the second order, the name of the evil spirit shall
be extracted from the order of the Princes and Governours; but if
we enter the table with the name of a good spirit of the third order,
or with the name of an evil spirit a Governour, after what maner
soever they are extracted, whether by this table, or from a celestial

---

[1] This section is an abridged explanation of the rules given for generating
the names of spirits in Agrippa's *Three Books of Occult Philosophy*, Book III,
chapters xxiv – xxviii. The method given there is much clearer than Agrippa's
summary here in the *Fourth Book of Occult Philosophy*.

[2] The table can be found in Book III, chapter xxvii of Agrippa's *Three Books
of Occult Philosophy*. To "enter the table" means to read off the resultant
name from either the left or right side.

figure, the names which do proceed from hence, shall be the names of the evil spirits, the Ministers of the inferiour order.

It is further to be noted, That as often as we enter this table with the good spirits of the second order, the names extracted are of the second order: and if under them we extract the name of an evil spirit, he is of the superiour order of the Governours. The same order is, if we enter with the name of an evil spirit of the superiour order. If therefore we enter this table with the names of the spirits of the third order, or with the names of the ministring spirits, as wel[l] of the good spirits, as of the evil, the names extracted shall be the names of the ministring spirits of the inferiour order.

But many Magicians, men of no small Authority, will have the tables of this kinde to be extended with Latine letters:[3] so that by the same tables also, out of the name of any office or effect, might be found out the name of any spirit, as wel[l] good as evil, by the same maner which is above delivered, by taking the name of the office or of the effect, in the columne of letters, in their own line, under their own star.[4] And of this practice *Trismegistus* is a great Author, who delivered this kinde of calculation in Egyptian letters: not unproperly also may they be referred to other letters of other tongues, for the reasons assigned to the signes; for truly he only is extant[5] of all men, who have treated concerning the attaining to the names of spirits.

Therefore the force, secrecy and power, in what maner the sacred names of spirits are truly and rightly found out, consisteth in the disposing of vowels, which do make the name of a spirit, and wherewith is constituted the true name, and right word.[6] Now this art is thus perfected and brought to pass: first, we are to take heed of the placing the vowels of the letters, which are found by the calculation of the celestial figure, to finde the names of the spirits of the second order, Presidents and Governours. And this

---

[3] Agrippa's tables are in Hebrew characters, which is appropriate as many of the names of spirits are derived from Hebrew. In this sentence he suggests that it might be proper to construct similar tables with Roman (English) letters, but does not himself do so.

[4] In other words, take the qualities or Latin name of the "office" of the spirit, and by reading the right columns and lines of the table, generate its proper name.

[5] "Excellent" is meant rather than "extant."

[6] As Hebrew words were basically made up of consonants (with a few exceptions) it is necessary to complete the name by adding in the correct vowels in order to pronounce it correctly.

in the good spirits, is thus brought to effect, by considering the stars which do constitute and make the letters, and by placing them according to their order.[7] First, let the degree of the eleventh House be subtracted from the degree of that star which is first in order; and that which remaineth thereof, let it be projected from[8] the degree of the ascendent, and where that number endeth, there is a part of the vowel of the first letter.[9] Begin therefore to calculate the vowels of these letters, according to their number and order; and the vowel which falleth in the place of the star, which is the first in order, the same vowel is attributed to the first letter.

Then afterwards thou shalt finde the part of the second letter, by subtracting the degree of a star which is the second in order from the first star; and that which remaineth, cast[10] from the ascendant. And this is the part from which thou shalt begin the calculation of the vowels; and that vowel which falleth upon the second star, the same is the vowel of the second letter. And so consequently maist thou search out the vowels of the following letters alwaies, by subtracting the degree of the following star, from the degree of the star next preceding and going before. And so also all calculations and numerations in the names of the good spirits, ought to be made according to the succession of the signes.[11] And in calculating the names of the evil spirits, where in the names of the good spirits is taken the degree of the eleventh House, in these ought to be taken the degree of the twelfth House. And all numerations and calculations may be made with the succession of the signes, by taking the beginning from the degree of the tenth House.

But in all extractions by tables, the vowels are placed after another maner. In the first place therefore is taken the certain number of letters making the name it self, and is thus numbred from the beginning of the columne of the first letter, or whereupon the name is extracted; and the letter on which this number falleth, is referred to the first letter of the name, extracted by taking the distance of the one from the other, according to the order of the Alphabet. But the number of that distance is projected from the

---

[7] I have inserted a sentence break here to facilitate comprehension; a colon occurs here in the original. Further sentence breaks will be referred to as "SB."

[8] In other words, added to.

[9] SB. A colon occurs here in the original.

[10] Count from the ascendant.

[11] Zodiacal signs.

beginning of his columne; and where it endeth, there is part of the first vowel.[12] From thence therefore thou shalt calculate the vowels themselves, in their own number and order, in the same columne; and the vowel which shall fall upon the first letter of a name, the same shall be attributed to that name.

Now thou shalt finde the following vowels, by taking the distance from the precedent vowel to the following: and so consequently according to the succession of the Alphabet.[13] And the number of that distance is to be numbered from the beginning of his own columne; and where he shall cease,[14] there is the part of the vowel sought after. From thence therefore must you calculate the vowels, as we have above said; and those vowels which shall fall upon their own letters, are to be attributed unto them: if therefore any vowel shall happen to fall upon a vowel, the former must give place to the latter: and this you are to understand only of the good spirits. In the evil also you may proceed in the same way; except only, that you make the numerations after a contrary and backward order, contrary to the succession of the Alphabet, and contrary to the order of the columnes (that is to say) in ascending.

The name of good Angels, and of every man, which we have taught how to finde out, in our third book of Occult Philosophy, according to that maner, is of no little Authority, nor of a mean foundation. But now we will give unto thee some other ways, illustrated with no vain reasons. One [method] whereof is, by taking in the figure of the nativity, the five places of Hylech:[15] which being noted, the characters of the letters are projected in their order and number from the beginning of *Aries*; and those letters which fall upon the degrees of the said places, according to their order and dignity disposed and aspected, do make the name of an Angel.

---

[12] SB. A colon occurs here in the original.

[13] In other words, count off that number of letters in the alphabet. When doing this, remember that the alphabet then was not as large as it is today. So "I" and "J" are considered the same letter, and "V," "U," and "W" are also the same letter (following Latin practice).

[14] Where the count reaches.

[15] Sometimes spelled "hyleg." There are five hylegical "parts" or places in the astrological chart. The parts, of which there are a number, formed an important part of Arab and mediaeval astrology. Each part was a position in the heavens, calculated by reference to the position of various planets. The best known was the Part of Fortune. Here they are used to select appropriate letters.

There is also another way, wherein they do take Almutel,[16] which is the ruling and governing stars over the aforesaid five places; and the projection[17] is to be made from the degree of the ascendant; which is done by gathering together the letters falling upon Almutel: which being placed in order, according to their dignity, do make the name of an Angel.

There is furthermore another way used, and very much had in observation from the Egyptians, by making their calculation from the degree of the ascendant, and by gathering together the letters according to the Almutel of the eleventh House; which House they call a good *Dæmon*:[18] which being placed according to their dignities, the names of the Angels are constituted.

Now the names of the evil Angels are known after the like maner, except only that the projections must be performed contrary to the course and order of the succession of the signes, so that whereas in seeking the names of good spirits, we are to calculate from the beginning of *Aries*; contrariwise, in attaining the names of the evil, we ought to account from the beginning of *Libra*. And whereas in the good spirits we number from the degree of the ascendant; contrarily, in the evil, we must calculate from the degree of the seventh House. But according to the Egyptians, the name of an Angel is collected according to the Almutel of the twelfth House, which they call an evil spirit.

[GENERATING THE CHARACTERS AND IMAGES OF THE SPIRITS]

Now all those rites, which are elsewhere already by us delivered in our third book of Occult Philosophy, may be made by the characters[19] of any language. In all which (as we have abovesaid) there is a mystical and divine number, order and figure; from whence it cometh to pass, that the same spirit may be called by divers names. But others are discovered from the name of the spirit himself, of the good or evil, by tables formed to this purpose.[20]

---

[16] Or Almutez, the prevailing or ruling planet in a horoscope, also called the Lord of the Figure. It is through this calculation that the name of your personal guardian angel may be derived.

[17] The count around the horoscopic circle.

[18] The House of the Daemon. Note the spelling "daemon" in the sense of the guardian angel or daemon of Plato, rather than "demon," or fallen angel.

[19] Any alphabet may be used; not just Hebrew.

[20] Texts often show variants or even completely different names for the same

Now these celestial characters do consist of lines and heads: the heads are six, according to the six magnitudes of the stars, whereunto the planets also are reduced. The first magnitude holdeth a Star, with the Sun, or a Cross. The second with Jupiter a circular point. The third holdeth with Saturn, a semicircle, a triangle, either crooked, round, or acute. The fourth with Mars, a little stroke penetrating the line, either square, straight, or oblique. The fifth with Venus and Mercury, a little stroke or point with a tail, ascending or descending. The sixth with the Moon, a point made black. All which you may see in the ensuing table. The heads then being posited according to the site of the Stars in the figure of Heaven, then the lines are to be drawn out, according to the congruency or agreement of their natures. And this you are to understand of the fixed Stars. But in the erecting of the Planets, the lines are drawn out, the heads being posited according to their course and nature amongst themselves.

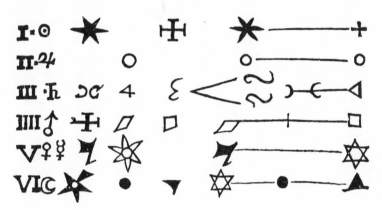

When therefore a character is to be found of any celestial Image ascending in any degree or face of a signe, which do consist of Stars of the same magnitude and nature; then the number of these Stars being posited according to their place and order, the lines are drawn after the similitude of the Image signified, as copiously as the same can be done.

---

spirit. These names are often generated from tables of letters. This is one of the reasons why John Dee was so obsessed with large tables of letters given him through the scrying of Edward Kelley, because he hoped this would give him the keys to words of power and specific angel and spirit names.

But the Characters which are extracted according to the name of a spirit, are composed by the table following, by giving to every letter that name which agreeth unto him, out of the table; which although it may appear easie to those that apprehend it, yet there is herein no small difficulty.[21] To wit, when the letter of a name falleth upon the line of letters or figures, that we may know which figure or which letter is to be taken. And this may be thus known: for if a letter falleth upon the line of letters, consider of what number this letter may be in the order of the name; as the second, or the third; then how many letters that name containeth; as five or seven; and multiply these numbers one after another by themselves, and treble the product: then cast[22] the whole (being added together) from the beginning of the letters, according to the succession of the Alphabet: and the letter upon which that number shall happen to fall, ought to be placed for the character of that spirit. But if any letter of a name fall on the line of figures, it is thus to be wrought. Take the number how many this letter is in order of the name, and let it be multiplied by that number of which this letter is in the order of the Alphabet; and being added together, divide it by nine, and the remainder sheweth the figure or number to be placed in the character: and this may be put either in a Geometrical or Arithmetical figure of number; which notwithstanding ought not to exceed the number of nine, or nine Angles.[23]

---

[21] This technique uses the letters of the spirit's name to help compose its seal. SB.

[22] Count.

[23] The following table shows the 24 constituent parts of a typical spirit's character. They are also alphabetic equivalences for the letters of the names of good spirits. The second table shows the 27 constituent parts of the characters of evil spirits (some images corresponding to the description of such spirits. They also function as alphabetic equivalences for the letters of the names of evil spirits.

THE CHARACTERS OF GOOD SPIRITS.

A simple point.

Round.

Starry.

Straight standing line.

Lying.

Oblique.

Line crooked like a bow.

Like waves.

Toothed.

Intersection right.

Inherent.

Adhering Separate.

Obliq[ue]; intersection simple.

[Mixed].

Manifold.

Perpendicular right dexter

Sinister.†

Neuter.

A whole figure.

Broken.

Half.

A letter inhering.

Adhering.

Separate.

---

† Left-handed.

The Characters of evil Spirits.

A right line.

Crooked.

Reflexed.

A simple figure.

Penetrate.

Broken.

A right letter.

Retrograde.

Invers'd.

Flame.

Winde.

Water.

A mass.

Rain.

Clay.

A flying thing.

A creeping thing.

A serpent.

An eye.

A hand.

A foot.

A crown.

A crest.

Horns.

A scepter.   A sword.   A scourge.

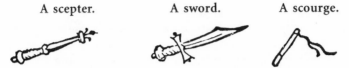

But the Characters which are understood by the revelation of Spirits, take their vertue from thence; because they are, as it were, certain hidden seals, making the harmony of some divinity: either they are signes of a Covenant entred into, and of promised and plighted faith, or of obedience. And those Characters cannot by any other means be searched out.

[The Visible Appearance of Spirits]

Moreover, besides these Characters, there are certain familiar Figures & Images of evil Spirits, under which forms they are wont to appear, and yield obedience to them that invoke them. And all these Characters or Images may be seen by the table following, according to the course of the letters constituting the names of Spirits themselves: so that if in any letter there is found more then the name of one Spirit, his Image holdeth the pre-eminence, the others imparting their own order.[24] So that they which are the first orders, to them is attributed the head, the upper part of the body, according to their own figure: those which are the lowest, do possess the thighs and feet; so also the middle letters do attribute like to themselves the middle parts of the body, or give the parts that fit. But if there happen any contrariety, that letter which is the stronger in the number shall bear rule: and if they are equal, they all impart equal things. Furthermore, if any name shall obtain any notable Character or Instrument out of the Table, he shall likewise have the same character in the Image.

We may also attain to the knowledge of the dignities[25] of the evil Spirits, by the same Tables of Characters and Images: for upon what spirit soever there falleth any excellent signe or instrument out of the Table of Characters, he possesseth that dignity. As if there shall be a Crown, it sheweth a Kingly dignity; if a Crest or Plume, a Dukedome; if a Horn, a County; if without these there be a Scepter, Sword, or forked Instrument, it sheweth Rule and Authority. Likewise out of the Table of Images you shall finde

---

[24] SB. A colon occurs here in the original.
[25] Office or place in the hierarchy of spirits.

them which bear the chief Kingly dignity: from the Crown judge dignity;[26] and from the Instruments, Rule and Authority. Lastly, they which bear an humane shape and figure, have greater dignity then those which appear under the Forms and Images of Beasts; they also who ride, do excel them which appear on foot. And thus according to all their commixtures, you may judge the dignity and excellency of Spirits, one before another. Moreover, you must understand, that the Spirits of the inferiour order, of what dignity soever they be, are alwaies subject to the Spirits of the superiour order: so also, that it is not incongruent for their Kings and Dukes to be Subject and Minister to the presidents of the superiour order.

The Shapes Familiar to the Spirits of Saturn.

ħ

They appear for the most part with a tall, lean, and slender body, with an angry countenance, having four faces; one in the hinder part of the head, one on the former part of the head, and on each side nosed or beaked: there likewise appeareth a face on each knee, or a black shining colour: their motion is the moving of the winde, with a kinde of earthquake: their signe is white earth, whiter then any Snow.[27]

The particular forms are,

- A King having a beard, riding on a Dragon.
- An Old man with a beard.
- An Old woman leaning on a staffe.
- A Hog.
- A Dragon.
- An Owl.
- A black Garment.
- A Hooke or Sickle.
- A Juniper-tree.

---

[26] In other words, a spirit who appears wearing a crown, or has this image as part of his seal, indicates that he is a king.

[27] The importance of these descriptions is that it enables the magician or karcist to readily identify the type of spirit from its appearance, because the spirit who appears is not always the spirit that has been called.

The Familiar Forms to the Spirits of Jupiter.

$$\text{♃}$$

The Spirits of Jupiter do appear with a body sanguine and choler-ick,[28] of a middle stature, with a horrible fearful motion; but with a milde countenance, a gentle speech, and of the colour of Iron. The motion of them is flashings of Lightening and Thunder; their signe is, there will appear men about the circle, who shall seem to be devoured of Lions.[29]

Their particular forms are,

- A King with a Sword drawn, riding on a Stag.
- A Man wearing a Mitre in long rayment.[30]
- A Maid with a Laurel-Crown adorned with Flowers,
- A Bull.
- A Stag.
- A Peacock.
- An azure Garment.[31]
- A Sword.
- A Box-tree.[32]

The Familiar Forms of the Spirits of Mars.

$$\text{♂}$$

They appear in a tall body, cholerick, a filthy countenance, of colour brown, swarthy or red, having horns like Harts horns, and Griphins claws, bellowing like wilde Bulls. Their Motion is like fire burning; their signe Thunder and Lightning about the Circle.

Their particular shapes are,

- A King armed riding upon a Wolf.
- A Man armed.

---

[28] Literally "bloody and fiery," but here referring to the four "humours" of mediaeval European medicine.

[29] Traditionally the spirits attempt to frighten the occupants of the circle with fearsome sights.

[30] Margin note: *Homo mitratus.*

[31] Margin note: *Azurino vestis.*

[32] Margin note: *Buxus.*

- A Woman holding a buckler[33] on her thigh.
- A Hee-goat.
- A Horse.
- A Stag.
- A red Garment.
- Wool.
- A Cheeslip.[34]

Shapes Familiar to the Spirits of the Sun.

The Spirits of the Sun do for the most part appear in a large, full and great body sanguine and gross, in a gold colour, with the tincture of blood. Their motion is as the Lightning of Heaven; their signe is to move the person to sweat that calls them.

But their particular forms are,

- A King having a Scepter riding on a Lion.
- A King crowned.
- A Queen with a Scepter.
- A Bird.
- A Lion.
- A Cock.
- A yellow or golden Garment.
- A Scepter.
- Caudatus.

Familiar Shapes of the Spirits of Venus.

They do appear with a fair body, of middle stature, with an amiable and pleasant countenance, of colour white or green, the upper part golden. The motion of them is as it were a most clear Star. For their signe, there will seem to be maids playing without the Circle,[35] which will provoke and allure him that calleth them to play.

---

[33] Shield.
[34] Margin note: *Multiceps.*
[35] Outside the circle.

But their particular forms are,

- A King with a Scepter riding upon a Camel.[36]
- A Maid clothed and dressed beautifully.
- A Maid naked.
- A Shee-goat.
- A Camel.
- A Dove.
- A white or green Garment.
- Flowers.
- The herb Savine.[37]

The Familiar Forms of the Spirits of Mercury.

The Spirits of *Mercury* will appear for the most part in a body of a middle stature, cold, liquid and moist, fair, and with an affable speech; in a humane shape and form, like unto a Knight armed; of colour clear and bright. The motion of them is as it were silver-coloured clouds. For their signe, they cause and bring horror and fear unto him that calls them.

But their particular shapes are,

- A King riding upon a Bear.
- A fair Youth.
- A Woman holding a distaffe.[38]
- A Dog.
- A Shee-bear.
- A Magpie.
- A Garment of sundry changeable colours.
- A Rod.
- A little staffe.

---

[36] The number of references to the camel in these descriptions suggests a Middle Eastern origin for these spirit descriptions.

[37] A kind of juniper.

[38] A weaving staff, part of a spinning wheel.

The Forms Familiar to the Spirits of the Moon.

☽

They will for the most part appear in a great and full body, soft and phlegmatique,[39] of colour like a black obscure cloud, having a swelling countenance, with eyes red and full of water, a bald head, and teeth like a wilde boar. Their motion is as it were an exceeding great tempest of the Sea. For their signe, there will appear an exceeding great rain about the Circle.

And their particular shapes are,

- A King like an Archer riding upon a Doe.
- A little Boy.
- A Woman-hunter with a bow and arrows.[40]
- A Cow.
- A little Doe.
- A Goose.
- A Garment green or silver-coloured.
- An Arrow.
- A Creature having many feet.

[MAKING PENTACLES AND SIGILS]

But we now come to speak of the holy and sacred Pentacles and Sigils. Now these pentacles, are as it were certain holy signes preserving us from evil chances and events, and helping and assisting us to binde, exterminate, and drive away evil spirits, and alluring the good spirits, and reconciling them unto us. And these pentacles do consist either of Characters of the good spirits of the superiour order, or of sacred pictures of holy letters or revelations, with apt and fit versicles,[41] which are composed either of Geometrical figures and holy names of God, according to the course and maner of many of them; or they are compounded of all of them, or very many of them mixt.

And the Characters which are useful for us to constitute and make the pentacles, they are the Characters of the good Spirits, especially and chiefly of the good spirits of the first and second

---

[39] Sluggish. One of the four "humours" or temperaments.

[40] Diana the huntress.

[41] Verses, liturgy, or conjurations.

order, and sometimes also of the third order. And this kinde of Characters are especially to be named holy; and then those Characters which we have above called holy. What Character soever therefore of this kinde is to be instituted, we must draw about him a double circle, wherein we must write the name of his Angel:[42] and if we will adde some divine name congruent with his Spirit and Office, it will be of the greater force and efficacy. And if we will draw about him any angular figure, according to the maner of his numbers, that also shall be lawful to be done. But the holy pictures which do make the pentacles, are they which everywhere are delivered unto us in the Prophets and sacred Writings, as well of the old as of the new Testament. Even as the figure of the Serpent hanging on the cross,[43] and such-like; whereof very many may be found out of the visions of the Prophets, as of *Esaias*,[44] *Daniel*, *Esdras*[45] and others, and also out of the revelation of the *Apocalypse*. And we have spoken of them in our third book of Occult Philosophy, where we have made mention of holy things.

Therefore when any picture is posited of any of these holy Images, let the circle be drawn round about it on each side thereof, wherein let there be written some divine name, that is apt and conformed to the effect of that figure, or else there may be written about it some versicle taken out of part of the body of holy Scripture, which may desire to ascertain or deprecate the desired effect. As, if a pentacle were to be made to gain victory or revenge against ones enemies, as wel[l] visible as invisible, The figure may be taken out of the second book of the *Macchabees:* that is to say, a hand holding a golden Sword drawn, about which let there be written the versicle there contained; To wit, *Take the holy Sword, the gift of God, wherewith thou shalt slay the adversaries of my people Israel.*[46] Or also there may be written about it a versicle of the fifth *Psalm: In this is the strength of thy arm: before thy face there is death*; or some other such-like versicle.

But if you will write any divine name about the figure, then let some name be taken that signifies Fear, a Sword, Wrath, the Revenge of God, or some such-like name congruent and agree-

---

[42] His controlling angel.

[43] Margin note: *The brazen serpent set up in the wilderness.*

[44] Isaiah.

[45] One of the books of the Apocrypha.

[46] Margin note: *Accipe gladium sanctum munus a Deo, in quo concides adversarios populi mei Israel.* Quoted from 2 Maccabees 15:16.

ing with the effect desired. And if there shall be written any Angular figure, let him be taken according to the reason and rule of the numbers, as we have taught in our second book of Occult Philosophy, where we have treated of the numbers, and of the like operations. And of this sort there are two pentacles of sublime vertue and great power, very useful and necessary to be used in the consecration of experiments and Spirits: one whereof is that in the first chapter of *Apocalypse*.[47] To wit, a figure of the Majesty of God sitting upon a Throne, having in his mouth a two-edged Sword, as there it is written, about which let there be written, *I am Alpha & Omega, the beginning and the end, which is, and which was, and which is to come, the Almighty. I am the first and the last, who am living, and was dead, and behold I live for ever and ever; and I have the keys of death and hell.*[48] Then there shall be written about it these three versicles.

> *Manda Deus virtuti tuæ*, &c.[49]
> *Give commandment, O God, to thy strength.*
> *Confirm, Oh God, thy work in us.*
> *Let them be as dust before the face of the winde. And let the Angel of the Lord scatter them. Let all their wayes be darkness and uncertain. And let the Angel of the Lord persecute them.*

Moreover, let there be written about it the ten general names, which are, *El, Elohim, Elohe, Zebaoth, Elion, Escerchie, Adonay, Jah, Tetragrammaton, Saday.*[50]

There is another pentacle, the figure whereof is like unto *a Lambe slain, having seven eyes, and seven horns, and under his feet a book sealed with seven seals*, as it is said in the 5. *chap*. of the

---

[47] SB. A semicolon occurs here in the original.

[48] Margin note: *Ego sum primus & novissimus, vivus & sui mortuus: & ecce sum vivens in secula seculorum; & habeo claves mortis & inferni.*

[49] All biblical quotes are from the Vulgate, the Latin version of the Bible which was the standard version used by Agrippa and his contemporaries, and not superseded in the English speaking world until the King James English translation of 1611. In many ways, the Vulgate is more accurate than the King James version. For example, the Vulgate does not confuse the word *demon* with *diabolus*, a confusion in the King James version that led to much unjustified persecution and pain.

[50] All of these are Hebrew names of god, although "Escerchie" is rather corrupted.

Apocalypse.[51] Whereabout let there be written this versicle: *Behold the Lion hath overcome of the Tribe of Judah, the root of David. I will open the book, and unloose the seven seals thereof.* And one other versicle: *I saw Satan like lightning fall down from heaven. Behold, I have given you power to tread upon Serpents and Scorpions, and over all the power of your enemies, and nothing shall be able to hurt you.*[52] And let there be also written about it the ten general names, as aforesaid.

But those Pentacles which are thus made of figures and names, let them keep this order: for when any figure is posited, conformable to any number, to produce any certain effect or vertue, there must be written thereupon, in all the several Angles, some Divine name, obtaining the force and efficacie of the thing desired.[53] Yet so nevertheless, that the name which is of this sort do consist of just so many letters, as the Figure may constitute a number; or of so many letters of a name, as joyned together amongst themselves, may make the number of a Figure; or by any number which may be divided without any superfluity or diminution.[54] Now such a name being found, whether it be onely one name or more, or divers names, it is to be written in all the several Angles in the Figure: but in the middle of the Figure let the revolution of the name be whole and totally placed, or at least principally.

Oftentimes also we constitute Pentacles, by making the revolution of some kinde of name, in a square Table,[55] and by drawing about it a single or double Circle, and by writing therein some holy Versicle competent and befitting this name, or from which that name is extracted. And this is the way of making the Pentacles, according to their several distinct forms and fashions, which we may as we please either multiply or commix[56] together by course among themselves, to work the greater efficacie, and extension and enlargement of force and vertue.

As, if a deprecation should be made for the overthrow and destruction of ones enemies, then we are to minde and call to remembrance how God destroyed the whole face of the earth in

---

[51] Revelation 5:6.

[52] The use of biblical texts, particularly in Latin, to give magical power was quite common.

[53] SB. A colon occurs here in the original.

[54] In other words, divided evenly without any fraction left over.

[55] Using a table of letters to trace out the name.

[56] Add or mix together.

the deluge of waters; and the destruction of Sodom and Gomorrha, by raining down fire and brimstone; likewise, how God overthrew Pharaoh and his host in the Red-Sea: and to call to minde if any other malediction or curse be found in holy Writ.[57] And thus in things of the like sort. So likewise in deprecating and praying against perils and dangers of waters, we ought to call to remembrance the saving of Noah in the deluge of waters, the passing of the children of Israel thorow[58] the Red-sea; and also we are to minde how Christ walked upon the waters, and saved the ship in danger to be cast away with the tempest; and how he commanded the windes and the waves, and they obeyed him; and also, that he drew *Peter* out of the water, being in danger of drowning: and the like.

And lastly, with these we invoke and call upon some certain holy names of God, God; to wit, such as are significative to accomplish our desire, and accommodated to the desired effect: as, if it be to overthrow enemies, we are to invoke and call upon the names of wrath, revenge, fear, justice, and fortitude of God: and if we would avoid and escape any evil or danger, we then call upon the names of mercy, defence, salvation, fortitude, goodness, and such-like names of God. When also we pray unto God that he would grant unto us our desires, we are likewise to intermix therewith the name of some good spirit, whether one onely, or more, whose office it is to execute our desires: and sometimes also we require some evil spirit to restrain or compel, whose name likewise we intermingle; and that rightly especially, if it be to execute any evil work; as revenge, punishment, or destruction.

Furthermore, if there be any Versicle in the Psalms, or in any other part of holy Scripture, that shall seem congruent and agreeable to our desire, the same is to be mingled with our prayers. Now after Prayer hath been made unto God, it is expedient afterwards to make an Oration to that executioner whom in our precedent prayer unto God we have desired should administer unto us, whether one or more, or whether he be an Angel, or Star, or Soul, or any of the noble Angels. But this kinde of Oration ought to be composed according to the Rules which we have delivered in the second book of Occult Philosophy, where we have treated of the manner of the composition of Inchantments.

---

[57] Using appropriate verses from scripture to achieve your ends.
[58] Through.

[BINDING SPIRITS]

You may know further, that these kinde of bonds[59] have a threefold difference: for the first bond is, when we conjure by Natural things: the second is compounded of Religious mysteries, by Sacraments, Miracles, and things of this sort: and the third is constituted by Divine names, and holy Sigils. And by these kinde of bonds, we may binde not onely spirits, but also all other creatures whatsoever; as animals, tempests,[60] burnings, floods of water, and the force and power of Arms. Oftentimes also we use these bonds aforesaid, not onely by Conjuration, but sometimes also using the means of Deprecation and Benediction. Moreover, it conduceth much to this purpose, to joyn some sentence of holy Scripture, if any shall be found convenient hereunto: as, in the Conjuration of Serpents, by commemorating the curse of the Serpent in the earthly Paradise, and the setting up of the Serpent in the wilderness; and further adding that Versicle, *Thou shalt walk upon the Asp and the Basilisk,* &c.[61] Superstition also is of much prevalency herein, by the translation of some Sacramental Rites, to binde that which we intend to hinder; as, the Rites of Excommunication, of Sepulchres, Funerals, Buryings,[62] and the like.

[CONSECRATION OF RITUAL EQUIPMENT]

And now we come to treat of the Consecrations which men ought to make upon all instruments and things necessary to be used in this Art: and the vertue of this Consecration most chiefly consists in two things; to wit, in the power of the person consecrating, and by the vertue of the prayer by which the Consecration is made. For in the person consecrating, there is required holiness of Life, and power of sanctifying: both which are acquired by Dignification[63] and Initiation. And that the person himself should with a firm and undoubted faith believe the vertue, power, and efficacie hereof. And then in the Prayer it self by which this Consecration is made, there is required the like holiness; which either solely consisteth in

---

[59] Binding is an important stage in the procedure of evoking spirits.

[60] Margin note: *Incendia*; Envie and Malice.

[61] Margin note: *Super aspidem & basiliscum ambulabis, &c.* Quoted from the Psalms.

[62] In this sense funeral rites were designed to bind the spirit of the deceased so that it did not interfere with the living.

[63] Ennoblement of the office conferred upon someone such as a priest.

the prayer it self, as, if it be by divine inspiration ordained to this purpose, such as we have in many places of the holy Bible; or that it be hereunto instituted through the power of the Holy Spirit, in the ordination of the Church. Otherwise there is in the Prayer a Sanctimony, which is not onely by it self, but by the commemoration[64] of holy things; as, the commemoration of holy Scriptures, Histories, Works, Miracles, Effects, Graces, Promises, Sacraments and Sacramental things, and the like. Which things, by a certain similitude, do seem properly or improperly to appertain to the thing consecrated.

There is used also the invocation of some Divine names, with the consignation of holy Seals, and things of the like sort, which do conduce to sanctification and expiation; such as are the Sprinkling with Holy-Water, Unctions with holy Oyl,[65] and odoriferous Suffumigations[66] appertaining to holy Worship. And therefore in every Consecration there is chiefly used the Benediction and Consecration of Water, Oyl, Fire, and Fumigations, used everywhere with holy Wax-lights or Lamps burning: for without Lights no Sacrament is rightly performed. This therefore is to be known, and firmly observed, That if any Consecration be to be made of things profane, in which there is any pollution of defilement, then an exorcising and expiation of those things ought to precede the consecration. Which things being so made pure, are more apt to receive the influences of the Divine vertues.

We are also to observe, that in the end of every Consecration, after that the prayer is rightly performed, the person consecrating ought to bless the thing consecrated, by breathing out some words, with divine vertue and power of the present Consecration, with the commemoration of his vertue and authority, that it may be the more duely performed, and with an earnest and intentive minde. And therefore we will here lay down some examples hereof, whereby the way to the whole perfection hereof may the more easily be made to appear unto you.

So then, in the consecration of water, we ought to commemorate how that God hath placed the firmament in the midst of the waters, and in what maner that God placed the fountain of waters in the earthly Paradise, from whence sprang four holy rivers, which watered the whole earth. Likewise we are to call to remembrance in

---

[64] The repetition and telling of great myths or holy stories.

[65] Oil.

[66] Burning of incense.

what manner God made the water to be the instrument of executing his justice in the destruction of the Gyants[67] in the general deluge over all the earth, and in the overthrow of the host of Pharaoh in the Red-sea; also, how God led his own people thorow[68] the midst of the Sea on dry ground, and through the midst of the river of Jordan; and likewise how marvelously he drew forth water out of the stony rock in the wilderness; and how at the prayer of Samson, he caused a fountain of running water to flow out of the cheek-tooth of the jaw-bone of an ass:[69] and likewise, how God hath made waters the instrument of his mercy, and of salvation, for the expiation of Original sin: also, how Christ was baptized in Jordan, and hath hereby sanctified and cleansed the waters. Moreover, certain divine names are to be invocated, which are conformable hereunto; as, that God is a living fountain, living water, the fountain of mercy; and names of the like kinde.

And likewise in the consecration of fire, we are to commemorate how that God hath created the fire to be an instrument to execute his justice, for punishment, vengeance, and for the expiation of sins: also, when God shall come to judge the world, he will command a conflagration of fire to go before him. And we are to call to remembrance in what manner God appeared to Moses in the burning bush; and also, how he went before the children of Israel in a pillar of fire; and that nothing can be duely offered, sacrificed, or sanctified, without fire; and how that God instituted fire to be kept continually burning in the Tabernacle of the Covenant; and how miraculously he re-kindled the same, being extinct, and preserved it elsewhere from going out, being hidden under the waters: and things of this sort. Likewise the Names of God are to be called upon which are consonant hereunto; as, it is read in the Law and the Prophets, that God is a consuming fire: and if there be any of the Divine names which signifies fire, or such-like names; as, the glory of God, the light of God, the splendor and brightness of God.

And likewise in the consecration of Oyl and Perfumes, we are to call to remembrance such holy things as are pertinent to this purpose, which we read in *Exodus* of the holy anoynting oyl, and divine names significant hereunto, such as is the name Christ,

---

[67] Giants, sometimes seen as the offspring of the "sons of god and the daughters of men" (Genesis 6:2–4).

[68] Through.

[69] Judges 15:19.

which signifies anoynted: and what mysteries there are hereof; as that in the *Revelation*,[70] of the two Olive-trees distilling holy oyl into the lamps that burn before the face of God: and the like.

And the blessing of the lights, wax, and lamps, is taken from the fire, and the altar which containeth the substance of the flame: and what other such similitudes as are in mysteries; as that of the seven candlesticks and lamps burning before the face of God.

These therefore are the Consecrations which first of all are necessary to be used in every kinde of devotion, and ought to precede it, and without which nothing in holy Rites can be duely performed.

In the next place now we shall shew unto you the consecration of Places, Instruments, and such-like things.

Therefore when you would consecrate any Place or Circle, you ought to take the prayer of Solomon used in the dedication of the Temple:[71] and moreover, you must bless the place with the sprinkling of Holy-water, and with Fumigations; by commemorating in the benediction holy mysteries; such as these are: The sanctification of the throne of God, of mount Sinai, of the Tabernacle of the Covenant, of the Holy of holies,[72] of the temple of Jerusalem. Also, the sanctification of mount Golgotha, by the crucifying of Christ; the sanctification of the Temple of Christ; of mount Tabor, by the transfiguration and ascension of Christ: and the like. And by invocating divine names which are significant hereunto; such as the Place of God, the Throne of God, the Chayr[73] of God, the Tabernacle of God, the Altar of God, the Habitation of God, and such-like divine names of this sort, which are to be written about the Circle or place to be consecrated.

And in the consecrations of instruments, and of all other things whatsoever that are serviceable to this Art, you shall proceed after the same manner, by sprinkling the same with Holy-water, perfuming the same with holy Fumigations, anoynting it with holy Oyl, sealing it with some holy Sigil, and blessing it with prayer; and by commemorating holy things out of the sacred Scriptures, Religion, and Divine names which shall be found agreeable to the thing that is to be consecrated: as for examples sake, in consecrating a sword, we are to call to remembrance that in the Gospel, *He that*

---

[70] Revelation 11:4.

[71] 2 Chronicles 6:12–42.

[72] Margin note: *Sanctum sanctorum.*

[73] Chair or throne.

hath two coats, &c.[74] and that place in the second [Book] of the *Macchabees*,[75] That a sword was divinely and miraculously sent to *Judas Macchabeus*. And if there be any thing of the like in the Prophets; as that place, *Take unto you two-edged Swords*, &c.[76]

In like maner you shall consecrate experiments and books, and whatsoever of the like nature, as is contained in writings, pictures, and the like, by sprinkling, perfuming, anointing, sealing, and blessing with holy commemorations, and calling to remembrance the sanctifications of mysteries; As, the sanctifying of the Tables of the ten Commandments, which were delivered to *Moses* by God in Mount *Sinai*; The sanctification of the Testaments of God, the Old and New; The sanctification of the Law, and of the Prophets, and Scriptures, which are promulgated by the holy Ghost. Moreover, there is to be commemorated such divine names as are fit and convenient hereunto; as these are: The Testament of God, The book of God, The book of life, The knowledge of God, The wisdom of God; and the like. And with such kinde of Rites is the personal consecration performed.

There is furthermore, besides these, another Rite of consecration, of wonderful power, and much efficacy; And this is out of the kindes of superstitions: That is to say, when the Rite of consecration or collection of any Sacrament in the Church is transferred to that thing which we would consecrate.

It is to be known also, that Vowes, Oblations,[77] and Sacrifice, have the power of consecration, as wel[l] real as personal; and they are as it were certain covenants and conventions between those names with which they are made, and us who make them, strongly cleaving to our desire and wished effect: As, when we dedicate, offer, and sacrifice, with certain names or things; as, Fumigations, Unctions,[78] Rings, Images, Looking-glasses;[79] and things less material, as Deities, Sigils, Pentacles, Inchantments, Orations, Pictures, and Scriptures: of which we have largely spoken in our third book of Occult Philosophy.

---

[74] Margin note: *Qui habet duas tunicas.* Matthew 10:10.

[75] One of the books of the *Apocrypha*.

[76] Margin note: *Accipte vobis gladios bis acutos.*

[77] An offering to God, specifically of wine and bread.

[78] Anointing with oil for religious or ceremonial purposes.

[79] Here Agrippa means scrying glasses and stones rather than bedroom furniture.

[THE LIBER SPIRITUUM OR BOOK OF SPIRITS]

There is extant amongst those Magicians (who do most use the ministery of evil spirits) a certain Rite of invocating spirits by a Book to be consecrated before to that purpose; which is properly called, A book of Spirits;[80] whereof we shall now speak a few words. For this book is to be consecrated, a book of evil spirits, ceremoniously to be composed, in their name and order: whereunto they binde with a certain holy Oath, the ready and present obedience of the spirit[s] therein written.

Now this book is to be made of most pure and clean paper, that hath never been used before; which many do call *Virgin-paper*. And this book must be inscribed after this maner: that is to say, Let there be placed on the left side the image of the spirit, and on the right side his character, with the Oath above it, containing the name of the spirit, and his dignity and place, with his office and power. Yet very many do compose this book otherwise, omitting the characters or image: but it is more efficacious not to neglect any thing which conduceth to it.

Moreover, there is to be observed the circumstances of places, times, hours, according to the Stars which these spirits are under, and are seen to agree unto, their site, rite, and order being applied.

Which book being so written, and well bound, is to be adorned, garnished, and kept secure, with Registers and Seals, lest it should happen after the consecration to open in some place not intented, and indanger the operator.[81] Furthermore, this book ought to be kept as reverently as may be: for irreverence of minde causeth it to lose its vertue, with pollution and profanation.

Now this sacred book being thus composed according to the maner already delivered, we are then to proceed to the consecration thereof after a twofold way: one whereof is, That all and singular the spirits who are written in the book, be called to the Circle, according to the Rites and Order which we have before taught; and the book that is to be consecrated, let it be placed without[82] the Circle in a triangle. And in the first place, let there be read in the presence of the spirits all the Oathes which are written in that book; and then the book to be consecrated being placed without the Circle in a triangle there drawn, let all the spirits be compelled

---

[80] Margin note: *Liber Spirituum.*

[81] By inadvertently calling up the spirit bound to that page.

[82] Outside the circle.

to impose their hands where their images and characters are drawn, and to confirm and consecrate the same with a special and common Oath. Which being done, let the book be taken and shut, and preserved as we have before spoken, and let the spirits be licensed to depart, according to due rite and order.

There is another maner of consecrating a book of spirits, which is more easie, and of much efficacie to produce every effect, except that in opening this book the spirits do not always come visible. And this way is thus: Let there be made a book of spirits as we have before[83] set forth; but in the end thereof let there be written Invocations and Bonds, and strong Conjurations, wherewith every spirit may be bound. Then this book must be bound between two Tables[84] or Lamens,[85] and in the inside thereof let there be drawn the holy Pentacles of the Divine Majestie, which we have before set forth and described out of the *Apocalypse*: then let the first of them be placed in the beginning of the book, and the second at the end of the same.

This book being perfected after this maner, let it be brought in a clear and fair time, to a Circle prepared in a cross way,[86] according to the Art which we have before delivered; and there in the first place the book being opened, let it be consecrated to the rites and ways which we have before declared concerning Consecration. Which being done, let all the spirits be called which are written in the book, in their own order and place, by conjuring them thrice by the bonds described in the book, that they come unto that place within the space of three days, to assure their obedience, and confirm the same, to the book so to be consecrated. Then let the book be wrapped up in clean linen, and buried in the middle of the Circle,[87] and there fast stopped up: and then the Circle being destroyed, after the spirits are licensed, depart before the rising of the sun.[88]

And on the third day, about the middle of the night, return, and new make the Circle, and with bended knees make prayer and giving thanks unto God, and let a precious perfume be made, and open the hole, and take out the book; and so let it be kept, not

---

[83] Duplicate word "before" in original omitted here.

[84] Tables of letters, not wooden tables.

[85] A protective talisman to be worn as a breastplate.

[86] Crossroad.

[87] This seems a rather dubious procedure. The circle is designed to keep the spirits out. Its destruction and the subsequent request by the operator that the spirits come into its previous location, appears to destroy the "fortress" nature of the circle.

[88] SB. A colon occurs here in the original text.

opening the same. Then you shall license the spirits in their order, and destroying the Circle, depart before the sun rise. And this is the last rite and maner of consecrating, profitable to whatsoever writings and experiments, which do direct to spirits, placing the same between two holy Lamens or Pentacles, as before is shewn.

But the Operator, when he would work by the book thus consecrated, let him do it in a fair and clear season, when the spirits are least troubled; and let him place himself [89] towards the region of the spirits. Then let him open the book under a due Register; let him invoke the spirits by their Oath there described and confirmed, and by the name of their character and image, to that purpose which you desire: and, if there be need, conjure them by the bonds placed in the end of the book. And having attained your desired effect, then you shall license the spirits to depart.

[THE INVOCATION OF GOOD AND EVIL SPIRITS]

And now we shall come to speak concerning the invocation [90] of spirits, as well of the good spirits as of the bad.

The good spirits may be invocated of us, divers ways, and in sundry manners do offer themselves unto us. For they do openly speak to those that watch, and do offer themselves to our sight, [91] or do inform us in dreams by oracle of those things which are desired.

Whosoever therefore would call any good spirit, to speak or appear in sight, it behoveth them especially to observe two things: one whereof is about the disposition of the invocant; the other about those things which are outwardly to be adhibited [92] to the invocation, for the conformity of the spirits to be called. It behoveth therefore that the invocant himself be religiously disposed for many days to such a mystery. [93] In the first place therefore, he

---

[89] Facing toward the compass point from which the spirit is expected to come. The direction from which each spirit is expected to come is well documented in some grimoires.

[90] Although nowadays it is more common to speak of the invocation of gods/goddesses as opposed to the evocation of spirits, Agrippa's contemporaries used the two terms almost interchangeably.

[91] Invocation to visible appearance or their appearance in dreams were the two typical methods of communicating with spirits.

[92] Added or applied.

[93] In the sense of a mystical or religious rite.

ought to be confessed and contrite, both inwardly and outwardly, and rightly expiated, by daily washing himself with holy water. Moreover, the invocant ought to conserve himself all these days, chaste, abstinent, and to separate himself as much as may be done, from all perturbation of minde, and from all maner of forraign and secular business. Also, he shall observe fastings all these days, as much as shall seem convenient to him to be done. Also, let him daily between sun-rising and sun-setting, being clothed with a holy linen garment, seven times call upon God, and make a deprecation[94] to the Angels to be called according to the rule which we have before taught. Now the number of days of fasting and preparation, is commonly the time of a whole Lunation.[95] There is also another number observed amongst the Caballists, which is fourty days.

[PREPARATION OF THE PLACE OF WORKING]

Now concerning those things which do appertain to this Rite of Invocation, the first is, That a place be chosen, clean, pure, close, quiet, free from all maner of noise, and not subject to any strangers sight. This place must first be exorcised and consecrated: and let there be a table or altar placed therein, covered with clean white linen, and set towards the east: and on each side thereof, let there be set two consecrated wax-lights burning, the flame whereof ought not to go out all these days. In the middle of the altar, let there be placed Lamens, or the holy paper which we have before described, covered with pure fine linen; which is not to be opened until the end of these days of the Consecration. You shall also have in readiness a precious perfume, and pure anointing oyl; and let them be both kept consecrated. There must also a Censer be set on the head of the altar, wherein you shall kindle the holy fire, and make a perfume every day that you shall pray.

You shall also have a long garment of white linen, close before and behinde, which may cover the whole body and the feet, and girt about you with a girdle. You shall also have a veil of pure clean linen, and in the fore-part thereof let there be fixed golden or gilded Lamens, with the inscription of the name Tetragrammaton;[96] all which things are to be sanctified and consecrated in order. But you must not enter into the holy place, unless it be first washed,

---

[94] Plead or prayer.

[95] A lunar month or 28 days.

[96] The name of god, Yod-He-Vav-He.

and arayed with a holy garment; and then you shall enter into it with your feet naked. And when you enter therein, you shall sprinkle it with holy water: then you shall make a perfume upon the altar, and afterwards with bended knees pray before the altar as we have directed.

But in the end of these days, on the last day, you shall fast more strictly: and fasting on the day following, at the rising of the sun, you may enter into the holy place, using the ceremonies before spoken of, first by sprinkling your self, then with making a perfume, you shall signe[97] your self with holy oyl in the forehead, and anoint your eyes; using prayer in all these Consecrations. Then you shall open the holy Lamen, and pray before the altar upon your knees, as abovesaid: and then an invocation being made to the Angels, they will appear unto you, which you desire; which you shall entertain with a benign and chaste communication, and license them to depart.

[THE HOLY TABLE AND LAMEN]

Now the Lamen which is to be used to invoke any good spirit, you shall make after this maner; either in metal conformable, or in new wax, mixt with species and colours conformable: or it may be made in clean paper, with convenient colours: and the outward form or figure thereof may be square, circular, or triangular, or of the like sort, according to the rule of the numbers: in which there must be written the divine names, as well the general names as the special. And in the centre of the Lamen, let there be drawn a character of six corners;[98] in the middle whereof, let there be written the name and character of the Star, or of the Spirit his governour, to whom the good spirit that is to be called is subject. And about this character, let there be placed so many characters of five corners,[99] as the spirits we would call together at once. And if we shall call only one spirit, nevertheless there shall be made four Pentagones, wherein the name of the spirit or spirits, with their characters, is to be written. Now this table ought to be composed when the Moon in increasing, on those days and hours which then agree to the Spirit. And if we take a fortunate star herewith, it will

---

[97] Make the sign of the cross upon yourself, by touching forehead, belly and both shoulders in order.

[98] Margin note: *Hexagonus.*

[99] Margin note: *Pentagonus.*

be the better. Which Table being made in this manner, it is to be consecrated according to the rules above delivered.

And this is the way of making the general Table, serving for the invocation of all good spirits whatsoever. Nevertheless we may make special Tables congruent to every spirit, by the rule which we have above spoken of concerning holy Pentacles.

[ANOTHER RITE FOR CALLING FORTH SPIRITS]

And now we will declare unto you another Rite more easie to perform this thing: that is to say, Let the man that is to receive any Oracle from the good spirits, be chaste, pure, and confess'd. Then a place being prepared pure and clean, and covered everywhere with white linen, on the Lords day in the new of the moon let him enter into that place, clothed with clean white garments; and let him exorcize the place, and bless it, and make a Circle therein with a sanctified cole;[100] and let there be written in the uttermost part of the Circle the names of the Angels, and in the inner part thereof let there be written the mighty names of God: and let him place within the Circle, at the four angles of the world, the Censers for the perfumes.

Then let him enter the place fasting, and washed, and let him begin to pray towards the east this whole Psalm: *Beati inmaculati in via*, &c. *Blessed are the undefiled in the way*, &c.[101] by perfuming; and in the end deprecating the Angels, by the said divine names, that they will daign[102] to discover and reveal that which he desireth: and that let him do for six days, continuing washed and fasting. And on the seventh day, which is the Sabbath, let him, being washed and fasting, enter the Circle, and perfume it, and anoint himself with holy anointing oyl, by anointing his forehead, and upon both his eyes, and in the palms of his hands, and upon his feet. Then upon his knees let him say the Psalm aforesaid, with Divine and Angelical names.

Which being said, let him arise, and let him begin to walk about in a circuit within the said Circle from the east to the west, until he is wearied with a dizziness of his brain: let him fall down in the Circle, and there he may rest; and forthwith he shall be wrapt up in an ecstasie, and a spirit will appear unto him, which will inform him of

---

[100] Piece of coal used as a chalk.

[101] Margin note: Psal[m] 119.

[102] Deign.

all things. We must observe also, that in the Circle there ought to be four holy candles burning at the four parts of the world, which ought not to want light for the space of a whole week. And the maner of fasting must be such, that he abstain from all things having a life of Sense, and from those things which do proceed from them:[103] and let him onely drink pure running water: neither let him take any food till the going down of the sun. And let the perfume and the holy anointing oyl be made, as is set forth in *Exodus* and the other holy books of the Bible. It is also to be observed, that always as often as he enters into the Circle, he have upon his forehead a golden Lamen, upon which there must be written the name *Tetragrammaton*, as we have before spoken.

[ORACLES AND DREAMS]

But natural things, and their commixtures, do also belong unto us, and are conducing to receive Oracles from any spirit by a dream: which are either Perfumes, Unctions, and Meats or Drinks: which you may understand in our first book of Occult Philosophy.

But he that is willing always and readily to receive the Oracles of a Dream, let him make unto himself a Ring of the Sun or of Saturn for this purpose. There is also an Image to be made, of excellent efficacie and power to work this effect; which being put under his head when he goeth to sleep, doth effectually give true dreams of what things soever the minde hath before determined or consulted on. The Tables of Numbers do likewise confer to receive an Oracle, being duly formed under their own Constellations. And these things thou mayst know in the third book of Occult Philosophy.

Holy Tables and Papers do also serve to this effect, being specially composed and consecrated: such as is the Almadel of *Solomon*,[104] and the Table of the Revolution of the name *Tetragrammaton*. And those things which are of this kinde, and written unto these things, out of divers figures, numbers, holy pictures, with the inscriptions of the holy names of God and of Angels; the composition whereof is taken out of divers places of the holy Scriptures, Psalms, and Versicles, and other certain promises of the divine Revelation and Prophecies.

To the same effect do conduce holy prayers and imprecations,[105] as well unto God, as to the holy Angels and Heroes: the impre-

---

[103] Animal or animal products.

[104] An important grimoire which forms part of the *Lemegeton*.

[105] Invocations.

cations of which prayers are to be composed as we have before shewn, according to some religious similitude of Miracles, Graces, and the like, making mention of those things which we intend to do: as, out of the Old Testament, of the dream of *Jacob, Joseph, Pharaoh, Daniel,* and *Nebuchadnezzar:* if out of the New Testament, of the dream of *Joseph* the husband of the blessed virgin *Mary;* of the dream of the three Wise-men; of *John* the Evangelist sleeping upon the brest of our Lord: and whatsoever of the like kinde can be found in Religion, Miracles, and Revelations; as, the revelation of the Cross to *Helen,* the revelations of *Constantine* and *Charles* the Great, the revelations of *Bridget, Cyril, Methodius, Mechtild,*[106] *Joachim,*[107] *Merhir,* and such-like. According to which, let the deprecations be composed, if when he goeth to sleep it be with a firm intention: and the rest well disposing themselves, let them pray devoutly, and without doubt they will afford a powerful effect.

Now he that knoweth how to compose those things which we have now spoken of, he shall receive the most true Oracles of dreams. And this he shall do; observe those things which in the second book of Occult Philosophy are directed concerning this thing. He that is desirous therefore to receive an Oracle, let him abstain from supper and from drink, and be otherwise well disposed, his brain being free from turbulent vapours; let him also have his bed-chamber fair and clean, exorcised and consecrated if he will; then let him perfume the same with some convenient fumigation; and let him anoint his temples with some unguent efficacious hereunto,[108] and put a ring upon his finger, of the things above spoken of.[109] Let him take either some image, or holy table, or holy paper, and place the same under his head: then having made a devout prayer, let him go unto his bed, and meditating upon that thing which he desireth to know, let him so sleep; for so shall he receive a most certain and undoubted oracle by a dream, when the Moon goeth through that signe which was in the ninth House of his nativity, and also when she goeth through the signe of the ninth House of the Revolution of his nativity; and when she is in the ninth signe from the sign of perfection. And this is the way and means whereby we may obtain all Sciences and Arts

---

[106] A German saint (1207–1294) who wrote a commentary on the teachings of Joachim of Flores (ca 1145–1202).

[107] Joachim of Flores.

[108] The temples are particularly susceptible to psychoactive unguents.

[109] SB. A colon occurs here in the original.

whatsoever, suddenly and perfectly, with a true Illumination of our understanding;[110] although all inferiour familiar Spirits whatsoever do conduce to this effect; and sometimes also evil Spirits sensibly informing us Intrinsecally or Extrinsecally.

[CALLING FORTH SPIRITS TO A MAGIC CIRCLE]

But if we would call any evil Spirit to the Circle, it first behoveth us to consider, and to know his nature, to which of the Planets it agreeth, and what Offices[111] are distributed to him from that Planet; which being known, let there be sought out a place fit and proper for his invocation, according to the nature of the Planet, and the quality of the Offices of the said Spirit, as near as the same may be done: as, if their power be over the Sea, Rivers or Flouds, then let the place be chosen in the Shore; and so of the rest.

Then let there be chosen a convenient time, both for the quality of the Air, serene, clear, quiet, and fitting for the Spirits to assume bodies; as also of the quality and nature of the Planet, and of the Spirit, as to wit, on his day, or the time wherein he ruleth: he may be fortunate or infortunate, sometimes of the day, and sometimes of the night, as the Stars and Spirits do require. These things being considered, let there be a Circle framed in the place elected, as wel[l] for the defence of the Invocant, as for the confirmation of the Spirit.

And in the Circle it self there are to be written the divine general names, and those things which do yeild defence unto us; and with them, those divine names which do rule this Planet, and the Offices of the Spirit himself; there shall also be written therein, the names of the good Spirits which bear rule, and are able to binde and constrain that Spirit which we intend to call. And if we will any more fortifie and strengthen our Circle, we may adde Characters and Pentacles agreeing to the work; then also if we will, we may either within or without the Circle, frame an angular figure, with the inscription of such convenient numbers, as are congruent amongst themselves to our work; which are also to be known, according to maner of numbers and figures: of which in the second book of Occult Philosophy it is sufficiently spoken. Further, He is to be provided of lights, perfumes, unguents and medicines,[112] compounded according to the nature of the Planet

---

[110] This is also the objective of the *Notary Art*.

[111] In other words: What are his functions?

[112] Herbs.

and Spirit; which do partly agree with the Spirit, by reason of their natural and coelestial vertue; and partly are exhibited to the Spirit for religious and superstitious worship. Then he must be furnished with holy and consecrated things, necessary as wel[l] for the defence of the Invocant, and his fellows, as also serving for bonds to binde and constrain the Spirits; such as are either holy Papers, Lamens, Pictures, Pentacles, Swords, Scepters, Garments of convenient matter and colour, and things of the like sort.

Then when all these things are provided, and the Master and his fellows being in the Circle, in the first place let him consecrate the Circle, and all those things which he useth; which being performed with a convenient gesture and countenance, let him begin to pray with a loud voice, after this manner. First let him make an Oration unto God, and then let him intreat the good Spirits: and if he will read any Prayers, Psalms, or Gospel for his defence, they ought to take the first place. After these Prayers and Orations are said, then let him begin to invocate the Spirit which he desireth, with a gentle and loving Inchantment, to all the coasts of the World, with the commemoration of his own Authority and power. And then let him rest a little, looking about him; to see if any Spirit do appear; which if he delay, then let him repeat his invocation, as abovesaid, until he hath done it three times; and if the Spirit be pertinacious, obstinate, and will not appear, then let him begin to conjure with divine power; so also that the conjurations and all his commemorations do agree with the Nature and Offices of the Spirit himself, and reiterate the same three times, from stronger to stronger, using Objurgations,[113] Contumeries,[114] Cursings, & Punishments, and suspension from his Office and power, and the like.

And after all the courses are finished, then cease a little; and if any Spirit shall appear, let the Invocant turn himself towards the Spirit, and courteously receive him, and earnestly intreating him, let him first require his name, and if he be called by any other name: and then proceeding further, let him ask him whatsoever he will: and if in any thing the Spirit shall shew himself obstinate or lying, let him be bound by convenient conjurations: and if you doubt of any lye,[115] make without the Circle with the consecrated Sword, the figure of a triangle or ∗ *Pentagone*,[116] and compel the

---

[113] Scoldings.
[114] Reproachful language.
[115] If you feel he is lying.
[116] Margin note: A Character with five corners.

Spirit to enter into it; and if thou receivest any promise which thou wouldst have to be confirmed with an Oath, let him stretch the sword out of the Circle, and swear the Spirit, by laying his hand upon the Sword.

[THE LICENSE TO DEPART]

Then having obtained of the Spirit that which you desire, or are otherwise contented, license him to depart with courteous words, giving command unto him, that he do no hurt: and if he will not depart, compel him by powerful conjurations; and if need require, expel him by Exorcismes, and by making contrary fumigations.[117] And when he is departed, go not out of the Circle, but make a stay, making prayer, and giving of thanks unto God and the good Angels, and also praying for your defence and conservation: and then all those things being orderly performed, you may depart.

But if your hope be frustrated, and no Spirits will appear, yet for this do not despair; but leaving the Circle, return again at other times, doing as before. And if you shall judge that you have erred in any thing, then that you shall amend, by adding or diminishing; for the constancy of Reiteration doth often increase your authority and power, and striketh terror into the Spirits, and humbleth them to obey.

And therefore some use to make a Gate in the Circle, whereby they may go in and out, which they open and shut as they please, and fortifie it with holy Names and Pentacles.

This also, we are to take notice of, That when no Spirits will appear, but the Master being wearied hath determined to cease and give over; let him not therefore depart without licensing the Spirits: for they that do neglect this, are very greatly in danger, except they are forified with some sublime defence.

Often [t]imes also the Spirits do come, although they appear not visible, (for to cause terror to him that calls them) either in the things which he useth, or in the operation it self. But this kinde of licensing is not given simply, but by a kinde of dispensation with suspension, until in the following terms they shall render themselves obedient. Also without a Circle these Spirits may be

---

[117] Burning incense contrary to the nature of the spirit, to encourage them to leave. One example of this is the burning of fish intestines to banish Asteroth.

called to appear, according to the way which is above delivered about the consecration of a book.

But when we do intend to execute any effect by evil Spirits, when an Apparition is not needful; then that is to be done, by making and forming that thing which is to be unto us as an instrument, or subject of the experiment it self; as, whether it be an Image, or a Ring, or a Writing, or any Character, Candle, or Sacrifice, or any thing of the like sort; then the name of the Spirit is to be written therein, with his Character, according to the exigency of the experiment, either by writing it with some blood, or otherwise using a perfume agreeable to the Spirit. Oftentimes also making Prayers and Orations to God and the good Angels before we invocate the evil Spirit, conjuring him by the divine power.

[NATURE SPIRITS]

There is another kinde of Spirits, which we have spoken of in our third book of Occult Philosophy, not so hurtful, and neerest unto men; so also, that they are effected with humane passions, and do joy in the conversation of men, and freely do inhabit with them: and others do dwell in the Woods and Desarts: & others delight in the company of divers domestique Animals and wilde Beasts; and othersome do inhabit about Fountains and Meadows. Whosoever therefore would call up these kinde of Spirits, in the place where they abide, it ought to be done with odoriferous perfumes, and with sweet sounds and instruments of Musick, specially composed for the business, with using of Songs, Inchantments and pleasant Verses, with praises and promises.

But those which are obstinate to yield to these things, are to be compelled with Threatnings, Comminations, Cursings, Delusions, Contumelies, and especially by threatning them to expel them from those places where they are conversant.

Further, if need be, thou maist betake thee to use Exorcismes; but the chiefest thing that ought to be observed, is, constancy of minde, and boldness, free, and alienated from fear.

Lastly, when you would invocate these kinde of Spirits, you ought to prepare a Table in the place of invocation, covered with clean linen; whereupon you shall set new bread, and running water or milk in new earthen vessels, and new knives. And you shall make a fire, whereupon a perfume shall be made. But let the Invocant go unto the head of the Table, and round about it let there be seats placed for the Spirits, as you please; and the Spirits being called, you shall invite them to drink and eat. But if perchance you shall fear any evil Spirit, then draw a Circle about it, and let that part of the Table at which the Invocant sits, be within the Circle, and the rest of the Table without the Circle.[118]

[NECROMANCY]

In our third book of Occult Philosophy, we have taught how and by what means the Soul is joyned to the Body; and, what hapeneth to the Soul after death.

Thou maist know further, That those Souls do still love their relinquished Bodies after death, as it were a certain affinity alluring them; such as are the Souls of noxious men, which have violently relinquished their Bodies, and Souls wanting a due burial, which do still wander in a liquid and turbulent Spirit about their dead carkasses; for these Souls by the known means by which heretofore they were conjoyned to their Bodies, by the like vapors, liquors, and favours, are easily drawn unto them.[119]

From hence it is, that the Souls of the dead are not to be called up without blood, or by the application of some part of their relict Body.

In raising up these shadows, we are to perfume with new Blood, with the Bones of the dead, and with Flesh, Egges, Milk, Honey and Oile, and such-like things, which do attribute to the Souls a means apt to receive their Bodies.

It is also to be understood, That those who are desirous to raise up any Souls of the dead, they ought to do it in those places, wherein these kinde of Souls are most known to be conversant, or for some alliance alluring those souls into their forsaken Body; or for some kinde of affection in times past, impressed in them in their life, drawing the said Soul to certain places, things, or persons; or for the forcible nature of some place fitted and prepared for to purge or punish these Souls. Which places for the most part are to be known by the experience of visions, mighty incursions, and apparitions, and such-like prodigies seen.

Therefore the places most befitting for these things, are Church-yards. And better then them, are those places wherein there is the

---

[118] Outside the circle.

[119] Presumably this, along with the section on nature spirits, is added for the sake of completeness. On the whole this book is not concerned with evoking the spirits of the dead, which was seen as a much lower grade operation.

execution of criminal judgements. And better then these, are those places, in which of late yeers there have been some publike slaughters of men. Furthermore, that place is better then there, where some dead carkass, that came by a violent death, is not yet expiated, nor ritely buried, and was lately buried; for the expiation of those places, is also a holy Rite duly to be adhibited to the burial of the bodies, and oftentimes prohibiteth the souls to come unto their bodies, and expelleth them far off unto the places of judgment.[120]

And from hence it is, That the Souls of the dead are not easily to be raised up, except it be the Souls of them whom we know to be evil, or to have perished by a violent death, and whose bodies do want[121] a right and due burial.

Now although we have spoken concerning such places of this kinde, it will not be safe or commodious to go unto them; but it behoveth us to take to what place soever is to be chosen, some principal part of the body that is relict, and therewith to make a perfume in due maner, and to perform other competent Rites.

It is also to be known, That because the Souls are certain spiritual lights, therefore artificial lights, especially if they be framed out of certain competent things, compounded according to a true rule, with congruent inscriptions of Names and Seals, do very much avail to the raising up of departed Souls.

Moreover, these things which now are spoken of, are not alwaies sufficient to raise up Souls, because of an extranatural portion of understanding and reason, which is above, and known onely to the Heaven and Destinies, and their power.

We ought therefore to allure the said Souls, by supernatural and coelestial[122] powers duely administred, even by those things which do move the very harmony of the Soul, as wel[l] imaginative, as rational and intellectual; as are Voices, Songs, Sound, Inchantments: and Religious things; as Prayers, Conjurations, Exorcismes, and other holy Rites, which may very commodiously be administred hereunto.

The end of the fourth book of Agrippa.

---

[120] A proper burial or funeral rite should prevent the return of the soul to the body. Necromancers need a body not buried with the usual rites.

[121] Lack.

[122] Celestial.

Heptameron:

or,

Magical Elements

of

Peter de Abano

Philosopher

[Introduction by the Translator]

 N the former book, which is the fourth book of *Agrippa*, it is sufficiently spoken concerning Magical Ceremonies, and Initiations.

But because he[1] seemeth to have written to the learned, and well-experienced in this art; because he doth not specially treat of the Ceremonies, but rather speaketh of them in general, it was therefore thought good to adde hereunto the Magical Elements of *Peter de Abano*: that those who are hitherto ignorant, and have not tasted of Magical Superstitions,[2] may have them in readiness, how they may exercise themselves therein. For we see in this book, as it were a certain introduction of Magical vanity; and as if they were in present exercise, they may behold the distinct functions of spirits, how they may be drawn to discourse and communication; what is to be done every day, and every hour; and how they shall be read, as if they were described sillable by sillable.

In brief, in this book are kept the principles of Magical conveyances. But because the greatest power is attributed to the Circles; (For they are certain fortresses to defend the operators safe from

---

[1]   Agrippa.
[2]   Superstitions here means "beliefs" rather than the modern-day derogatory meaning.

the evil Spirits;) In the first place we will treat concerning the composition of a Circle.

OF THE CIRCLE, AND THE COMPOSITION THEREOF.

The form of Circles is not alwaies one and the same; but useth to be changed, according to the order of the Spirits that are to be called, their places, times, daies and hours.[3] For in making a Circle, it ought to be considered in what time of the year, what day, and what hour, that you make the Circle; what Spirits you would call, to what Star and Region they do belong, and what functions they have.

Therefore let there be made three Circles of the latitude[4] of nine foot, and let them be distant one from another a hands breadth; and in the middle Circle, first, write the name of the hour wherein you do the work. In the second place, Write the name of the Angel of the hour. In the third place, The Sigil of the Angel of the hour. Fourthly, The name of the Angel that ruleth that day wherein you do the work, and the names of his ministers. In the fifth place, The name of the present time. Sixthly, The name of the Spirits ruling in that part of time, and their Presidents. Seventhly, The name of the head of the Signe ruling in that part of time wherein you work. Eighthly, The name of the earth, according to that part of time wherein you work. Ninthly, and for the compleating of the middle Circle, Write the name of the Sun and of the Moon, according to the said rule of time; for as the time is changed, so the names are to be altered. And in the outermost Circle, let there be drawn in the four Angles, the names of the presidential Angels of the Air, that day wherein you would do this work; to wit, the name of the King and his three Ministers.

Without[5] the Circle, in four Angles, let *Pentagones*[6] be made. In the inner Circle let there be written four divine names with crosses interposed in the middle of the Circle; to wit, towards the East let there be written *Alpha*, and towards the West let there be written

---

[3] Many grimoires, like the *Goetia*, suggest just one design for the magician's protective circle. Here de Abano clearly states that the circle must be appropriate to the time and spirit or angel invoked.

[4] Diameter.

[5] Outside the circle.

[6] De Abano probably meant pentagrams (5-pointed figures) rather than pentagons (5-sided figures).

Omega;[7] and let a cross divide the middle of the Circle. When the Circle is thus finished, according to the rule now before written, you shall proceed.

OF THE NAMES OF THE HOURS, AND THE ANGELS RULING THEM.

It is also to be known, that the Angels do rule the hours in a successive order, according to the course of the heavens, and Planets unto which they are subject; so that that Spirit which governeth the day, ruleth also the first hour of the day; the second from this governeth the second hour; the third; the third hour, and so consequently: and when seven Planets and hours have made their revolution, it returneth again to the first which ruleth the day.[8] Therefore we shall first speak of the names of the hours.

Hours of the day.	Hours of the night.
1. Yayn.	1. Beron.
2. Janor.	2. Barol.
3. Nasnia.	3. Thami.
4. Salla.	4. Athar.
5. Sadedali.	5. Mathon.
6. Thamur.	6. Rana.
7. Ourer.	7. Netos.
8. Thamic.	8. Tafrac.
9. Neron.	9. Sassur.
10. Jayon.	10. Aglo.
11. Abai.	11. Calerva.
12. Natalon.	12. Salam.

Of the names of the Angels and their Sigils, it shall be spoken in their proper places. Now let us take a view of the names of the times. A year therefore is fourfold, and is divided into the Spring, Summer, Harvest and Winter; the names whereof are these.

The Spring.   *Talvi.*

---

[7] Alpha and omega, the first and last letters of the Greek alphabet, which therefore have the meaning "the beginning and the end," referring by extension to God.

[8] In other words, the cycle begins again with the eighth hour, which is ruled by the same planet as the first hour.

The Summer.	*Casmaran.*
Autumne.	*Ardarael.*
Winter.	*Farlas.*

The Angels of the Spring.

Caratasa.
Core.
Amatiel.
Commissoros.

The head of the Signe of the Spring.

Spugliguel.

The name of the earth in the Spring.

Amadai.

The names of the Sun and Moon in the Spring.

The Sun.	The Moon.
Abraym.	*Agusita.*

The Angels of the Summer.

Gargatel.
Tariel.
Gaviel.

The head of the Signe of the Summer.

Tubiel.

The name of the earth in Summer.

Festativi.

The names of the Sun and Moon in Summer.

The Sun.	The Moon.
Athemay.	*Armatus.*

The Angels of Autumne.

Tarquam.
Guabarel.

The head of the signe of Autumne.

Torquaret.

The name of the earth in Autumne.

Rabianara.

The names of the Sun and Moon in Autumne.

The Sun.	The Moon.
Abragini.	*Matasignais.*

The Angels of the Winter.

Amabael.
Ctarari.

The head of the sign[e] of Winter.

Altarib.

The name of the Earth in Winter.

Geremiah.

The names of the Sun and Moon in Winter.

The Sun.	The Moon.
Commutaff.	*Affaterim.*

THE CONSECRATIONS AND BENEDICTIONS: AND FIRST OF THE BENEDICTION OF THE CIRCLE.

When the Circle is ritely perfected, sprinkle the same with holy or purging water, and say, *Thou shalt purge me with hysop, (O Lord,) and I shall be clean: Thou shalt wash me, and I shall be whiter then snow.*[9]

THE BENEDICTION OF PERFUMES.

The God of Abraham, God of Isaac, God of Jacob, bless here the creatures of these kindes, that they may fill up the power and vertue of their odours; so that neither the enemy, nor any false imagination, may be able to enter into them: through our Lord Jesus Christ, &c. Then let them be sprinkled with holy water.

THE EXORCISME OF THE FIRE UPON WHICH THE PERFUMES ARE TO BE PUT.

The fire which is to be used for suffumigations,[10] is to be in a new vessel of earth[11] or iron; and let it be exorcised after this manner.

I exorcise thee, O thou creature of fire, by him by whom all things are made, that forthwith thou cast away every phantasme from thee, that it shall not be able to do any hurt in any thing.

Then say, *Bless*, O Lord, *this creature of fire, and sanctifie it, that it may be blessed to set forth the praise of thy holy name, that no hurt may come to the Exercisers or Spectators: through our Lord Jesus Christ*, &c.

OF THE GARMENT AND PENTACLE.

Let it be a Priests Garment, if it can be: but if it cannot be had, let it be of linen, and clean. Then take this Pentacle made in the day and hour of *Mercury*, the Moon increasing,[12] written in parchment made of a kids skin. But first let there be said over it the Mass of the holy Ghost, and let it be sprinkled with water of baptism.

---

[9] Taken from the Psalms. This rubric is used in the Catholic Mass, as well as many other grimoires, as a purification by water.

[10] Burning incense.

[11] Pottery.

[12] During the 14 days of the waxing Moon.

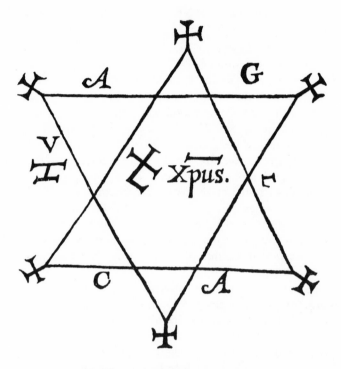

An Oration to be said,
when the Vesture is put on.

Ancor, Amacor, Amides, Theodonias, Anitor, by the merits of thy Angel, O Lord, I will put on the Garment of Salvation, that this which I desire I may bring to effect: through thee the most holy Adonay, whose kingdom endureth for ever and ever. Amen.[13]

---

[13] Peterson points out that this oration occurs widely in magical texts (Joseph Peterson, *The Lesser Key of Solomon* [York Beach, Weiser, 2001], p. xiv). For example, the version in the *Lemegeton* is almost identical, and was probably taken directly from the *Heptameron*, along with other invocations. Compare also with the version in *The Sworn Book* of Honorius and the example in *Ars Notoria*.

OF THE MANNER OF WORKING.

Let the *Moon* be increasing and equal,[14] if it may then be done, and let her not be combust.[15]

The Operator ought to be clean and purified by the space of nine daies before the beginning of the work, and to be confessed, and receive the holy Communion. Let him have ready the perfume appropriated to the day wherein he would perform the work. He ought also to have holy water from a Priest, and a new earthen vessel with fire, a Vesture[16] and [a] Pentacle; and let all these things be rightly and duly consecrated and prepared. Let one of the servants carry the earthen vessel full of fire, and the perfumes, and let another bear the book, another the Garment and Pentacle, and let the master carry the Sword; over which there must be said one mass of the Holy Ghost; and on the middle of the Sword, let there be written this name *Agla* +, and on the other side thereof, this name + *On* +.

And as he goeth to the consecrated place, let him continually read Letanies,[17] the servants answering. And when he cometh to the place where he will erect the Circle, let him draw the lines of the Circle, as we have before taught: and after he hath made it, let him sprinkle the Circle with holy water, saying, *Asperges me Domine*, &c.[18]

The Master therefore ought to be purified with fasting, chastity, and abstinency from all luxury the space of three whole dayes before the day of the operation. And on the day that he would do the work, being clothed with pure garments, and furnished with Pentacles, Perfumes, and other things necessary hereunto, let him enter the Circle, and call the Angels from the four parts of the world, which do govern the seven Planets the seven dayes of the week, Colours and Metals; whose name you shall see in their places. And with bended knees invoking the said Angels particularly, let him say, "*O Angels supradicti, estote adjutores meæ petitioni, & in adjutorium mihi, in meis rebus & petitionibus.*"

---

[14] Waxing an even number of days, e.g. on the 2nd, 4th, or 6th day of the waxing Moon.

[15] Combust is within three degrees of the Sun's longitude, in other words, where the Moon is overwhelmed by the "heat" of the Sun's influence.

[16] The correct clothing or robes.

[17] Litanies, where the master repeats aloud a petition or prayer to god (or the angels), and his disciples (or servants) answer with a set response.

[18] Margin note: Wash me O Lord, &c.

Then let him call the Angels from the four parts of the world, that rule the Air the same day wherein he doth the work or experiment. And having implored specially all the Names and Spirits written in the Circle, let him say, "*O vos omnes, adjuro atque contestor per sedem Adonay, per Hagios, ò Theos, Ischyros, Athanatos, Paracletos, Alpha & Omega, & per hæc tria nomina secreta, Agla, On, Tetragrammaton, quòd hodie debeatis adimplere quod cupio.*"[19]

These things being performed, let him read the Conjuration assigned for the day wherein he maketh the experiments, as we have before spoken; but if they shall be partinacious[20] and refractory, and will not yield themselves obedient, neither to the Conjuration assigned to the day, nor to the prayers before made, then use the Conjurations and Exorcismes following.

An Exorcisme of the Spirits of the Air

"*Nos facti ad imaginem Dei,dotats potentia Dei, & ejus facti voluntate, per potentissimum & corroboratum nomen Dei El, forte & admirabile vos exorcizamus* (here he shall name the Spirits he would have appear, of what order soever they be) *& imperamus per eum qui dixit, & factum est, & per omnia nomina Dei, & per nomen Adonay, El, Elohim, Elohe, Zebaoth, Elion, Escerchie, Jah, Tetragrammaton, Sadai, Dominus Deus, excelsus, exorcizamus vos, atque potenter imperamus, ut appareatis statim nobis hic juxta Circulum in pulchra forma, vide licet humana, & sine deformitate & tortuositate aliqua. Venite vos omnes tales, quia vobis imperamus, per nomen Y & V quod Adam audivit, & locutus est: & per nomen Y & V quod Adam audivit, & locutus est: & per nomen Dei Agla, quod Loth audivit, & factus salvus cum sua familia: & per nomen Joth, quod Jacob audivit ab Angelo secum luctantes, & liberatus est de manu fratris sui Esau:* and by the name *Anephexeton, quod Aaron audivit, & loquens, & sapiens factus est: & per nomen Zebaoth, quod Moses nominavit, & omnia flumina & paludes de terra ægypti, versæ fuerunt in sanguinem: & per nomen Ecerchie Oriston, quod Moses nominavit, & omnes flu vis ebullierunt ranas, & ascenderunt in domos ægyptiorum,*

---

[19] "I adjure and call you all forth, by the seat of Adonay, by Hagios, O Theos, Iscyros, Athanatos, Paracletos, Alpha & Omega, and by these three secret names: Agla, On, Tetragrammaton, that you at once fulfill what I desire." This is almost identical to part of the second conjuration of the *Goetia*.

[20] Obstinate.

omnia destruentes: & per nomen Elion, quod Moses nominavit, & fuit grando talis, qualis non fuit ab initio mundi: & per nomen Adonay, quod Moses nominavit, & fuerunt locustae, & apparuerunt super terram ægyptiorum, & comederunt quæ residua erant grandinis: & per nomen Schemes amathia, quod Joshua vocavit, & remoratus est Sol cursum: & per nomen Alpha & Omega, quod Daniel nominavit, & destruxit Beel, & Draconem interferit: & in nomine Emmanuel, quod tres pueri, Sidrach, Misach & Abednago, in camino ignis ardentis, cantaverunt, & liberati fuerunt: & per nomen Hagios, & sedem Adonay, & per ò Theos, Iscyros, Athanatos, Paracletus; & per hæs tria secreta nomina, Agla, On, Tetragrammaton, adjuro, contestor, & per hæc nomina, & per alia nomina Domini nostri Dei Omnipotentis, vivi & veri, vos qui vestra culpa de Coelis ejecti fuistis usque ad infernum locum, exorcizamus, & viril[i]ter imperamus, per eum qui dixit, & factum est, cui omnes obediunt creaturæ, & per illud tremendum Dei judicium: & per mare omnibus incertum, vitreum, quod est ante conspectum divinæ majestatis gradiens, & potentiale: & per quatuor divina animalia T. aniè sedem divinæ majesta is gradientia, & oculos antè & retrò habentia: & per ignem ante ejus thronum circumstantem: & per sanctos Angelos Cælorum, T. & per eam quæ Ecclesia Dei nominatur: & per summam sapientiam Omnipotentis Dei viriliter exorcizamus, ut nobis hic ante Circulum appareatis, ut faciendam nostram voluntatem, in omnibus prout placuerit nobis: per sedem Baldachiæ, & per hoc nomen Primeumaton, quod Moses nominavit, & in cavernis abyssi fuerunt profundati vel absorpti, Datan, Corah & Abiron: & in virtute istius nominis Primeumaton, tota Coeli militia compellente, maledicimus vos, privamus vos omni officio, loco & gaudio vestro, usque in profundum abyssi, & usque ad ultimum diem judicii vos ponimus, & relegamus in ignem æternum, & in stagnum ignis & sulphuris, nisi statim appareatis hic coram nobis, inte Circulum, ad faciendum voluntatem nostram. In omnibus venite per hæc nomina, Adonay Zebaoth, Adonay Amioram. Venite, venite, imperat vobis Adonay, Saday, Rex regum potentissimus & tremendissimus, cujus vires nulla subterfugere potest creatura vobis pertinacissimis futuris nisi obedieritis, & appareatis ante hunc Circulum, affabiles subito, tandem ruina flebilis miserabilisque, & ignis perpetuum inextinguibilis vos manet. Venite ergo in nomine Adonay Zebaoth, Adonay Amioram: venite, venite, quid tardatis? festinate imperat vobis Adonay, Saday, Rex regum, El, Aty, Titcip, Azia, Hyn, Jen, Minosel, Achadan: Vay, Vaa, Ey, Haa, Eye, Exe, à, El, El, El, à, Hy, Hau, Hau, Hau, Va, Va, Va, Va."

[**Translation**:[21] "We being made after the image of God, endued with power from God and made after his will, do exorcise you, by the most mighty and powerful name of God, *El*, strong and wonderful (*here he shall name the Spirit[s] he would [have] appear, of what Order soever they be[long] to*), and we command you by Him who spoke the word and it was done, and by all the names of God, and by the name Adonai, El, Elohim, Elohe, Zebaoth, Elion, Escerchie [Eskerie or Eskeriel], Jah, Tetragrammaton, Sadai, Lord God Most High: we exorcise you, and powerfully command you that you forthwith appear unto us here before this circle in a fair human shape, without any deformity or tortuosity; come ye all such, because we command you by the name Y[od] and V[au], which Adam heard and spoke; and by the name of God, Agla, which Lot heard, and was saved along with all his family; and by the name Joth which Jacob heard from the angel wrestling with him, and was delivered from the hand of his brother Esau; and by the name Anephexeton, which Aaron heard and spoke, and was made wise; and by the name Zebaoth, which Moses named, and all the rivers were turned into blood; and by the name Ecerchie [Eskerie or Eskeriel] Oriston, which Moses named, and all the rivers brought forth frogs, and they ascended into the houses of the Egyptians, destroying all things; and by the name Elion, which Moses named, and there was great hail, such as had not been since the beginning of the world; and by the name Adonai, which Moses named, and there came up locusts, which appeared upon the whole land of Egypt, and devoured all which the hail had left; and by the name Schemes Amathia,[22] which Joshua called upon, and the sun stayed his course; and by the name Alpha and Omega, which Daniel named, and destroyed Bel and slew the dragon; and in the name Emmanuel, which the three children, Shadrach, Meshach, and Abednego,[23] sung in the midst of the fiery furnace, and were delivered; and by the name Hagios; and by the seal of Adonai; and by Theos, Iscyros,[24] Athanatos, Paracletos; and by these three secret names, Agla, On, Tetragrammaton, I do adjure and contest you; and by these names, and by all the other names of the living and true God, our Lord Almighty, I exorcise and command you, by Him who spoke the word and it was done, to whom all creatures are obedient; and by the dreadful judgment of God; and by the uncertain sea

---

[21] This is very similar to the second conjuration of the *Goetia*.

[22] Sometimes rendered as "Schema Amathia."

[23] "Sidrach, Misach & Abednego" in the Latin text.

[24] "Iscytos" in the original. Sometimes rendered "O Theos Iscyroa Thanatos Paracletos."

of glass, which is before the divine Majesty, mighty and powerful; by
the four beasts before the throne, having eyes before and behind; and
by the fire round about his throne; and by the holy angels of heaven;
by the mighty wisdom of God, we do powerfully exorcise you, that
you appear here before this circle, to fulfil our will in all things which
shall seem good unto us; by the seal of Baldachiæ, and by this name
Primeumaton, which Moses named, and the earth opened and swal-
lowed up Datan, Corah and Abiron: and in the power of that name
Primeumaton, commanding the whole host of heaven, we curse you,
and deprive you of your office, joy, and place, and do bind you in the
depth of the bottomless pit, there to remain until the dreadful day of
the last judgment; and we bind you into eternal fire, and into the lake
of fire and brimstone, unless you forthwith appear before this circle
to do our will: therefore, come ye, by these names, Adonai Zebaoth,
Adonai Amioram; come ye, come ye, come ye, Adonai commandeth;
Saday, the most mighty and potent King of Kings, whose power no
creature is able to resist, be unto you most dreadful, unless ye obey,
and forthwith affably appear before this circle, let miserable ruin and
fire unquenchable remain with you; therefore come ye, in the name
of Adonai Zebaoth, Adonai Amioram; come, come, why do you delay?
Hasten, Adonai, Sadai, the King of Kings commands you: El, Aty, Titcip,
Azia, Hyn, Jen, Minosel, Achadan, Vay, Vaa, Ey, Haa, Eye, Exe, a, El, El,
El, a, Hy, Hau, Hau, Hau, Va, Va, Va, Va."[25]]

A PRAYER TO GOD,
TO BE SAID IN THE FOUR PARTS OF THE WORLD,
IN THE CIRCLE.

"Amorule, Taneha, Latisten, Rabur, Taneha, Latisten. Escha, Aladia,
Alpha & Omega, Leyste, Oriston, Adonay: O my most merciful heav-
enly Father, have mercy upon me, although a sinner; make appear
the arm of thy power in me this day (although thy unworthy child)
against these obstinate and pernicious Spirits, that I by thy will may
be made a contemplator of thy divine works, and may be illustrated[26]
with all wisdom, and alwaies worship and glorifie thy name. I hum-
bly implore and beseech thee, that these Spirits which I call by thy
judgement, may be bound and constrained to come, and give true
and perfect answers to those things which I shall ask them, and that
they may declare and shew unto us those things which by me or us

---

[25] Obviously a corrupt list of Hebrew letters.
[26] Illuminated.

*shall be commanded them, not hurting any creature, neither injuring
nor terrifying me or my fellows, nor hurting any other creature, and
affrighting no man; but let them be obedient to my requests, in all
these things which I command them."*

Then let him stand in the middle of the Circle, and hold his hand
towards the Pentacle, and say, *"Per Pentaculum Salomonis advocavi,
dent mihi responsum verum."*[27]

Then let him say, *"Beralanensis, Baldachiensis, Paumachiæ & Apologiæ
sedes, per Reges potestaiesiá magnanimas, ac principes præpotentes, genio,
Liachidæ, ministri tartareæ sedes: Primac, hic princeps sedis Apologiæ
nona cohorte: Ego vos invoco, & invocando vos conjure, atque supernæ
Majestatis munitus virtute, potenter impero, per eum qui dixit, & factum est, & cui obediunt omnes creaturæ: & per hoc nomen ineffabile,
Tetragrammaton IHVH Jehovah, in quo est plasmatum omne seculum,
quo audito elementa corruunt, aër concutitur, mare retrograditur, ignis
extinguitur, terra tremit, omnesque exercitus Coelestium, Terrestrium,
& Infernorum tremunt, turbantur & corruunt: quatenus citò & sine
mora & omni occasione remota, ab universis mundi partibus veniatis,
& rationabiliter de omnibus quæcunque interrogavero, respondeatis vos,
& veniatis pacifice, visibiles, & affabiles: nunc & sine mora manifestantes
quod cupimus: conjurati per nomen æterni vivi & veri Dei Helioren,
& mandata nostra per ficientes, persistentes semper usque ad finem, &
intentionem meam, visibiles nobis, & affabiles, clara voce nobis, intel-
ligibile, & sine omni ambiguitate."*

[Translation: "Beralanensis, Baldachiensis, Paumachiæ, and Apologiæ
Sedes, by the most mighty kings and powers, and the most powerful princes, genii, Liachidæ, ministers of the Tartarean seat,[28] chief
prince of the seat of Apologiæ, in the ninth legion, I invoke you,
and by invocating, conjure you; and being armed with power from
the supreme Majesty, I strongly command you,[29] by Him who spoke
and it was done, and to whom all creatures are obedient; and by
this ineffable name, Tetragrammaton IHVH Jehovah, which being
heard the elements are overthrown, the air is shaken, the sea runneth back, the fire is quenched, the earth trembles, and all the host
of the Celestial, Terrestrial, and Infernal [Spirits] do tremble together,

---

[27] By the pentacle of Solomon I have called you; give me a true answer.
[28] Tartaros (*sic*) is the abyss below Hades where the Titans were chained.
[29] It is usual to insert the name of the spirit being conjured at this point.

and are troubled and confounded: wherefore, forthwith and without delay, do you come from all parts of the world, and make rational answers unto all things I shall ask of you; and come ye peaceably, visibly and affably now, without delay, manifesting what we desire, being conjured by the name of the living and true God, Helioren,[30] and fulfill our commands, and persist unto the end, and according to our intentions, visibly and affably speaking unto us with a clear voice, intelligible, and without any ambiguity."[31]]

VISIONS AND APPARITIONS.

Quibus ritè peractis, apparebunt infinitæ visiones, & phantasmata pulsantia organa & omnis generis instrumenta musica, idque fit à spiritibus, ut terrore compulsi socii abeant à Circulo, quia nihil adversus magistrum possunt. Post hæc videbis infinitos sagittarios cum infinita multitudine bestiarum horribilem: quæ ita se componunt, ac si vellent devorare socios: & tamen nil timeant. Tunc Sacerdos sive Magister, adhibens manum Pentaculo, dicat:

"Fugiat hinc iniquitas vestra, virtute vexilli Dei. Et tunc Spiritus obedire magistro coguntur, & socii nil amilius videbunt."

[**Translation:** These things being duly performed, there will appear infinite visions, apparitions, phantasms, &c. beating of drums, and the sound of all kinds of musical instruments; which is done by the spirits, that with the terror they might force some of the companions out of the circle, because they can effect nothing against the exorcist himself: after this you shall see an infinite company of archers, with a great multitude of horrible beasts, which will arrange themselves as if they would devour your companions; nevertheless, fear nothing. Then the exorcist or Master, holding the Pentacle in his hand, let him say:

"Avoid hence these iniquities, by virtue of the banner of God. Then will the spirits be compelled to obey the exorcist, and the company shall see them no more."]

---

[30] May be derived from Helios, Greek god of the Sun.

[31] This is very similar to the first conjuration in the *Goetia*.

Then let the Exorcist say, stretching out his hand to the Pentacle,

"Ecce Pentaculum Salomonis, quod ante vestram adduxi præsentiam: ecce personam exorcizatoris in medio Exorcismi, qui est optimè à Deo munitus, intrepidus, providus, qui viribus potens vos exorcizando invocavit & vocat. Venite ergo cum festinatione in virtute nominum istorum, Aye, Saraye, Aye, Saraye, Aye Saraye, ne differatis venire, per nomina æterna Dei vivi & veri Eloy, Archima, Rabur: & per hoc præsens Pentaculum, quod super vos potenter imperat: & per virutem coelestium Spirituum dominorum vestrorum: & per personam exorcizatoris, conjurati, festinati venire & obedire præceptori vestro, qui vocatur Octinomos."

[**Translation:** "Behold the Pentacle of Solomon, which I have brought into your presence; behold the person of the exorcist in the middle of the exorcism, who is armed by God, without fear, and well provided, who potently invocateth and calleth you by exorcising; come, therefore, with speed, by the virtue of these names; Aye Saraye, Aye Saraye; defer not to come, by the eternal names of the living and true God, Eloy, Archima, Rabur, and by the Pentacle of Solomon here present, which powerfully reigns over you; and by the virtue of the celestial spirits, your lords; and by the person of the exorcist, in the middle of the exorcism: being conjured, make haste and come, and yield obedience to your master, who is called Octinomos."]

His peractis, sibiles in quatuor angulis mundi. Et videbis immediate magnos motus: & cum videris, dicas:

"Quid tardatis? quid moramini? quid facitis? præparate vos & obedite præceptori vestro, in nomine Domini Bathat, vel Vachat super Abrac ruens, super veniens, Abeor super Aberer."

[**Translation:** This being performed, immediately there will be hissings in the four parts of the world, and then immediately you shall see great motions; which when you see, say:

"Why stay you? Wherefore do you delay? What do you? Prepare yourselves to be obedient to your master in the name of the Lord Bathat or Vachat rushing upon Abrac, Abeor coming upon Aberer."[32]]

---

[32] See the address to the spirit in the *Goetia*.

Tunc immediatè venient in sua forma propria. Et quando videbis eos juxta Circulum, ostende illis Pentaculum coopertum syndone sacro, & discooperiatur, & dicat:

"Ecce conclusionem vestram, nolite fieri inobedientes."

[**Translation:** Then they will immediately come in their proper forms; and when you see them before the circle, shew them the pentacle covered with fine linen; uncover it, and say:

"Behold your conclusion (fate) if you refuse to be obedient."]

Et subito videbis eos in pacifica forma: & dicent tibi, Pete quid vis, quia nos sumus parati complere omnia mandata tua, quia dominus ad hæc nos subjugavit. Cum autem apparuerint Spiritus, tunc dicas:

"Bene veneritis Spiritus, vel reges nobilissimi, quia vos vocavi per illum cui omne genu flectitur, coelestium, terrestrium & infernorum: cujus in manu omnia regna regum sunt, nec est qui suæ contrarius esse possit Majestati. Quatenus constringo vos, ut hic ante circulum visibiles, affabiles permanetis, tamdiu tamque constantes, nec sint licentia mea recedatis, donec meam sine fallacia aliqua & veredicè perficiatis voluntatem, per potentiæ illius virtutem, qui mare posuit terminum suum, quem præterire non potest, & lege illius potentiæ, non pertransit fines suos, Dei scilicet altissimi, regis, domini, qui cuncta creavit, Amen."

[**Translation:** And suddenly they will appear in a peaceable form, and will say, Ask what you will, for we are prepared to fulfil all your commands, for the Lord hath subjected us hereunto. Then let the exorcist say,

"Welcome spirits, or most noble princes, because I have called you through Him to whom every knee doth bow, both of things in heaven, and things in earth, and things under the earth; in whose hands are all the kingdoms of kings, neither is there any able to contradict his Majesty. Wherefore, I bind you, that you remain affable and visible before this circle, so long and so constant; neither shall you depart without my licence, until you have truly and without any fallacy performed my will, by virtue of his power who hath set the sea her bounds, beyond which it cannot pass, nor go beyond the law of his providence, viz. of the Most High God, Lord, and King, who hath created all things. Amen."]

Then command what you will, and it shall be done. Afterwards license them thus:

"+ *In nomine Patris,* + *Filii,* & + *Spiritus sancti, ite in pace ad loca vestra:* & *pax sit inter nos* & *vos, parati sitis venire vocati."*

[**Translation:** "In the name of the Father, and of the Son, and of the Holy Ghost, go in peace unto your places; peace be between us and you; be ye ready to come when you are called."]

These are the things which *Peter de Abano* hath spoken concerning Magical Elements.[33]

[ADDITIONAL CONSIDERATIONS, CONJURATIONS AND TIMES]

But that you may the better know the manner of composing a Circle, I will set down one Scheme; so that if any one would make a Circle in Spring-time for the first hour of Lords day, it must be in the same manner as is the figure following.[34]

The figure of a Circle for the
first hour of the Lords day, in Spring-time.

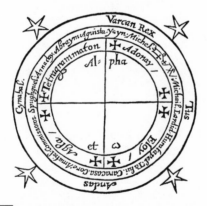

---

[33] This is the actual end of de Abano's work. The following appendices are now, however, always included in the *Heptameron.*

[34] Remember this is just a sample circle for the first hour after dawn on a Sunday, and its constituents will be different for different times and days. This and the following material may not have been part of the original *Magical Elements* of de Abano.

It remaineth now, That we explain the week, the several dayes thereof: and first of the Lords day.

CONSIDERATIONS OF THE LORDS DAY.

The Angel of the Lords day,[35] his Sigil, Planet, Signe of the Planet, and the name of the fourth heaven.[36]

The Angels of the Lords day.

Michael, Dardiel, Huratapal.

The Angels of the Air ruling on the Lords day.

Varcan, King.

His Ministers.

Tus, Andas, Cynabal.

The winde which the Angels of the Air abovesaid are under.[37]

The North-winde.

The Angel of the fourth heaven, ruling on the Lords day, which ought to be called from the four parts of the world.

---

[35] Sunday.

[36] The diagram on this page (and the next 6 diagrams) each contain 5 parts for each day. For each day the engraved figures show five separate things: the angel (Michael), his sigil (directly below his name), the planet (in this case the Sun symbolized by a circle with a dot), the astrological sign (the sign for Leo), and the name of the appropriate heaven (here Machen, the fourth heaven).

[37] This is also the direction from which to call them.

At the East.

Samael.	Baciel.	Atel.
Gabriel.	Vionairaba.	

At the West.

Anael.	Pabel.	Ustael.
Burchat.	Suceratos.	Capabili.

At the North.

Aiel.	Aniel, vel Aquiel.	Masgabriel.
Sapiel.	Matuyel.	

At the South.

Haludiel.	Machasiel.	Charsiel.
Uriel.	Naromiel.	

The perfume of the Lords day.

Red Wheat.[38]

THE CONJURATION OF THE LORDS DAY

"*Conjuro & confirmo super vos Angeli fortes Dei, & sancti, in nomine Adonay, Eye, Eye, Ey[e], qui est ille, qui fuit, est & erit, Eye, Abraye: & in nomine Sad[a]y, Cados, Cados, Cados, alie sendentis super Cherub[i]n, & per nomen magnum ipsius Dei fortis & potentis, exaltatique super omnes coelos, Eye, Saraye, plasmatoris seculorum, qui creavit mundum, coelum, terram, mare, & omnia quæ in eis sunt in primo die, & sigillavit ea sancto nomine suo Phaa: & per nomina sanctorum Angelorum, qui dominantur in quarto exercitu, & serv[i]unt coram potentissimo Salamia,[39] Angelo magno & honorato: & per nomen stellæ, quæ est Sol, & per signum, & per immensum nomen Dei vivi, & per nomina omnia prædicta, conjuro te Michael[40] an[g]ele magne, qui es præposi[t]us Dei Dominicæ: & per nomen*

---

[38] Probably should be "red sandal."

[39] The angel Salamian appeared to Kelley and Dee on 15 March 1582.

[40] Michael is the Strength of God.

Adona[y], Dei Israel, qui creavit mundum & quicquid in eo est, quod pro melabores, & ad moleas omnem meam petitionem, juxta meum velle & votum meum, in negotio & causa mea."

[**Translation:** "I conjure and confirm upon you, ye strong and holy angels of God, in the name Adonai, Eye, Eye, Eya, which is he who was, and is, and is to come, Eye, Abraye; and in the name Saday, Cados, Cados, sitting on high upon the cherubim; and by the great name of God himself, strong and powerful, who is exalted above all the heavens; Eye, Saraye, who created the world, the heavens, the earth, the sea, and all that in them is, in the first day, and sealed them with his holy name Phaa; and by the name of the angels who rule in the fourth heaven, and serve before the most mighty Salamia, an angel great and honorable; and by the name of his star, which is Sol, and by his sign, and by the immense name of the living God, and by all the names aforesaid, I conjure thee, Michael, O great angel! who art chief ruler of this day; and by the name Adonai, the God of Israel, I conjure thee, O Michael! that thou labor for me, and fulfill all my petitions according to my will and desire in my cause and business."]

And here thou shalt declare thy cause and business, and for what thing thou makest this Conjuration.

The Spirits of the Air of the Lords day, are under the North-winde; their nature is to procure Gold, Gemmes, Carbuncles, Riches; to cause one to obtain favour and benevolence; to dissolve the enmities of men; to raise men to honors; to carry or take away infirmities. But in what manner they appear, it's spoken already in the former book of Magical Ceremonies.

CONSIDERATIONS OF MUNDAY

The Angel of Munday, his Sigil, Planet, the Signe of the Planet, and name of the first heaven.

Gabriel.

Shamain.

The Angels of Munday.

Gabriel. *Michael.* *Samael.*

The Angels of the Air ruling on Munday.

Arcan, King.

His Ministers.

Bilet. *Missabu.* *Abuzaha.*

The winde which the said Angels of the Air are subject to.

The West-winde.

The Angels of the first heaven, ruling on Munday, which ought to be called from the four parts of the world.

From the East.

Gabriel. *Gabrael.* *Madiel.*
Deamiel. *Janael.*

From the West.

Sachiel. *Zaniel.* *Habaiel.*
Bachanael. *Corabael.*

From the North.

Mael. *Vuael.* *Valnum.*
Baliel. *Balay.* *Humastrau.*

From the South.

Curaniel. *Dabriel.* *Darquiel.*
Hanun. *Anayl.* *Vetuel.*

The perfume of Munday.

Aloes.

THE CONJURATION OF MUNDAY.

"Conjuro & confirmo super vos Angeli fortes & boni, in nomine Adonay, Adonay, Adonay, Eie, Eie, Eie, Cados, Cados, Cados, Achim, Achim, Ja, Ja, Fortis, Ja, qui apparuis monte Sinai, cum glorificatione regis Adonay, Saday, Zebaoth, Anathay, Ya, Ya, Ya, Marinata, Abim, Jeia, qui maria creavit stagna & omnes aquas in secundo die, quasdam super coelos, & quosdam in terra. Sigillavit mare in al[i]o nomine suo, & terminum, quam sibi posuit, non præter b[i]t: & per nomina Angelorum, qui dominantur in primo exercitu, qui serviunt Orphaniel Angelo magno, precioso & honorato: & per nomen Stellæ, quæ est Luna: & per nomina prædicta, super te conjuro, scilicet Gabriel, qui es præpositus diei. Lunæ secundo quòd pro me labores & adimpleas," &c. As in the Conjuration of Sunday.[41]

[**Translation:** "I conjure and confirm upon you, ye strong and good angels, in the name Adonai, Adonai, Adonai, Adonai, Eye, Eye, Eye, Cados, Cados, Cados, Achim, Achim, Ja, Ja, strong Ja, who appeared in Mount Sinai with the glorification of king Adonai, Saday, Zebaoth, Anathay, Ya, Ya, Ya, Marinata, Abim, Jeia, who created the sea, and all lakes and waters, in the second day, which are above the heavens and in the earth, and sealed the sea in his high name, and gave it its bounds beyond which it cannot pass; and by the names of the angels who rule in the first legion, and who serve Orphaniel, a great, precious, and honorable Angel, and by the name of his star which is Luna, and by all the names aforesaid, I conjure thee, Gabriel, who art chief ruler of Monday, the second day, that for me thou labor and fulfill," &c.]

The Spirits of the Air of Munday, are subject to the West-winde, which is the winde of the Moon: their nature is to give silver; to convey things from place to place; to make horses swift, and to disclose the secrets of persons both present and future: but in what manner they appear, you may see in the former book.

CONSIDERATIONS OF TUESDAY.

The Angel of Tuesday, his sigil, his Planet, the Signe governing that Planet, and the name of the fifth heaven.

---

[41] The rest to be the same as the conjuration for Sunday.

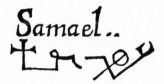

Samael.. **of ♉ ♏.**
Machon.

The Angels of Tuesday.

Samael.   Satael.   Amabiel.

The Angels of the Air ruling on Tuesday.

Samax, King.

His Ministers.

Carmax.   Ismoli.   Paffran.

The winde to which the said Angels are subject.

The East-winde.

The Angels of the fifth heaven ruling on Tuesday, which ought to be called from the four parts of the world.

At the East

Friagne.   Guael.   Damael.
Calzas.   Arragon.

At the West.

Lama.   Astagna.   Lobquin.
Soncas.   Jazel.   Isiael.
Irel.

At the North.

Rahumel.   Hyniel.   Rayel.
Seraphiel.   Mathiel.   Fraciel.

At the South.

Sacriel.	*Janiel.*	*Galdel.*
Osael.	*Vianuel.*	*Zaliel.*

The perfume of Tuesday.

Pepper.

THE CONJURATION OF TUESDAY.

"*Conjuro & confirmo super vos, Angeli fortes & sancti, per nomen Ya, Ya, Ya, He, He, He, Va, Hy, Hy, Ha, Ha, Ha, Va, Va, Va, An, An, An, Aie, Aie, Aie, El, Ay, Elibra, Eloim, Eloim: & per nomina ipsius alti Dei, qui fecit aquam aridam apparere, & vocavit terram, & produxit arbores, & herbas de ea, & sigillavit super eam cum precioso, honorato, metuendo & sancto nomine suo: & per nomen angelorum dominantium in quinto exercitu, qui serviunt Acimoy Angelo magno, forti, potenti, & honorato: & per nomen Stellæ, quæ est Mars: & per nomina præd[i]cta conjuro super te Samael, Angele magne, qui præpositus es diei Martis: & per nomina Adonay, Dei vivi & veri, quod pro me labores, & adimpleas,*" &c. As in the Conjuration of Sunday.[42]

[**Translation:** "I conjure and call upon you, ye strong and good angels, in the names Ya, Ya, Ya; He, He, He; Va, Hy, Hy, Ha, Ha, Ha; Va, Va, Va; An, An, An; Aia, Aia, Aia; El, Ay, Elibra, Elohim, Elohim; and by the names of the high God, who hath made the sea and dry land, and by his word hath made the earth, and produced trees, and hath set his seal upon the planets, with his precious, honored, revered, and holy name; and by the name of the angels governing in the fifth house, who are subservient to the great angel Acimoy, who is strong, powerful, and honored, and by the name of his star which is called Mars, I call upon thee, Samael, by the names above mentioned, thou great angel! who presides over the day of Mars, and by the name Adonai, the living and true God, that you assist me in accomplishing my labors," &c.]

---

[42] The rest to be same as per the conjuration for Sunday.

The Spirits of the Air of Tuesday are under the East-winde: their nature is to cause wars, mortality, death and combustions; and to give[43] two thousand Souldiers at a time; to bring death, infirmities or health.[44] The manner of their appearing you may see in the former book.

CONSIDERATIONS OF WEDNESDAY.

The Angel of Wednesday, his Sigil. Planet, the Signe governing that Planet, and the name of the second heaven.

The Angels of Wednesday.

Raphael.   *Miel.*   *Seraphiel.*

The Angels of the Air ruling on Wednesday.

Mediat, or Modiat, Rex.[45]

Ministers.

Suquinos,   *Sallales.*

The winde to which the said Angels of the Air are subject.

The Southwest-winde.

The Angels of the second heaven governing Wednesday, which ought to be called from the four parts of the world.

---

[43] To give to the magician.
[44] In almost every case the angel is able to bring positive or negative results, to cure illness or to inflict illness.
[45] King.

At the East.

Mathlai.   *Tarmiel.*   *Baraborat.*

At the West.

Jeresous.   *Mitraton.*

At the North.

Thiel.   *Rael.*   *J[a]riahel.*
Venahel.   *Velel.*   *Abuiori.*
Ucirnuel.

At the South.

Milliel.   *Nelapa.*   *Babel.*
Caluel.   *Vel.*   *Laquel.*

The Fumigation of Wednesday.

Mastick.

THE CONJURATION OF WEDNESDAY.

"*Conjuro & confirmo vos angeli fortes, sancti & potentes, in nomine fortis, metuendissimi & ben[e]dicti Ja, Adonay, Eloim, Saday, Saday, Saday, Eie, Eie, Eie, Asamie, Asaraie: & in nomine Adonay Dei Israel, qui creavit luminaria magna, ad distinguendum diem à nocte: & per nomen omnium Angelorum deservientium in exercitu secundo coram Tetra Angelo majori, atque forti & potenti: & per nomen Stellæ, quæ est Mercurius: & per nomen Sigilli, quæ sigillatur a Deo fortissimo & honoratio: per omnia prædicta super te Raphael*[46] *Angele magne, conjuro, qui es præpositus die: quartæ: & per no[m]en sanctum quod erat scrip[t]um in fronte Aaron sacerdotis alt[i]ssimi creatoris: & per nomina Angelorum qui in gratiam Salvatoris confirmati sunt: & per nomen sedis Animalium, habentium senas alas, quòd pro me labo, et,*" &c. As in the Conjuration of Sunday.

---

[46] Raphael is sometimes termed the "Medicine of God."

[**Translation:** "I conjure and call upon you, ye strong and holy angels, good and powerful, in a strong name of fear and praise, Ja, Adonay, Eloim, Saday, Saday, Saday; Eie, Eie, Eie; Asamie, Asaraie; and in the name of Adonay, the God of Israel, who hath created the great lights, and distinguished day from night; and by the names of all the discerning Angels, governing openly in the second house before the great Angel, Tetra, strong and powerful; and by the name of his star which is Mercury; and by the name of his seal, which is that of a powerful and honored God; and I call upon thee, great Angel Raphael, and by the names above mentioned, who presidest over the fourth day: and by the holy name which is written in the front of Aaron, created the most high priest, and by the names of all the Angels who are constant in the grace of Christ, and by the name and place of Animalium, that you assist me in my labors," &c.]

The Spirits of the Air of Wednesday are subject to the South-west-winde: their nature is to give all Metals; to reveal all earthly things past, present and to come; to pacifie judges, to give victories in war, to re-edifie, and teach experiments and all decayed Sciences, and to change bodies mixt of Elements conditionally out of one into another:[47] to give infirmities or health; to raise the poor, and cast down the high ones; to binde or lose Spirits; to open locks or bolts: such-kinde of Spirits have the operation of others, but not in their perfect power, but in virtue or knowledge. In what manner they appear, it is before spoken.

CONSIDERATIONS OF THURSDAY.

The Angel of Thursday, his Sigil, Planet, the Signe of the Planet, and the name of the sixth heaven.

---

47 Transmutation.

The Angels of Thursday.

Sachiel,   *Castiel,*   *Asasiel.*

The Angels of the Air governing Thursday.

Suth, Rex.

Ministers.

Maguth,   *Gutrix.*

The winde which the said Angels of the Air are under.

The South-winde.

But because there are no Angels of the Air to be found above the fifth heaven, therefore on Thursday say the prayers following in the four parts of the world.

At the East.

O Deus magne & excelse, & honorate, per infinita secula.[48]

At the West.

O Deus sapiens, & clare, & juste, ac divina clementia: ego rogo te prissime Pater, quòd meam petitionem, quòd meum opus, & meum laborem hodie debeam complere, & perfectè intelligere. Tu qui vivis & regnas per infinita secula seculorum, Amen.[49]

At the North.

O Deus potens, fortis, & sine principio.[50]

---

[48] O great and most high God, honored be thy name, world without end.

[49] O wise, pure and just God, divine in clemency, I beseech thee, most holy Father, that this day I may perfectly understand and accomplish my petitions, work and labour and perfect knowledge, you who lives and reigns forever, world without end, Amen.

[50] O powerful God, strong, and without beginning.

At the South.

O Deus potens & misericors.[51]

The Perfume of Thursday.

Saffron.

THE CONJURATION OF THURSDAY.

"*Conjuro & confirmo super vos, Angeli sancti, per nomen, Cados, Cados, Cados, Eschereie, Eschereie, Eschereie, Hatim ya, fortis firmator seculorum, Cantine, Jaym, Janic, Anic, Calbat, Sabbac, Berisay, Alnaym: & per nomen Adonay, qui creavit pisces reptilia in aquis, & aves super faciem terræ, volantes versus coelos die quinto: & per nomina Angelorum serventium in sexto exercitu coram pastore Angelo sancto & magno & potenti principe: & per nomen stellæ, quæ est Jupiter: & per nomen Sigilli sui: & per nomen Adonay, summi Dei, omnium creatoris: & per nomen omnium stellarum, & per vim & virtutem earum: & per nomina prædicta, conjuro te Sachiel Angele magne, qui es præpositus diei Jovis, ut pro me labores,*" &c. As in the Conjuration of the Lords day.

[**Translation:** "I conjure and confirm upon you, ye strong and holy angels, by the names Cados, Cados, Cados, Eschereie, Eschereie, Eschereie, Hatim, Ya, strong founder of the worlds; Cantine, Jaym, Janic, Anic, Calbot, Sabbac, Berisay, Alnaym; and by the name Adonai, who created fishes and creeping things in the waters, and birds upon the face of the earth, flying toward heaven, in the fifth day; and by the names of the angels serving in the sixth host before Pastor, a holy Angel, and a great and powerful prince and by the name of his star, which is Jupiter, and by the name of his seal, and by the name of Adonai, the great God, Creator of all things, and by the name of all the stars, and by their power and virtue, and by all the names aforesaid, I conjure thee, Sachiel, a great Angel, who art chief ruler of Thursday, that for me thou labor," &c.]

The Spirits of the Air of Thursday, are subject to the South-winde; their nature is to procure the love of women; to cause men to be merry and joyful; to pacifie strife and contentions; to appease

---

[51] O powerful and merciful God.

enemies; to heal the diseased, and to disease the whole;[52] and procureth losses, or taketh them away. Their manner of appearing is
spoken of already.

CONSIDERATIONS OF FRIDAY.

The Angel of Friday, his Sigil, his Planet, the Signe governing that
Planet, and name of the third heaven.

The Angels of Friday.

Anael.   Rachiel.   Sachiel.

The Angels of the Air reigning on Friday.

Sarabotes, King.

Ministers.

Amabiel.   Aba.   Abalidoth.
Flaef.

The winde which the said Angels of the Air are under.

The West-winde.

Angels of the third heaven, ruling on Friday, which are to be called
from the four parts of the world.

At the East.

Setchiel.   Chedusitaniel.   Corat.
Tamael.   Tenaciel.

---

[52] The Spirits can either bring disease, or take it away: there does not seem
to be a strong inclination one way or the other.

At the West.

Turiel.   Coniel.   Babiel.
Kadie.   Maltiel.   Huphaltiel.

At the North.

Peniel.   Penael.   Penat.
Raphael.[53] Raniel.   Doremiel.

At the South.

Porna.   Sachiel.[54] Chermiel.
Samael.   Santanael.   Famiel.

The Perfume of Friday.

Pepperwort.

THE CONJURATION OF FRIDAY.

"*Conjuro & confirmo super vos Angeli fortes, sancti atque potentes, in nomine On, Hey, Heya, Ja, Je, Adonay, Saday, & in nomine Saday, qui creavit quadrupedia & anamalia reptilia, & homines in sexto die, & Adæ dedit potestatem super omnia animalia: unde benedictum sit nomen creatoris in loco suo: & per nomina Angelorum servientium in tertio exercitu, coram Dagiel Angelo magno, principe forti atque potenti: & per nomen Stellæ quæ est Venus: & per Sigillum ejus, quod quidem est sanctum: & per nomina prædicta conjuro super te Anael, qui es præpositus diei sextæ, ut pro me labores,*" &c. As before in the Conjuration of Sunday.

[Translation: "I conjure and confirm upon you, ye strong and holy angels, by the names On, Hey, Heya, Ja, Je, Saday, Adonai, and in the name Saday, who created quadrupeds, and creeping things, and man, in the sixth day, and gave to Adam power over all creatures; wherefore blessed be the name of the Creator in his place; and by the name of the angels serving in the third host, before Dagiel, a

---

[53] It does not seem to matter that Raphael is also the main angel of Wednesday.

[54] Also the main angel of Thursday.

great angel, and a strong and powerful prince, and by the name of his star, which is Venus, and by his seal which is holy; and by all the names aforesaid, I conjure upon thee, Anael, who art the chief ruler this day, that thou labor for me," &c.]

The Spirits of the Air of Friday are subject to the West-winde; their nature is to give silver: to excite men, and incline them to luxury; to reconcile enemies through luxury; and to make marriages; to allure men to love women; to cause, or take away infirmities; and to do all things which have motion.

CONSIDERATIONS OF SATURDAY, OR THE SABBATH DAY.

The Angel of Saturday,[55] his Seal, his Planet, and the Signe governing the Planet.

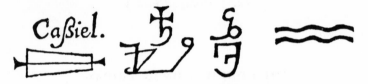

The Angels of Saturday.

Cassiel.   Machatan. Uriel.

The Angels of the Air ruling on Saturday.

Maymon, King.

Ministers.

Abumalith. Assaibi.   Balidet.

The winde which the said Angels of the Air aforesaid are under.

The Southwest-winde.

---

[55] Mentioning Saturday as the Sabbath day tends to suggest Jewish origins for this work. Of course all the angels with their "–iel" endings are obviously from Hebrew sources. The angel of Saturday named in the diagram is Cassiel.

The Fumigation of Saturday.

Sulphur.[56]

It is already declared in the Consideration of Thursday, That there are no Angels ruling the Air, above the fifth heaven: therefore in the four Angles of the world, use those Orations which you see applied to that purpose on Thursday.

THE CONJURATION OF SATURDAY.

"*Conjuro & confirmo super vos Caphriel vel Cassiel, Machatori, & Seraquiel Angeli fortes & potentes: & per nomen Adonay, Adonay, Adonay, Eie, Eie, Eie, Acim, Acim, Acim, Cados, Cados, Ina vel Ima, Ima, Saclay, Ja, Sar, Domini formatoris seculorum, qui in septimo die quieu[i]t: & per illum qui in beneplacito suo filiis Israel in hereditatem observandum dedit, ut eum firmiter custodirent, & sanctificarent, ad habendem inde bonam in alio seculo remunerationem: & per nomina Angelorum servientium in exercitu septimo Pooel Angelo magno & potenti principi: & per nomen stellæ quæ est Saturnus: & per sanctum Sigillum ejus: & per nomina prædicta conjuro super te Caphriel, qui præpositus es diei septimæ, quæ est dies Sabbati, quòd pro me labores,*" &c. As is set down in the Conjuration of the Lords day.

[**Translation:** "I conjure and confirm upon you, Caphriel, or Cassiel, Machatori, and Seraquiel, strong and powerful angels; and by the name Adonai, Adonai, Adonai, Eie, Eie, Eie; Acim, Acim, Acim; Cados, Cados; Ina or Ima, Ima; Saclay, Ja, Sar, Lord and Maker of the World, who rested on the seventh day; and by him who of his good pleasure gave the same to be observed by the children of Israel throughout their generations, that they should keep and sanctify the same, to have thereby a good reward in the world to come; and by the names of the angels serving in the seventh host, before Pooel, a great Angel, and powerful prince; and by the name of his star, which is Saturn; and by his holy seal, and by the names before spoken, I conjure upon thee, Caphriel, who art chief ruler of the seventh day, which is the Sabbath, that for me thou labor," &c.]

---

[56] "Fumigation" refers to the incense to be burned. Sulphur is traditional for Saturn, but very dangerous to burn in a confined space.

The Spirits of the Air of Saturday are subject to the Southwest-winde: the nature of them is to sow discords, hatred, evil thoughts and cogitations; to give leave freely, to slay and kill every one, and to lame or maim every member. Their manner of appearing is declared in the former book.

TABLES OF THE ANGELS OF THE HOURS, ACCORDING TO THE COURSE OF THE DAYES.[48]

SUNDAY.

Hours of the day.	Angels of the [day] hours.	Hours of the night.	Angels of the [night] hours.
1. Yayn.	Michael.	1. Beron.	Sachiel.
2. Janor.	Anael.	2. Barol.	Samael.
3. Nasnia.	Raphael.	3. Tha[n]u.	Michael.
4. Salla.	Gabriel.	4. Athir.	Anael.
5. Sadedali.	Cassiel.	5. Mathun.	Raphael.
6. Thamur.	Sachiel.	6. Rana.	Gabriel.
7. Ourer.	Samael.	7. Netos.	Cassiel.
8. Tanic.	Michael.	8. Tafrac.	Sachiel.
9. Neron.	Anael.	9. Sassur.	Samael.
10. Jayon.	Raphael.	10. Aglo.	Michael.
11. Abay.	Gabriel.	11. Calerna.	Anael.
12. Natalon.	Cassiel.	12. Salam.	Raphael.

MUNDAY.

Hours of the day.	Angels of the [day] hours.	Hours of the night.	Angels of the [night] hours.
1. Yayn.	Gabriel.	1. Beron.	Anael.
2. Janor.	Cassiel.	2. Barol.	Raphael.
3. Nasnia.	Sachiel.	3. Thaun.[49]	Gabriel.
4. Salla.	Samael.	4. Athir.	Cassiel.
5. Sadedali.	Michael.	5. Mathon.	Sachiel.
6. Thamur.	Anael.	6. Rana.	Samael.
7. Ourer.	Raphael.	7. Netos.	Michael.
8. Tanic.	Gabriel.	8. Tafrac.	Anael.
9. Neron.	Cassiel.	9. Sassur.	Raphael.
10. Jayon.	Sachiel.	10. Aglo.	Gabriel.
11. Abay.	Samael.	11. Calerna.	Cassiel.
12. Natalon.	Michael.	12. Salam.	Sachiel.

---

[57] This is the second appendix that was probably not in de Abano's original work. The tables for Sunday have been slightly redesigned to clarify them.

[58] This is likely an error and should be "Thanu."

TUESDAY.

Hours of the day.	Angels of the [day] hours.	Hours of the night.	Angels of the [night] hours.
1. Yayn.	Samael.	1. Beron.	Cassiel.
2. Janor.	Michael.	2. Barol.	Sachiel.
3. Nasnia.	Anael.	3. Thanu.	Samael.
4. Salla.	Raphael.	4. Athir.	Michael.
5. Sadedal[i].	Gabriel.	5. Mathon.	Anael.
6. Thamur.	Cassiel.	6. Rana.	Raphael.
7. Ourer.	Sachiel.	7. Netos.	Gabriel.
8. Tanic.	Samael.	8. Tafrac.	Cassiel.
9. Neron.	Michael.	9. Sussur.[59]	Sachiel.
10. Jayon.	Anael.	10. Aglo.	Samael.
11. Abay.	Raphael.	11. Calerna.	Michael.
12. Natalon.	Gabriel.	12. Salam.	Anael.

WEDNESDAY.

Hours of the day.	Angels of the [day] hours.	Hours of the night.	Angels of the [night] hours.
1. Yayn.	Raphael.	1. Beron.	Michael.
2. Janor.	Gabriel.	2. Barol.	Anael.
3. Nasnia.	Cassiel.	3. Thanu.	Raphael.
4. Salla.	Sachiel.	4. Athir.	Gabriel.
5. Sadedali.	Samael.	5. Mathon.	Cassiel.
6. Thamur.	Michael.	6. Rana.	Sachiel.
7. Ourer.	Anael.	7. Netos.	Samael.
8. Tanic.	Raphael.	8. Tafrac.	Michael.
9. Neron.	Gabriel.	9. Sassur.	Anael.
10. Jayon.	Cassiel.	10. Aglo.	Raphael.
11. Abay.	Sachiel.	11. Calerna.	Gabriel.
12. Neron.[60]	Samael.	12. Salam.	Cassiel.

---

[59] This appears in the original text but should probably read "Sassur."
[60] This appears in the original text but should probably read "Natalon."

THURSDAY.

Hours of the day.	Angels of the [day] hours.	Hours of the night.	Angels of the [night] hours.
1. Yayn.	Sachiel.	1. Beron.	Gabriel.
2. Janor.	Samael.	2. Barol.	Cassiel.
3. Nasnia.	Michael.	3. Thanu.	Sachiel.
4. Salla.	Anael.	4. Athir.	Samael.
5. Sadedali.	Raphael.	5. Mathon.	Michael.
6. Thamur.	Gabriel.	6. Rana.	Anael.
7. Ourer.	Cassiel.	7. Netos.	Raphael.
8. Tanic.	Sachiel.	8. Tafrac.	Gabriel.
9. Neron.	Samael.	9. Sassur.	Cassiel.
10. Jayon.	Michael.	10. Aglo.	Sachiel.
11. Abay.	Anael.	11. Calerna.	Samael.
12. Natalon.	Raphael.	12. Salam.	Michael.

FRIDAY.

Hours of the day.	Angels of the [day] hours.	Hours of the night.	Angels of the [night] hours.
1. Yayn.	Anael.	1. Beron.	Samael.
2. Janor.	Raphael.	2. Barol.	Michael.
3. Nasnia.	Gabriel.	3. Thanu.	Anael.
4. Salla.	Cassiel.	4. Athir.	Raphael.
5. Sadedali.	Sachiel.	5. Mat[h]on.	Gabriel.
6. Thamur.	Samael.	6. Rana.	Cassiel.
7. Ourer.	Michael.	7. Netos.	Sachiel.
8. Tanic.	Anael.	8. Tafrac.	Samael.
9. Neron.	Raphael.	9. Sassur.	Michael.
10. Jayon.	Gabriel.	10. Aglo.	Anael.
11. Abay.	Cassiel.	11. Calerna.	Raphael.
12. Natalon.	Sachiel.	12. Salam.	Gabriel.

SATURDAY.

Hours of the day.	Angels of the [day] hours.	Hours of the night.	Angels of the [night] hours.
1. Yayn.	Cassiel.	1. Beron.	Raphael.
2. Janor.	Sachiel.	2. Barol.	Gabriel.
3. Nasnia.	Samael.	3. Thanu.	Cassiel.
4. Salla.	Michael.	4. Athir.	Sachiel.
5. Sadedali.	Anael.	5. Mat[h]on.	Samael.
6. Thamur.	Raphael.	6. Rana.	Michael.
7. Ourer.	Gabriel.	7. Netos.	Anael.
8. Tanic.	Cassiel.	8. Tafrac.	Raphael.
9. Neron.	Sachiel.	9. Sussur.[61]	Gabriel.
10. Jayon.	Samael.	10. Aglo.	Cassiel.
11. Abay.	Michael.	11. Calerna.	Sachiel.
12. Natalon.	Anael.	12. Salam.	Samael.

But this is to be observed by the way, that the first hour of the day, of every Country, and in every season whatsoever, is to be assigned to the Sun-rising,[62] when he first appeareth arising in the horizon: and the first hour of the night is to be the thirteenth hour, from the first hour of the day. But of these things it is sufficiently spoken.

FINIS.

---

[61] This appears in the original text but should read "Sassur."

[62] These "hours" are usually referred to as "planetary hours." The start time of the first hour of the day will vary slightly from day to day, as the time of sunrise varies. It is more usual to count the first hour of the night from the time of sunset, not from a fixed 13 hours from the first hour of the day. The effect of calculating 12 "planetary hours" from sunrise to sunset is that each "day hour" will be shorter in winter and longer in summer. The reverse is true of the night hours.

ISAGOGE

An Introductory Discourse of the nature of such Spirits as are exercised in the sublunary Bounds; their Original, Names, Offices, Illusions, Power, Prophesies, Miracles; and how they may be expelled and driven away.

By *Geo. Pictorius Villinganus Dr.* in *Physick.*

in a Discourse between CASTOR and POLLUX.

astor. The Greeks do report, that *Castor & Pollux have both proceeded from one egge*; but this I scarcely credit, by reason of the difference of your mindes; for thou affectest the heavens, but she meditates upon the earth and slaughters.

Pollux. And from thence perhaps was derived that argument, *That liberty of lying was alwaies assigned to the Greeks.*

Castor. Principally.

Pollux. But it is not to be supposed, that the *Greeks* are vain in all things; but as many others, when they speak out of a three-footed thing;[1] whereof also the Poet *Ovid* speaks in verse,

Nec singunt omnia Graeci.

Castor. In this proverb I protest they are most true, without any exception, that is, ἀιθϵυπ & διθιώπυ δαιμόνιον.[2] that is, *One man to another is a devil.*

Pollux. Wherefore believest thou this to be most true, *Castor?*

---

[1] A tripod is the reference, by which he means the Classical Greek oracles.
[2] Margin note: *Homo homini Deus.*

Castor. Truely, that man to man is a devil[3] and a ravening wolf, daily events do most certainly prove, if we do but note the treacheries that one man invents daily against another, the robberies, thefts, plunderings, rapes, slaughters, deceits, adulteries, and an hundred vipers of this nature; the fathers persecute the son, with a serpentine and poisonous biting; one friend seeks to devour another, neither can the guest be safe with his host.

Pollux. I confess it is truth thou speakest; but for ought I hear, thou dost misunderstand the Etymologie of the word compared in this Proverb; for *Daemon* here is not an horrible or odious name, but the name of one that doth administer help or succor unto another, and whom *Pliny* calleth a God.[4]

Castor. Therefore dost thou affirm the word *Daemon* in this Proverb to signifie any other then a cunning and malicious accuser?

Pollux. Thou hast not shot besides the mark:[5] for, that there are more *Daemons* then that sublunary[6] one which thou understandest, every one may easily perceive, who hath not negligently read the opinions of the most excellent *Plato*.[7]

Castor. I desire therefore, that thou wouldst not conceal such [in] his writings; but that I may apprehend the marrow[8] thereof.

Pollux. I will embrace such thy desire, for truely I do delight to treat[9] with thee concerning this subject; mark therefore, and give attention.

---

[3]   Margin note: *Homo homini diabolus.*

[4]   Explaining that the meaning of the word "daemon" is quite different from "devil" which is a different word in the Vulgate, or Latin version of the Bible. Margin note: *Plin[y] lib[er] 2. chap[ter] 7.*

[5]   In other words, you have made a correct statement.

[6]   That is, "beneath the Moon," meaning existing in the atmosphere between the Earth and the Moon.

[7]   Plato's *daemon* is the most famous classical description of this kind of entities. In modern terms, Plato's *daemon* comes close to a sort of personal guardian angel, quite different to what was meant by the word "devil."

[8]   The "marrow" means the core of the meaning.

[9]   Discuss.

Plato divided the orders of Devils or Spirits into three degrees,[10] which as they are distinct in the greatness of their dignity, so also they are different in the distance and holding of their places. And the first order[11] he ascribeth to those Spirits whose bodies are nourished of the most pure element of Air, wrought and joyned together, in a manner, as it were with splendid threeds, not having so much reference to the element of fire, that they may be perspicuous to the sight;[12] neither do they so much participate of the earth, that they may be touched or felt.[13] And they do inhabit the Coelestial Theatre, attending and waiting on their Prince, not to be declared by any humane tongue, or beyond the commands of the most wise God.

But the other degree[14] is derived from those Spirits which *Apuleius* termeth rational animals, passive in their minde, and eternal in their time, understanding the apostate Spirits[15] spread abroad from the bounds and borders of the Moon, unto us under the dominion of their Prince *Beelzebub*, which before the fall of *Lucifer* had pure clarified bodies; and now, like unto the former, do wander up and down, after their transgression, in the form of an aiery quality.

Castor. These I do not conceive are underſtood in the *Greek* Proverb: for these do hurt, are the accusers and betrayers of men. But proceed.

Pollux. The third degree of Spirits[16] is of a divine deitie, which is called by *Hermes*, A divine miracle to man, if he do not degenerate from the Kingly habit of his first form; whom therefore of this kinde the *Greeks* and *Plato* have called *Daemons*, that is, God; and that man may be like unto God, and profitable and commodious one to another; and so also (the *Syrian* being witness) we have known *Plato* himself to have been called [a] *Daemon*,[17] because he had set forth very many things of very high matters, for the good

---

[10] Margin Note: Three degrees of Spirits.

[11] Margin note: The first degree of Spirits.

[12] Not having enough Fire Element to be visible.

[13] SB. A semicolon occurs here in the original.

[14] Margin note: The second degree.

[15] Those who deny God.

[16] Margin note: The third degree.

[17] Margin note: *Plato* called *daemon*, and *Aristotle* [also].

of the Commonwealth; and so likewise *Aristotle*, because he very largely disputed of sublunaries, and all such things as are subject to motion and sence. *Homer* calleth [both] God and evil Spirits, *Demons*, without putting a discrimination.

Castor. Thou hast committed the ship to the waves,[18] *Pollux*; therefore cease not to proceed, and declare something more concerning the Office[19] and imployment of these Spirits, to whom *Plato* attributeth the second degree, and calleth them Lunaries.[20]

Pollux. What shall I say?

Castor. In the first place, declare wherefore thou hast before termed these Spirits cunning and much knowing Accusers.

Pollux. Saint *Augustine* unfoldeth this difficulty, and saith, That a *Devil doth so far signifie the cunning and much knowing quickness and vivacity of his deceitful wit, that by the congruent and agreeable seminal permixtures of elements, he doth so know the secrets and unknown vertues of men, as those things which may be effected and wrought by themselves successively and leisurely according to the course of nature, he by a speedy hasting or forcing of the works of nature, or by his own art, sooner bringeth the same to pass.*[21]
An example hereof he giveth in the wise men of *Pharaoh*, who immediately brought forth frogs and serpents at the commandment of the King, which nature more slowly and leisurely procreateth.

Castor. Thou hast excellently answered to the question, *Pollux*; but adde some thing concerning the original of those Spirits which do refut[e] and refuse vertue; for oftentimes doubting, I have been perswaded that such Erynnes[22] as are from God, do not appear out of the earth.

Pollux. The Ecclesiastical Scripture everywhere maketh mention of the rising of them; but I will unfold such a doubt: and there do arise many and various opinions of writers, but more commonly

---

[18] In other words, begun your argument.
[19] Function.
[20] Of the Moon.
[21] Margin note: Why the devil is said to have much knowledge.
[22] Erinyes, Furies or avenging goddesses who punished crimes.

Peter Lombardus in his book of Sentences,[23] draweth his Allegations out of St. *Augustine* upon *Genesis*; to wit, That *the Divel was before his fall an Archangel, and had a fine tender body, composed by God, cut of the serenity and purest matter of the Skie and Air; but then after his fall from an Archangel, he was made an Apostate, and his body no more fine and subtil; but his body was made that it might suffer the effect of a more gross substance, from the quality of the more obscure, dark, and spissious Air, which body also was stricken and astonished with the raging madness of pride, did draw away very many which were then Angels with him into his service and bondage, that they might be made Devils, who for him in this troublesome world do exercise their servile courses for him, and they do compel the inhabitants therein, or rather entice them; and to this purpose they undertake various endeavours, and do attempt various and manifold horrible studies, that are abominable unto God, and they serve in slavery and thraldom to Beelzebub their Prince, and are held in most strong captivity.*

Castor. What? Have we the fall of this Archangel nowhere else in holy writ, but in the writings of St. *Augustine*?

Pollux. We have also the fall of other Angels.[24]

Castor. Where?

Pollux. In *Esaias*,[25] to whom thou shalt give the honour of an Evangelist, rather then a Prophet, because he so fully and plainly foretold of Christ and his kingdom: he maketh mention hereof in his 14th Chapter. And we have them also spoken of by the Apostle *Peter*, when he saith, *God spared not his Angels which sinned.* 2 Epist[le]. 2.

Castor. Have the Devils a select place appointed them by God, which they inhabit?

---

[23] The *Sentences* of Peter of Lombard (ca.1100–ca.1160) is a famous collection of theological opinions. Margin note: *Lib[er] 2. distinct. 7.*

[24] Margin note: The fall of *Lucifer* in Scripture.

[25] Isaiah 14:12–15; although Isaiah 14:16 reads as if the description pertains to an earthly king, rather than a fallen angel.

Pollux. Peter the head of the Church,[26] in the place before quoted, affirmeth *them to be cast headlong into bell, reserved in the chains of hell, from whence (as Cortesius saith) they never go out, unless it be to tempt, provoke. and delude men.*[27] But St. *Augustine* the Champion of Christ, in his book of *The Agony of a Christian*, teacheth, That *these kinde of Spirits do inhabit* [the Air] *in the sublunary region.* And in his 49th Epist[le]. he sets forth, That *the most dark and obscure part of the Air, is predestinated unto them as a prison, that they may the more nearly cast their nets of enticing and detaining.*

Castor. Origen hath taught, That *the punishments of the Devils are appointed for a time*; what saist thou to this?[28]

Pollux. What shall I say? unless I should bewail and deplore the opinion of so great a man.

Castor. Wherefore shouldst thou do so?

Pol[lux]. Truely if they have hardened themselves in wickedness, time cannot purge nor cleanse them; or if they never so much desire it, they can never be able to accomplish it; for there is no space of repentance, nor time to recal that which is past, given unto them.

Castor. Thou hast now declared that the Archangel that became an apostate, did draw away very many other Angels with him in his fall, that they might become Devils: could not he of his own proper inseparate malice after his fall sufficiently rule over his own Province, without the Angels that fell with him?

Pol[lux].[29] He could: but being allured by that pride, which made him so arrogantly affect the Majesty of God, he did so far strive to be like unto God, that he chose very many Ministers unto himself, to which in general he doth not commit all things he would have effected, but diverse things to divers Ministers, as may be gathered from the *Hebrew* Astronomers. Those which we call *Jovii*, &

---

[26] St. Peter.

[27] Margin note: What place the devils have appointed [for them].

[28] Margin note: The torments of the devils are everlasting.

[29] Margin note: Why the Devil hath familiars.

Antemeridianii,[30] which are false Gods, that is, lyers, which desire
to be esteemed and adored for Gods.[31] And they are appointed as
Servants and slaves to the Devil their Prince, that they might allure
the people of the earth into a common love of themselves, which
Plato saith, *Is the fountain of all wickedness, that they may aspire to
authority and greatness, covet to be gorgeously clothed, to be called
Monarchs of the earth in perpetual power, and Gods upon earth.* It
is said, That it was one of these that spoke to our Saviour, shewing
him all the Kingdoms of the earth, saying, *All these things will I
give thee, if thou wilt fall down and worship me.*[32]

Castor. Certainly these *Meridiani,*[33] I have almost declared to appear
a madness in *Libicus, Sappho,* and *Dioclesian* the Emperour, who
accounted, the utmost degree of blessedness was, to be reputed
for Gods.[34]

Pol[lux]. Truly, this is a certain natural foolishness of the minde,
and of humane nature: he began, having taken certain little birds
to teach them by little and little to pronounce humane words, &
say, μίγαι Θεὸς Ψisor , that is, *Sapho is a great God.* Which birds when
they could pronounce the words perfectly, he sent them abroad
for this end and purpose, that flying everywhere abroad, [in order
that] they might repeat those words; and the people which were
ignorant of his deceitful invention, were drawn to believe, that
those words were spoken by divine instinct, and thereupon adore
and worship him for a God. The other would compel his Subjects
hereunto, that prostrating themselves down, and lifting up their
hands, they should worship him as Almighty.

Castor. But are not they the captives of the Devil, who stir up wars,
which are called *bloody men* in Scripture?[35]

---

[30] Margin note: *Daemons Jovii* or *Antemerid.*

[31] SB. Originally a comma here.

[32] Margin note: Mat[thew] 4[:9]. It is interesting that the Bible accepts
that there were spirits upon Earth who were able to transport Christ up a
mountain, and who pretended or were really able to give the Earth and its
treasures to him.

[33] Margin note: The Southern Spirits.

[34] Margin note: *Libicus, Sapho* and *Dioclesian,* [say they are] Gods. The
Comment of *Sapho.*

[35] Margin note: *Psalm. 55.*

Pol[lux]. The Martialists of the North part of the world,[36] are called Executioners of vengeance, Authors of devastations, and sowers of evil, working and executing judgement with *Asmodeus*, for their King *Abaddon* or *Apollyon*, whom St. *John* in his *Revelation*, mentioneth to be banished and expelled; for these Spirits have committed to them rapines, hatred, envy, robberies, wrath, anger, the excitements and provocations to sin, war and fury; sometimes making the Meridional Spirits their Messengers.[37] And *Arioch* the Spirit of vengeance, whose work is to cause discord among brethren, to break wedlock, and dissolve conjugal love, that it's impossible to be renewed; of these mention is made in the 39th Chapter of *Ecclesiasticus*.[38] And *Esaias* the heavenly Prophet[39] speaketh of other Spirits sent from God to the *Aegyptians* to make them erre, which were Spirits of darkness, that is, of lyes; and this kinde of Spirit they call *Bolichim*.[40]

Castor. Is unlawful venery, and excessive gluttony, also to be imputed to [the action of] the Devils?

Pol[lux]. Yes chiefly; for *Iamblichus* doth assert, *That the Spirits of the water, of the western part of the world, and some meridional Spirits,*[41] are predestinated to this purpose; such as Nesrach *and* Kellen, *that do so frame and contrive unlawful loves, which produce shame and dishonesty. revellings and g[o]urmandizings, surfetings with excessive drunkenness, wanton dances, gluttony and vomiting: they wander about lakes, fish-ponds and rivers, and which are the worst, foul and most fraudulent kinde of Spirits: and by* Alcinach *an occidental Spirit, he causeth shipwracks, tempests, earthquakes, hail, rain, and frequently subverteth and overturneth ships: and if he will appear visible, he appeareth and is seen in the shape of a woman.* The *Hebrew* Astronomers before spoken of, do say, *That the Spirits of the Air do cause thunders, lightnings and thunderbolts, that so they might corrupt and infect the Air, and produce pestilence and destruction.*[42]

---

[36] Margin note: The Spirits of the North.
[37] Margin note: Meridian Spirit[s].
[38] Margin note: Eccl[esiatic]us. 39. 28.
[39] Isaiah.
[40] Margin note: Spirits of darkness.
[41] Margin note: Occidental Spirits.
[42] Margin note: The spirits of the air do infect the air.

Of such kinde of Spirits St. *John* makes mention in the 9[th] Chapter of the *Revelation*, having *Meceris* for their tutelar,[43] which is a Spirit causing heat in the time of noon. St. *Paul* calleth him, *The Prince of the power of the Air*, and *the Spirit that ruleth in the children of disobedience.*[44]

Castor. Are there so many monsters in *Phlegeton*,[45] *Pollux?*

Pol[lux]. And many more; for the same *Hebrew* Assertors do declare and maintain, That *there are Spirits of the fiery element,*[46] *raging about like the fierce Panthers, which are conversant under the lunary regions, that whatsoever is committed to them, they forthwith execute the same. And there are Spirits of the earth,*[47] *which inhabit in groves, woods and wildernesses, and are the plague and mischief of hunters; and sometimes they frequent open fields, endeavouring to seduce travellers and passengers out of their right way, or to deceive them with false and wicked illusions; or else they seek to afflict men with a hurtful melancholy, to make them furious or mad, that they may hurt them, and sometimes almost kill them.*

    The chief of these are Sanyaab *and* Achimael, *which are oriental Spirits,*[48] *a kinde unapt for wickedness, by reason of the constancy of their dispositions. There are also subterranean Spirits,*[49] *which do inhabit in dens and cavernes of the earth, and in remote concavities of [the] mountaines, that they might invade deep pits, and the bowels of the earth; these do dig up metals, and keep treasures, which oftentimes they do transport from one place to another, lest any man should make use thereof: they stir up windes with flashing flames of fire: they smite the foundations of buildings, acting frightful daunces in the night, from which they suddenly vanish away, with making a noise and sounds of bells, thereby causing fear in the beholders; and sometimes dissembling, and faining*[50] *themselves to be the Souls of the dead: notwithstanding they are ignorant in compassing their*

---

[43] Teacher.

[44] Margin note: *Ephes[ians].* 2[:2].

[45] One of the rivers of hell, a tributary of the Styx.

[46] Margin note: Spirits of fire.

[47] Margin note: Spirits of the earth.

[48] Spirits from the Eastern quarter, rather than Asian spirits.

[49] Margin note: Subterranean Spirits.

[50] Pretending.

deceits upon women; of which company the Negromancers[51] do say is *Gazael, Fegor and Anarazol,[which are] Meridian Spirits.*

Castor. How warily ought a man to walk, *Pollux*, amongst so many ginnes and snares?

Pol[lux]. A man never walketh safely,[52] unless he fortifie and strengthen himself with the armour of God, which is, *That his loynes be girt about with truth, and having on the breast-plate of righteousness, let him walk with his feet shod with the preparation of the Gospel of peace, and let him take the sheild of faith, and the helmet of salvation, whereby he shall dash in pieces all the darts of his adversary.*

But hear further: There are also besides these, other lying Spirits (although they are all lyers) yet these are more apt to lye; they are called *Pythons*,[53] from whence *Apollo* is called *Pythius*. They have a Prince, of whom mention is made in the book of the *Kings*,[54] where it is said, *I will be a lying Spirit in the mouth of all thy Prophets*; from whom the Spirits of iniquity do but a little differ, which also are called vessels of wrath. *Belial*, whom they have interpreted to be without any equal, and *Paul* calleth him an Apostate or transgessor, is filthily inservient for the worst inventions.

Plato affirmeth *Theut*[55] to have been such a one, who was the first that found out and invented Playes and Dice:[56] to whom we will joyne the Monk, who invented the use of Gunpowder, in his Engins of war.[57] Of these *Jacob* makes mention in *Genesis*, where he blesseth his Sons.[58] He saith, Simeon and Levi are bloody vessels or iniquity; Oh my soul, come not thou into their counsels.

---

[51] Necromancers.

[52] Margin note: A man never walketh safe. *Eph[esians]* 6.

[53] A reference to the ancient Greek priestess or sybil who sits upon the tripod of Apollo above a fissure in the Earth and prophesies. *Pytho* is the spirit who possesses the sybil who utters the prophecy.

[54] Margin note: 1 *Kings* 11.

[55] Maybe Thoth.

[56] Card and dice games and hence gambling.

[57] Roger Bacon (ca.1214–ca.1294) was reputed to be a sorceror, as well as being centuries ahead of his time and inventing the telescope and gunpowder. In 1265 Pope Clement IV commissioned Bacon to write three books which were to contain all that was then known about science.

[58] SB; originally a colon here. Margin note: *Pulvis pyrium. Gen[esis]* 49.

The *Psalmist* termeth these Spirits, *vessels of death;* *Esaias*[59] calleth them, *vessels of fury;* Jeremiah, *vessels of wrath;* and *Ezekiel* calleth them, *vessels of death and destruction.*

The Negromancers do call the said *Belial, Chodar, an oriental Spirit, which hath under him also the Spirits of Juglers,*[60] who do imitate and endeavour to act miracles, that they may seduce false Magicians and wicked persons.

It is apparently manifest, that the Serpent which deceived *Eve,* was such a seducer, and *Satan* is his Prince, of whom it is spoken in the *Revelation,* that *he should deceive the whole world.* And such a one was he, that at *Tubinga,*[61] in the sight of many people devoured a whole Chariot and some horses.

Castor. And what shall be the end of these false Prophets, and workers of wickedness? I can scarce believe that there is any angle or corner in the whole fabrick of the world, that is free from them.

Pol[lux]. Scarce the smallest mite that may be seen.

Castor. Therefore dost thou truely call the world the receptacle of those false lights.[62]

Pol[lux]. If it were not most safely purged with the Sword of the word of God, it would forthwith be worse.

Castor. Without doubt.

Pol[lux]. Nevertheless I have seen many that remain, whom I have not yet inscribed in this frantique Catalogue [of spirits].

Castor. Who are they?

Pol[lux]. False accusers and spies, obedient to *Astaroth,* who is called a Devil among the *Greeks;* and *John* calleth him [Astaroth] the accuser of the brethren.[63] Also there are tempters and deceivers that lie in wait to deceive, who are present with every man, and

---

[59] Isaiah.

[60] "Jugglers" meant tricksters or false magicians.

[61] Tubingen.

[62] Margin note: The world is the receptacle of [false prophets].

[63] Margin note: devils, false accusers, and spies.

these we term evil Angels, which have *Mammon* for their King, & they do affect men with an insatiable* avarice & thirsty desire after authority and dominion.

There are others called *Lucifugi*, which fly from the light,[64] never appearing in the day, but delighting in darkness, maliciously vexing and troubling men, and sometimes by Gods permission, either by some touching, breathing or inspiration, do hurt to them; but truely they are a kind which are unapt for to do much wickedness, because they eschew[65] & fly from any communication with men. *Pliny* the second relates, that *there was such a one at* Athens, *in a certain spacious house, which* Anthenodorus *the Philosopher happened to purchase.*[66] And *Suetonius* in his sixth book of *Caesar*, makes mention of another [spirit] to have long continued in the garden of *Lamianus*.

Castor. I desire, if it be not too irksome to thee, declare unto me what *Pliny* speaketh concerning this Spirit of *Anthenodorus*.

Pol[lux]. The story is something long and prolixious, yet it shall not much trouble me to relate it. It is thus: *Pliny* in the seventh book of his *Epistles* writeth, *Of a certain large spacious house at* Athens, *which no body would inhabit by reason of the nocturnal incursions of Spirits, which were so formidable to the inhabitants, that sometimes in the day-time, and when they were watching, they would cast them into dreams, so alwayes, that the shapes & forms which they then saw, were ever present in their memory.*

Where at length a certain Philosopher named Anthenodorus *happened to purchase that house, and prepared and furnished the same for himself to dwell in; and because all men had an evil suspition of that house, he forthwith commanded his servants to provide him a bed and tables, that after he had compleated and finished his study he might go to bed. He therefore* (saith Pliny[)] *when he went in (in the evening) and applied himself to his study, suddenly heard the locks to shake open, and the chains to be moved; nevertheless he did not lift up his eyes, nor stirred from his book, but stopped his ears with his fingers, lest that furious tumult might work a vain fear upon him;*

---

[64] Margin note: *Lucifugi*, fliers from the light.

[65] Avoid.

[66] Margin note: A horrible apparition of a Spirit in the house of Anthenodorus.

but the noise still approaching neerer unto to him, at length he looked up, and saw an effigies like unto a finger beckoning and calling unto him, which he little regarded, until it had touched him three times, and the noise drew neer unto the table; and then he looked up, and took a light, and beheld the Spirit, as it were an old man, worn away with withered leanness and deformity, his beard hanging down long, horrible and deformed hair, his legs and feet were as it were laden with chains and fetters: he went towards a gate which was bolted, and there left the Philosopher, and vanished away.

Castor. What fearful things thou relatest, *Pollux!* but what was the event of this sad spectacle?

Pol[lux]. The next day he related the whole matter to the Magistrates in order, as he had seen the same, admonishing them that they should dig diligently about the threshold of the door; for there it was probable they might finde something which might cause the house to he quiet and habitable.

Castor. What did they finde?

Po[lux]. Having digged up the earth, *Pliny* saith, *They found a dead carcass, bound and intangled in chains and fetters, his flesh being consumed with devouring time, which without delay they caused to be buried, according to the Christian ceremonies.*

Castor. But this being performed, did the house afterwards become quiet and habitable?

Pol[lux]. Yes, very well.

Castor. What madness therefore possesseth them who prophane and destroy Churchyards, where the sacred Organs of the holy and blessed Spirit do rest; and do give the bones of the dead for meat to the Spirit *Zazelus*, of whom mention is made in the 3[rd book] of the *Kings*; and we read in *Pausanias*, amongst the Histories of *Delphos*, that he was called *Eurynomus*.[67]

---

[67] Eurynomus was a Prince of hell who supposedly fed on corpses. Margin note: They are possessed with madness, that destroy Churchyards. The Spirit *Zazelus & Eurynomus.*

Pol[lux]. Thou shalt finde, that the Governours of Cities that were of the opinion and judgement of Christians; did subvert, destroy and prophane these holy places, that herein the youth might dance their mocking interludes, after the furious sound of the drum or taber, and sing, *Io paen*; or, there the poor inferiour old women did sell base trumpery or lupines, which God would have to be purged with holy prayers, for the salvation of souls, or breaking of bread to the hungry.

Castor. But it is in impious and heathenish thing so to have touched the anointed of God.

Pol[lux]. And worse then heathenish; for the heathens did highly esteem the Rites and Ceremonies of burials, as *Elpinor* is witness in *Homer*, where he yeildeth up his life; and in *Homer* he speaketh to Ulysses, *I intreat thee, O Ulysses, to be mindeful of me, and not depart away hence and leave me uninterred, left that, not being ritely buried, I shall be made the wrath of the Gods.*[68] And *Archita* the Philosopher in *Flaccus*, thus speaketh to the Mariner:

Me quoque divexi Rapidus comes rionis[69]
Illyrisis Notus obruit undis.
Artu Nauta vagae ne parce malignus harenae,
Ossibus & capiti inhumato.
Particulam dare; sic quocunque minabitur Eurus
Fluctibus Hesperiis, Venusinae
Plectantur siluae, te sospite muliaque merces
Unde potest tibi desluat aequo.
Ab Jove Neptuno, sacrs Custode Tarenti.
Negligis immeritis nocituram,
Post modo te natis frandem committere: fors &,
Debita Jura vicesass superbae
Te manent ipsum praecibus non linquar multis
Teque piacula nulla resolvent.

---

[68] Margin note: The Ceremony of burial was in great esteem amongst the Heathens.

[69] Margin note: *Horace* book of verses.

[70] Here "Gentiles" is used in the sense of both non-Jew and non-Christian. Margin note: The vain Religion of the *Gentiles*.

And *Palinurus* to *Aeneas* in the sixth book of *Virgils Aeneids*.

Nunc me fluctus habent versantque in littore venti,
Quodte per Coeli jucundum lumen & auras
Per genitorem oro, per spern surgentis Juli.
Eripe me his invicte malis, aut tu mihs terram
Injice namque potes.

Castor. Have the *Gentiles* so greatly esteemed the ceremony of burials?[70]

Pollux. Yes, very much; for their Religion did hold that the Soul of a body which was uninterred, was void of any intelligible essence, and left to the power and command of a raging furious phansie, and subject to the torment and affliction of corporal qualities; so that it being an airey body, sometimes the departed shadow would speak unto his remaining friends, and sometimes evilly vex and torment his enemies with revenge, as in the Poet, *Dido* threatneth *Aeneas*, saying,

Omnibus umbra locis adero dabis improbe penas.[71]

Suetoninus, as we have shown before, addeth the like concerning the dead body of *C. Caligula* the Emperour in the Garden of *Lamianus*, being not duly buried; for this body, because it was onely covered with a light turff, did very much disquiet and trouble the possessors of the Garden, with violent incursions in the night; until by his sisters, who were returned from banishment, it was taken up again and ritely and duly by them buried.[72]

Castor. And the house wherein the same Emperour died, could by no other way or means be freed from the fury of these shadows or spirits, as History makes mention, but by burning thereof.[73]

Pollux. Aristotle speaking of miracles, mentioneth a certain mountain in *Norway*, named *Hechelberg*, environed abour[74] with the Sea, that continually sent forth such lamentable voices, like the yelling

---

[71] Margin note: [Virgil's] *Aeneid* 4.
[72] Margin note: The History of C[aius] Caligula.
[73] Margin note: The house of *Caligula* burnt, because of Spirits.
[74] Probably should read "about."

& howling of infernal devils, insomuch that the noise & clamour of their terrible roaring might be heard almost a mile; and the flocking together of great Ravens and Vultures neer it, did prohibit any access thereunto.[75] And he reporteth that in *Lyppora* neer about the *Aeolian* islands, there was a certain Hill from whence in the night there was heard Cymbals, and sounds of tinkling instruments of brass, with certain secret & hidden screechings, laughings and roarings of Spirits.[76] But even now, *Castor*, thou didst make mention of Zazelus, whom also thou didst assert to have been called *Eurynomus* by *Pausania*; I desire thee to shew me something more largely concerning this Spirit.

Castor. They do declare that he lives altogether by the flesh of the dead; so as sometimes he doth not leave the bones.[77]

Pollux. The *Saxon* Grammarians, in the fifth book of the *Danish History*, do most truely subscribe their consents and agreements to this thy Assertion; for there they set before our eyes an admirable History of one *Asuitus* and *Asmundus*, which easily proveth all thy sayings.

Castor. I beseech thee declare this unto me, *Pollux.*

Pollux. Give attention; it is thus: *Asuitus* and *Asmundus* had sworn with mutual vows each to other, that he which should live longest of them, would entomb himself alive. Now sickness did consume away *Asuitus* before *Asmundus;* whereupon *Asmundus* for his Oath of friendship sake, with his dog & his horse entombed himself alive in a vast deep den; having carried with him some meat, whereupon a long time he fed.[78] And at length *Ericus* the King of *Suecia* came into that place with an Army, and broke open the tombe of *Asuitus;* (supposing there had been treasure hid therein) but when the cave was opened, he drew out *Asmundus*, and brought him into the light, who was covered with a deformed sharp countenance, a deadly deformity, and gored with blood flowing from his fresh wounds.

---

[75] Margin note: The mountain of *Hechelberg.*
[76] Margin note: A Hill in *Lyppora.*
[77] Margin note: *Zazelus* liveth by the flesh of the dead.
[78] Margin note: A wonderful History of *Asuitus* and *Asmundus.*

Castor. But this story pertaineth not to our purpose.

Pollux. Truely it doth, if you diligently mark these verses, which set forth the cause of his wounds.

Castor. Shew me these verses, if thou hast them.

Pollux. They are these which follow.

Quid stupetis qui relictum me Colore cernitis?
Obsoles it nempe vivus omnis inter mortuos,
Nescio quo Stygii numinis ausu,
Missus ab inferis Spiritus affluit
Savis alipedem dentibus edit,
Infandoque Canem praebuit ori,
Non contentus equi velcanis esu,
Mox in me rapidos transtulit ungues,
Discissaque gena sustulit aurem;
Huic laceri vultus horret imago,
Emicat inque fero vulnere sanguis
Haud impune tamen monstrifer egit,
Nam ferro servi mox caput ejus,
Persodique nocens stipite Corpus.[79]

Castor. I observe here, that *Asmundus* did cut the head of the Spirit *Zazelus* or *Eurynomus*, and struck and pierced his body with a club; what? have Spirits bodies, that may be seen and handled by men?

Pollux. Cortesius doth not deny, but that their natures may receive the habit and covering of vegetable bodies, and be transformed in several kindes of shapes, whereby they can the more craftily and subtilly delude and deceive the improvident wits of men.[80] *Basilius Magnus* also testifieth the same, and witnesseth, that they have bodies appropriate to themselves, as likewise also have the pure Angels. *Psellus* a Necromancer[81] doth also report the same;

---

[79] Margin note: *Asmundus* reports of himself, that a Spirit eat up his horse & his dog, and afterwards began to devour him, & that he beat and wounded the Spirit.

[80] Margin note: The devils have bodies.

[81] Not a very fair categorization of the eleventh-century scholar Michael Psellus, who wrote on daemons.

and he also teacheth, That sometimes they sleep or rest, and do change their places, and shew themselves visible to the sences of men. *Socrates* asserteth, That a Spirit did speak with him, which also sometimes he saw and felt;[82] but their bodies cannot be discerned to be different in sex.[83] But *Marcus Cherronesus*, an excellent searcher into the natures of Spirits, writeth, That they have simple bodies & that there doth belong a difference of sex to compound bodies; yet their bodies are easily drawn to motion and flexibility, and naturally apt to receive every configuration.

For, saith he, *even as the clouds do shew forth the apparition and resemblance of men, and sometimes of every thing you conceive; so likewise do the bodies of Spirits receive various shapes as they please, by reason whereof they transforme themselves into the forms sometimes of men, and sometimes of women. Nevertheless this is not free to them all, but onely to the fiery and aiery Spirits.*[84] For he teacheth, That the Spirits of the water have more slow and less active bodies, which by reason of the slowness and softness of that element, they do most especially resemble birds and women; of which kinde the *Naiades* and *Nereides* are, celebrated by the Poets.

Trimetius[85] testifies, That *the Devils do desire to assume the shapes of men rather then any other form; but when they cannot finde the matter of the air convenient and befitting for that purpose*. And he saith, That *they frame such kinde of apparences to themselves, as the contrary humour or vapour will afford; and so they are seen sometimes in the form and shape of a Lion, a Wolfe, a Sow, an Ass, a Centaure, of a Man horned, having feet like a Goat*: such as it is reported were seen in the mountain of *Thru[i]ngia*, where there was heard a terrible roaring.

Castor. *Porphyr[i]us* in Eusebius, in his fourth book of *Evangelical Preparations*, teacheth, That *some of these are good Spirits, and some bad*; but I have counted them to be all evil, *Pollux*.

Pollux. Then it seemeth that thou art not seduced with the assertions either of *Porphyrius*, or *Apuleus*, or *Proclus*, or of some other Platonicks, which are mentioned in St. *Augustines* book of *The City of God*, 1, 2, and 3 Chapter, who also do affirm that there are

---

[82] Socrates spoke of a *daemon* rather than a spirit.

[83] Margin note: The Spirits cannot be discerned by sex.

[84] Margin note: All Spirits cannot receive several shapes.

[85] Trithemius of Sponheim.

some of these Spirits good; for *Eusebius* in the said book and 6th Chapter; and St. *Augustine* concerning the same in his book of *The City of God*, the 9th Chapter and the 8th, with very great and strong Arguments do convince the Platonicks, that none of these *Daemons* are good, but all evil.[86]

And that we do also approve of from their names, which are every where set forth in holy Scripture; for the Devil is called *Diabolus*, that is, flowing downwards: that he which swelling with pride, determined to reign in high places, fell flowing down wards to the lowest parts, like the torrent of a violent stream, as *Cassiodorus* writeth.[87] And he is called *Sathan*, that is, an adversary; who as St. *Jerome* testifieth, by reason of the corruption of his own malice, he continually resisteth, and is an adversary against God, who is the chiefest good.[88] He is called *Behemoth* in the 40th Chapter of *Job*, which signifieth an Ox; for even as an Ox desireth hay, so he with the teeth of his suggestions, coveteth to destroy the upright lives of spiritual men.[89] And *Leviathan* in the same place, which signifies an addition, because the Devil alwaies endeavours to adde evil to evil, and punishment to punishment.[90]

He is also called in *Revelation* 15. *Apollyon*,[91] signifying a rooter out, for he rooteth out the vertues which God planteth in the Soul. He is called a *Serpent* in the 12th of the *Revelation*, by reason of his virulency.[92] A *Lion* in the 1 Epist[le of] *Peter* and the last Chapter, which roareth about seeking whom he may devour. He is called a cunning Workman *Isa[iah]* 55. because by his malice the vessels that are elected and approved. He is called, *Isa[iah]* 34. *Onocentaurus Erynus, Philosus, Syren, Lamia, Ulula, Struthio*. And by *David* in the 90th *Psal[m]* an *Aspe, Basiliske* and *Dragon*. In the Gospel Mammon, the Prince of this world, and Ruler of darkness.

Castor. Why therefore have the Divines declared, That the Almighty hath given two kindes of Spirits unto men; the one good, the keeper

---

[86] SB; originally a semicolon here. Margin note: There is no *Daemon* God.

[87] Margin note: Why he is called *Diabolus*.

[88] Margin note: *Sathan*.

[89] Margin note: *Behemoth*.

[90] Margin note: *Leviathan*.

[91] In the Greek version of *Revelation*. Margin note: *Apollyon*.

[92] Margin note: *A Serpent*.

and preserver of their lives, the other evil, resisting the good: if
they are all evil?   ·

Pollux. The holy Doctors do understand by the good Spirit a good
Angel, such as we read *Raphael* was to *Tobias*, who bound the evil
Spirit *Asmodeus* in the wilderness of the furthest parts of *Egypt*,
that he might be the more safe.

Castor. It had been more safe for every man to have been without
the evil Spirits; what therefore was the will of the heavenly Father
concerning them?

Pollux. That by the assistance of the good Spirits, we might cour-
agiously wage continual war against the evil Spirits; but being
clothed with the harness of righteousness, like valiant souldiers
we may gird our loyns with truth, and with the sheild of faith
resist and fight against all his darts.

Castor. If we condescend unto this warfare of Spirits, it seemeth
good to inquire whether the Devils have power of doing hurt,
granted unto them by God; or whether of themselves they can
hurt as much as they please?

Pollux. If the last were true, who could compare the end of their
hurting? but it is very manifest, that their authority from on high
is of so great existency, that *John* the Evangelist doubteth not to
name the Devils the Princes of the earth.[93]

Castor. In what manner therefore do they hurt?

Pollux. Although they be most mighty and powerful Spirits, yet
they can do no hurt unless it be by permission; or, as *Damascenus*
saith, *By dispensation.* And *Chrysostome* saith, *They have a limited
power; for truely without the will of God, they cannot touch a hair
of any mans head.* The Devil could not have deceived the Prophets
of *Ahab*, if he had not received power from God; neither could he
have brought any detriment upon *Job*, either unto his body or his
goods, but by the power God had given him. In the 7[th chapter]
of *Exodus* the Magicians made Frogs and Serpents by the power

---

[93] Margin note: The devils are the Princes of the earth.

of the Devil permissively; but Lice they could not bring forth, by reason of the greater power of God prohibiting them. Neither in the Gospel could the Devils hurt the Swine until Christ had given them leave.

Castor. Therefore the Devil is not so much to be feared, but the Lord our God, that either he would not suffer him to rage against us; or if at any time by his own determinate counsel he let loose his chains, that then he would defend and mercifully preserve us.

Pollux. Thou saiest well; for even as a wilde boare is not to be feared if he bound, and held with a strong chain by a powerful strong man, and who is able by his strength to restrain the fierceness of the boare; but the man is to be feared, and requested, that he would not let loose the boare: So also *Satan* is not to be feared, being bound with the cords of the Almighty; but the Almighty rather, who holdeth him with a cord, lest at any time he should let loose his cord, for to execute his will against us.

Castor. We know that the Devils, after incarnation of the Word, were called the Lords of the earth; but I wonder, where the Word is not yet incarnate, whether they have power also over men.[94]

Pollux. If it pleaseth God, they have very much; but take a demonstration thereof, *Castor*, from the *Caldeans*, amongst whom the Devil raged with so much power and dominion, that they made no esteem of the true God, but worshipped the elements. There needeth not a demonstration of the *Greeks*; for the fury of the Devil did so much reign amongst them, that by his Arguments, they accounted *Saturn* for a very great God, devouring their own proper Children; and *Jupiter*, an adulterer and father of all filthiness, they named to be the father of Gods and men; *Bacchus*, the most wicked example of all servitude and bondage, they called a free father; *Venus* a strumpet, they termed a pure virgin; and they worshipped *Flora* an harlot, as a type or example of virginity.

There is no man that is ignorant, that the *Egyptians* have been worse than the *Greeks*, when they made peculiar Gods to themselves, by the inanimate perswasions of the Devil; for one worshipped a sheep, another a goat, another a calfe, very many did worship hoggs, crows, hawkes, vultures, eagles, crocodiles, cats,

---

[94] Margin note: The devils seduce men where the word is not known.

dogs, wolves, asses, dragons; and things growing also, as onyons, garlick, and thornes; as every one that is covetous of reading, shall finde in *Damascenus*, in his History of *Josaphas*[95] and *Barlaas*, and in *Eusebius*, in the fourth book, and first Chapter of *Evangelical Preparations*; neither do I account the *Hebrews* (who glory in being the offspring of their father Abraham) to have been better then the former, when also by the instinct of the devil, after their coming up out of *Egypt*, with cruel hands they violently assaulted the Prophets and holy men of God, whom at length they also slew: that I may hold my peace, how diligently they have brought into their Religion the Gods, or rather Devils of the *Gentiles*.

Castor. I perceive by these thy assertions, that one Devil, and another Devil, hath been adored for Gods; for thou hast now said, That the *Greeks*, by the madness wherewith the Devil possessed them, have made unto themselves, *Saturn, Jupiter, Bacchus, Venus* and *Flora*, for Gods; which *Lactantius* in his fourth book *De vera Sapientia*, also accounteth for Devils.[96]

Pollux. Declare, I pray, thee the words of *Lactantius*.

Castor. Mark them; they are thus: *The same Devils are the gods of the Gentiles; but if any one will not believe these things of me; then let him credit* Homer, *who joyneth the great Jupiter to the great Devils; and the other Poets and Philosophers do call them sometimes Gods.*[97] And sometimes Devils whereof there is one true, and another false: for the most wicked Spirits when they are conjured, do confess themselves to be Devils; but where they are worshipped, they declare themselves to be Gods, that they may thrust men into errors, and draw them from the worship of the true God; through whom alone eternal death can be escaped.

Pollux. It is expedient for me now to be more inquisitive in this discourse; whether there be power given to the Devils to foretell things to come? concerning which thing hitherto I have not been able to dart at the right mark; for this question seemeth sufficiently doubtful unto me.

---

[95] Josephus.

[96] Lactantius was an early Christian father who flourished around A.D. 300.

[97] SB. Originally a semicolon here.

Castor. St. *Augustine* in his book *De Natura Daemonum*, dissolveth this *Gordoneus* knot,[98] and saith, That *the damned Spirits, being filled full of all manner of impiety and wickedness, do sometimes challenge to themselves power of foreseeing things to come;*[99] *because in the sense of their Aiery bodies, they have a far more strong and prevalent power of fore-knowing, then men of earthly bodies can have; or because of the incomparable swiftness of their aiery bodies, which wonderfully exceedeth not onely the celerity of men and wilde beasts, but also the flying of birds.*[100] *By which means, they are able to declare things long before they come to be known; which we, by reason of the earthly slowness of our sense, cease not to wonder at and admire: or because of the benefit of their continual life, they obtain this wonderful experience of things; which we cannot attain to, because of the shortness of our momentaneous life, which is but as it were a bubble.*

Poll[ux]. This last assertion of S[t]. *Augustine* seemeth unto me to be more true then the rest, because the Series of many yeers doth cause great experience.

Cast[or]. If any one shall deny these opinions of *Augustine*, as erroneous, *Damascenus* setteth a greater witness of these things, without all exception, before our eyes; who in his second book of *Orthodox Faith* saith thus: *That the devils cannot foreknow things to come, for that belongs onely unto God: but so much as they are able to know, they have from the disposition of the celestial and inferiour bodies.*[101]

Poll[ux]. Why therefore do the devils so willingly and of their own accord undertake Prophecies, and to answer Oracles? What benefit have they from hence?

Cast[or]. Nothing, but that hereby they seek to get great estimation, and covet to be counted worthy of admiration, and to be adored in stead of Gods.[102]

---

[98] A difficult problem. The Gordian knot was a supposedly unsolvable puzzle, until Alexander the Great cut through it with his sword.

[99] Margin note: The devils do foretel things to come.

[100] SB. Originally a colon here.

[101] A bit of special pleading here. Margin note: The devils themselves cannot foreknow things to come.

[102] Margin note: Why the devils desire to be counted Prophets.

Poll[ux]. We know that the devil is the father of lyes, *Castor:* from whence we are piously to believe, that those things which he fore-telleth, he extracteth from his own lyes.

Cast[or]. Furthermore, the Prophet *Esais* saith thus: *Shew the things that are to come hereafter, and tell us, that we may know that ye are gods.*[103] And the Apostle *Peter* also saith, *The prophecie came not in old time by the will of man, but holy men of God spake as they were moved by the holy Ghost.*[104]

Poll[ux]. No man therefore will deny that they do sometimes foretel things to come.

Cast[or]. No man, certainly: but for what cause that is attained to, *Chrysostome* doth most clearly teach, in these words: *It is granted,* he saith, *that sometimes the devil doth speak truth, that he might commend his own lying with rare verity: whereas, if he should never tell the truth, he could deceive no man, neither would his lying suffice him to tempt with.*[105] Thus far *Chrysostome.* Notwithstanding, if he understand that he hath not grace granted unto him of himself to foretel the truth, he foretelleth things nevertheless, but *so obscurely,* saith S[t]. *Augustine, that he always layeth the blame of the things by him so foretold, upon the interpreter thereof.*[106] *Porphyrius,* in his book of Oracles, although he be the greatest maintainer of devils, and the most expert teacher of diabolical Arts, nevertheless he saith with the aforesaid Doctors, that *the foreknowledge of things to come, is not onely intricate to men, but also uncertain to the gods; and full of many obscurities.*

Poll[ux]. Thou hast said, that the predictions of the devils are done in this maner, that they may gain authority to themselves amongst the credulous people, and be worshipped instead of Gods: for what end do the evil spirits work Miracles?

Cast[or]. What is a Miracle, *Pollux?*

---

[103] Margin note: *Isai[ah]* 41.
[104] Margin note: 2 *Pet[er]* 1.
[105] Margin note: Why the devil sometimes tell truth.
[106] Margin note: The Oracles of the devils are uncertain.

Poll[ux]. A new and unwonted accident, which cometh to pass contrary to its course and custome, and draweth men into admiration thereof.[107]

Cast[or]. But do they work Miracles?

Poll[ux]. They do: for whereby dost thou believe that *Aesculapius* was honoured in his Consecration for a god, but onely by the means of a Miracle, when he conveyed a Serpent from *Epidaurus* to *Rome*? What gave so great authority to *Juno*, but onely the working of a Miracle? when her Image of wood was asked by *Furius Camillus* whether it would he carried to *Rome*, and it answered with a humane voice, *It would.*

Also, from thence *Fortune* was made a goddess, because her *Statua*, in the way to *Latium*, in the hearing of many people, not once, but oftentimes spoke with a humane voice. In the 8th Chapter of the *Acts* of the Apostles, we read of Miracles done by *Simon* the son of *Rachel*; and in *Exod[us].* 8. of the Magicians of *Pharaoh*, who in the sight of many people brought forth frogs and serpents, and turned the waters into blood. *Apuleus* doth testifie the power of men to be so great in Inchantments, that the devils do not onely work Miracles by the means of men, but they are able also to subvert Nature, and with a Demoniacal Incantation, make violent streams to stay their course, To turn the windes, To make the sun stand still, To break the course of the moon, To lay impediments upon the stars, To prolong the day, and to shorten the night; as *Lucanus* excellently sheweth.[108]

Cessavere vices rerum, dilataque longa,
Haesit nocte dies, legi non paruit aether
Torruit & praeceps audito Carmine mundus.

And *Tibullus* of a certain Demoniacal Charm.

Hanc ego de coelo ducentem sydera vidi,
Fluminis ac rapidi Carmine vertitater,
Haec cantu funditque solum manesque sepulchris
Elicit, & tepido devorat ossa rogo.

---

[107] Margin note: What a Miracle is. The devils work miracles.
[108] Margin note: The Inchantments of the devils do subvert Nature.

Cum libet haec tristi depellit lumina coelo,
Cum libet astivo convocat orbe nives.

Cast[or]. I do not any more wonder that *Moses* called God *Wonderful,* that he doth so connive at this sink of wickedness, and most wicked seducers, that he granteth them power to act such things so freely.

Poll[ux]. *Firmianus* excellently sheweth why God doth so, in his last book but one *of the works of God, De opisicio Dei:* for he saith, that vertue is not vertue, unless it have some like, in ruling whereof it may shew and exercise its power: for he saith, *As Victory cannot stand without Vertue, so neither can Vertue subsist without an Enemy; which vertue no sooner had the Almighty indued man withal, but he forthwith added unto him an enemy, lest that vertue should lose its nature, being stupified with idleness.*[109] He saith, that *a man cannot otherwise attain to the highest step, unless he have always an active hand; and that he shall establish and build up his salvation with a continual warfare and contention: for God will not that mortal men shall come to immortal blessedness with an easie journey, but he, must wrestle and strive with sayls and oars against the author and inventor of all evils and errours, who causeth and worketh execrable things and miracles.*

Cast[or]. But sometimes it cometh to pass, that by reason of the subtil snares and stratagems of the devil, which he so craftily prepareth against us, and especially against simple persons, whom he intangleth with vain Religions, so that we cannot resist him;[110] or if we suppose our selves to be very able to withstand him, yet nevertheless we shall be very much deceived by him; as we read he oftentimes did to the good, but almost-foolish Pastor, of whom *Tritemius* maketh mention.

Poll[ux]. But what happened to this good Pastor, and whom thou termest simple?

Cast[or]. *Tritemius* saith, *Insomuch that he was not strong in faith, therefore he made more account of the name of Saint* Blaze, *and*

---

[109] Margin note: Why God permitteth the devils to work Miracles.
[110] Margin note: Sometimes it comes to pass, that the devil cannot be resisted.

attributed more power and custody unto it, then unto the name of God, the best and greatest good.[111]

Poll[ux]. In what maner?

Cast[or]. He had in his walkingstaff, or Pastoral Crook, a Schedule[112] inscribed with the name of St. *Blaze;* by the power and vertue of which staff, he did believe his swine were safely defended from the ravening of the wolves: and he did attribute so great a Deity to that Schedule, that he would leave his herd of swine to feed in the fields alone: notwithstanding, a certain time coming when the pastor was absent from his flock, and a certain man coming in the mean time, saw the devil keeping them; and he asked him what he kept here, who is the worst persecutor of the salvation of men? He answered, *I keep these swine.* The other replied, *By whose command?* The devil saith, *By the foolish confidence of the pastor: for he included a certain Schedule in his staff, unto which he ascribeth divine vertue, or to the inscription of the name of St. Blaze; and now, contrary to his own law, he believeth that his hogs are thereby defended from the injury of wolves; inhering to me with a false superstition; where when he hath been by me called again and again, and hath not appeared, I have taken this custody upon my self, instead of S[t]. Blaze: for I always freely stand instead of God and his Saints: so also most freely do I keep his swine for St. Blaze, that I may magnify and confirm the foolish man in his vain confidence; and thereby I may seduce him so, that he may esteem of this Schedule more then God.*

Poll[ux]. This is a pleasant story: but I do not wonder that, the devil should impose so much upon so simple a Pastor, when he doth in many things prevail over the more wise, if they do at themselves to his opportunities; which the Church contradicteth.

Poll[ux]. But are all things wrought and brought to pass by means of the devil which men call Miracles?

---

[111] St. Blaise is associated with miraculous cures, particularly of throat deseases and the rescuing of a pig from a wolf, at the request of its owner. Margin note: An admirable story of a swineherd.

[112] A written prayer or blessing.

Cast[or]. No: for we must give unto Nature that which seemeth to belong unto her, who is said to be the greatest worker of Miracles;[113] as that which we have experienced in the stone *Asbestos*, which, as *Solinus* witnesseth, being once set on fire, cannot be quenched: and the root *Baara*,[114] described by *Josephus* in the history of *Jerusalem*, which he testifieth to be of the colour of a flame of fire, splendent and shining in the night; but so difficult to be taken, that it always flies from under the hand of him that would take it, and deceiveth his eyes so long, until it be sprinkled with the urine of a menstrous woman.[115] And when it is retained by this means, it may not be gathered or plucked up with out danger; for present death followeth him that gathereth or plucketh it up, unless he shall be fortified with a Preservative about his neck, of the same root. For which cause, they who want the same root, do scarifie it round about; and having bound the root about with a bond, they tie the same to a dog, and suddenly depart away. Whereupon, the dog, too much endeavouring to follow after him, draweth up the root; and, as if the dog were to perform the turn of his master, he forthwith dies; and afterwards the same root may be taken and handled without any danger to any man. And the same *Josephus* teacheth, that the same root is of such present force for expiations, that also those who are vexed and tormented with unclean spirits, are immediately delivered, if they carry this root about them. Notwithstanding there is nothing hindereth, but that Art also may imitate Nature in the working of Miracles; as we may read in *Aristotle*, of the Greek fire that would burn in water: of which the said Author, in his singular Treatise concerning this, hath described very many compositions. And concerning the fire which is extinguished with oyl, and kindled with cold water, when it is besprinkled over therewith.[116]

Poll[ux]. It sometimes happeneth that the devils do clothe themselves, sometimes in more slender, and sometimes in more gross habits, that thereby they may very much affright and molest men with horrible phantasies, and terrible sights; with Ghosts appearing in divers and several shapes and aspects. What, cannot we be fortified with any thing to force and compel them to flie from us?

---

[113] Margin note: Some miracles are done naturally.

[114] This sounds as if he is describing the traditional fears surrounding the gathering of mandrake root.

[115] SB. Originally a colon here.

[116] Margin note: Art sometimes imitateth Nature in working Miracles.

Cast[or]. Origen, in his book against Celsus,[117] saith, that there is
no way more certain, then the naming of JESUS the true God.[118]
For he saith he hath oftentimes seen innumerable spirits so driven
away, both from the souls and bodies of men. St. Athanasius, in his
book de variis Quaestion, testifieth, that the most present remedy
against the insultation of evil spirits, is the beginning of the 67th
Psalm, Let God arise, and let his enemies be scattered. Cyprian, in his
book Quod idola demon sint, commandeth that the devils should
be conjured away by the true God.

Some men have declared, that Fire, which is the most holy of all
elements, and the Creed, and also the instrument whereon the fire
was carried, were very profitable for this purpose: from whence,
in their sacrifices about the sepulchres of the dead, they diligently
observed the use of lights: or else from thence that Pythagoras did
determine, that God could be in no wise truely worshipped without
lights burning. Some others do binde swords for this intent and
purpose, taking the same out of the 11th Ode of Homer, where
he writeth, that Ulysses, when he offered a sacrifice to his mother,
had a sword drawn present by him, wherewith he expelled and
drove away the spirits from the blood of his sacrifice.[119] And in
the sixth [Aeneid] of Virgil, when the Sybil led Aeneas into hell,
she saith thus:

. . . Procul, O procul este profani,
Tuque invade viam, vaginaque eripe ferrum.

Philostratus writeth, that he compelled Apollonius, a spirit, obvious[120] to him and his companions, to flight, with contumelies and
direful imprecations;[121] that the vision [of Apollonius was] making
a noise, and with great horrour vanished away from them. Very
many do much commend a Perfume of Calamint, Piony, Mint,

---

[117] The classical Roman writer (1st century A.D.) on medicine whose influence
on that art predominated in Europe until the Renaissance.

[118] Margin note: How the devils are to be driven away.

[119] That spirits fear iron, particularly swords, was a commonly held theory.
Margin note: The Spirits fear Swords.

[120] Visible.

[121] Philostratus was the main biographer of Apollonius of Tyana (1st century A.D.). Contumelies are invocations couched in reproachful language.
An imprecation is an invocation, which is sometimes a curse.

Palma Christi, and Parsley, to be used in this case.[122] Many do keep present with them Red Coral, Mugwort, Hypericon, Rue, or Vervain, for this purpose. Some do use for this business the tinkling of keys, sounding of consecrated bells, or the terrible ratling of Armour.

Poll[ux]. I have sometimes heard from our Elders, that they made them Sigils inscribed with Pentagones;[123] by vertue whereof, the spirits might be expelled and driven away. What sayst thou to these?

Cast[or]. *Averrois* Writing against *Algazelus,* affirmeth such things to be almost nothing worth, unless to them that have confederated with the spirits.[124] If therefore *Averrois* saith the truth, how then can the devils kingdom stand, divided against it self?

Poll[ux]. But we read that *Solomon,* a singular man with God, did make such Sigils.

Cast[or]. We do read truely that *Solomon* did make them; but it was at such time when he worshipped Idols, and not when be was in the state of salvation.[125] *Tertullian* offereth a more certain Antidote then all the former, and exhorteth us, as *Job,* the most strong champion of God, to fight against all the assaults of temptations: he admonisheth us to be clothed with the silken garment of Honesty, the purple robe of Modesty and Shamefac'dness,[126] and the cloak of Patience: and he perswadeth us to meditate upon all those things which the devil doth devise and invent, to overthrow our integrity; that his falling may be proved the glory of our constancy, and that we be willing constantly to war against all machinations, which are permitted by God for this end. And the Prophet *Jeremiah* teacheth the same, in these words: *The Lord of hosts is the approver of the just.*

D. *Maximus,* in his book *de charitate,* commandeth us to binde and kill the devils. He saith we do then binde them, when by dili-

---

[122] To dismiss a spirit.

[123] Pentagrams. Margin note: Characters do drive away Spirits.

[124] Margin note: Characters avail not.

[125] This consideration is hardly likely to determine if sigils work or not.

[126] Purple is a strange color to choose for modesty, it being more often associated with dissoluteness. The author at this point seems more interested in establishing his piety and Christian credentials than pursuing the topic.

gent observation of the Commandments of God, we do diminish and quash those affectations that do boyl up in us.[127] And we are said to kill them, when we so truely mortifie our lusts, that we cut him off from all occasions of accusing; saying with the Prop[h]et, *Depart, O homicide, the Lord the strong warriour is with me: thou shalt fall, and shalt be vanquished from me for ever.* Olympiadorus, 10[th] c[h]ap[ter] when he interpreteth the Ecclesiastical history, saith, that *all sensual appetites are to be shut out, and excluded, so that the devil may not be admitted, neither by the allurements of the eyes, nor by itching ears, nor by the petulancie and frowardness of a hurtful tongue*: for this he accounteth to be the most absolute seal against the power of the devils.

Some do admonish us, in our going forth to war against the devil, to use two sorts of weapons:[128] the one is pure Prayer, which may raise up our affections unto heaven; and true and perfect Knowledge, which may communicate and fill our understandings with wholesome doctrines, and may suggest unto us what we are to pray for, that we may pray ardently, according to St. *James*, and not doubtingly. In the Prophesie of *Isaiah*, and Epistles of St. *Paul*, we may finde the same things; *Isai[ah]* 59. *Eph[esians]* 6 and 1 *Thess[alonians]* 5. which may be as a remedy against vain Ghosts, that they may he expelled.

Poll[ux]. For a remedy against Ghosts? Dost thou conceive that a Ghost is diverse and different from a spirit?

Cast[or]. I know not truely what I may think hereof: for flowing in so spacious a sea of many opinions, I am so led in doubt, that I cannot easily attain to a certain Port of judgement: for there are some which do suppose that these Ghosts are devils, by reason of the great fear and terrour wherewith they ragingly molest men by night in their houses; and sometimes for their innate nature do[129] hurt. There are others that do believe these Spirits are deceitful fantasies, deceiving those that are of evil belief; who by their fallacious visions and imaginations do deceive and frighten the inhabitants

---

[127] SB. Originally a colon here.

[128] Margin note: We are to fight against the devil with two sorts of armor.

[129] Duplicate word "do" in original deleted here.

in their houses.[130] And [they] do deny that they are Spirits indeed, because [it is said that] the Spirits have a body without hands and feet; wherefore they can hurt no man, nor make any tumult: being ignorant that the Angel (who also hath a body without hands and feet) did carry *Habakkuk* with his whole dinner, by the hair of his head, into *Babylon*, and afterwards brought him back again, and set him in his own place; neither considering that the Spirit of the Lord, also without a body, snatched up *Philip*, and carried him to *Azotus*.[131]

That I may forbear to speak concerning a certain incorporeal Spirit, which did so disquiet the house of my Grandfather, that by the space of almost thirty yeers he caused it to be uninhabitable, unless it were when a Lamp was burning therein; neither did that then sufficiently quiet the same [Spirit]: for going out of the house, they did so molest them with stones from above in the streets, that they would cast out of their hands the hearts of Pine trees, which they used for torches.

Concerning the Ghost that haunted the house of *Anathenodorus* the Philosopher, and the tumultuous spirit of *C. Caligula*, there may more be spoken: but thou hast understood the relations of them already in the foregoing discourse. From all which, we may easily convince the opinions of those, who deny that the Spirits can walk, or make any motion; but of how much truth we may hold the assertions of them, who do suppose that these tumultuous Spirits are neither devils, nor phantasms, but the souls of the dead, now hearken unto.

Poll[ux]. Are there they who are of that opinion?

Cast[or]. There are they who are of both opinions: for they do declare that these are the souls of them who have departed from their bodies laden and clogged in their sins; which are therefore heard to be more or less turbulent in houses, according as they have any sensible ardent spark of that sin more or less; so that except in the mean time they are expelled and driven away from thence, or expiated by Alms or Intercessions, they are compelled to a certain bound of liberty, wandering thereabouts in expectation of the [day of the] last Judgement.

---

[130] SB. Originally a colon here.
[131] SB. Originally a colon here.

Poll[ux]. Wherefore?

Cast[or]. Because I believe that the souls of them which sleep in Christ, do live with Christ, and do not wander about the earth; and the souls of them who are oppressed and burdened with the grievous weight of their sins, since they are the members of Satan, are bound with Satan in the chains of darkness, expecting judgement in hell.[132]

Poll[ux]. But *Firmianus*, a Writer of no mean judgement, thinketh the contrary, in his Book which he hath written *de Divino premio.*

Cast[or]. How is that?

Poll[ux]. These are his words:[133] *Let not any man conceive that the souls of the dead are judged immediately after death: for they are all detained in one common custody, until the time shall come, wherein the Almighty Judge shall make examination and inquisition of their deeds. Then they who shall be found righteous, shalt receive the reward of immortality; but they whose sins and wickedness shall then be detected, shall not arise again, but shall be inclosed with the wicked in darkness, and destined to eternal punishments.*

Cast[or]. St. *Augustine* subscribeth to *Lactantius* in his *Enchiridion,* saying, *That the time which is intexposed between the death of mankinde and the last resurrection, containeth the souls in secret hidden receptacles, where every soul receiveth condigne rest or misery, for the good or evil which he did in the body while he lived.*[134]

Poll[ux]. Neither doth St. *Ambrose* disagree from this: in his second book of *Cain* and *Abel,* he saith, that *the soul is loosed from the body, and after the end of this life, is suspended to the ambiguous time of the last judgement.*

Cast[or]. So also some have declared, that the soul of *Trajanus Caesar* did wander about; but the soul of St. *George* Was freed from such suffrage.

---

[132] Margin note: *Lactant[us]* of the souls of the dead.

[133] Margin note: The opinion of *Firmianus.*

[134] A most unattractive doctrine.

Poll[ux]. Thou hast even now spoke, and that truely, that spacious is the sea of various opinions concerning these Spirits; for so indeed it is: but what Port thou touchest at, I desire thee it may not seem troublesome to thee to tell me: for I am not as yet satisfied of the certainty hereof by our discourse.

Cast[or]. That which thou desirest, I conceive to be this: I hold that these tumultuous Spirits are meer images of Satan; which are not to be feared, neither is there any credit to be given to their answers: and are in no wise the souls of the dead, which either live with Christ, if they have done well; or else are bound in chains with Satan, if they have done evil.

Poll[ux]. It remaineth that we sift out this, *Castor:* for it happeneth now sometimes, that my father appeareth to me in my sleep; perhaps that may also seem unto thee to be a Spirit.

Cast[or]. It may seem so: but I will not in any thing contradict thee beyond Reason: of my self I will adde nothing; but at leastwise I will annihilate thy opinion with the assertions of St. *Augustine.*

Poll[ux]. What assertions are those?

Cast[or]. In his 11th book, which he intituleth *De mortuorum cura,* he offereth them as a means, saying, *Humane infirmity doth so believe of himself, that when he seeth any one that is dead, in his sleep, he supposeth that he seeth the soul of that dead person; but when he dreameth of any one that is alive, he then is out of doubt, that neither his soul nor his body, but the similitude of the man appeared unto him: As if they could be ignorant, that the souls of dead men do not appear unto them in dreams, but onely the similitudes of the persons deceased.*

And he proveth both these to be done, by two examples which were at *Mediolames;* whereof the first he sheweth to have been the image of a certain father that was dead, who appeared to his son, admonishing him that he should not pay again a debt to an unjust Creditor, which the father had paid him before: for he saith the Case was thus [as follows].[135] The father had paid a debt to a certain Creditor, which after the death of the father, the Creditor endeavoured by force to recover the same again of his son, who was

---

[135] SB. Originally a colon here.

ignorant of the payment thereof: to whom the image of his father appeared when he was sleeping, and shewed him where the Writing was hid. Whereupon, the son awaking from his sleep, sought for the Paper in the place he was directed, and found it, and thereby overthrew the malice of his deceitful Creditor.

The second example is, whereby the same St. *Augustine* sheweth that the living do appear to the living, in their sleep: for he saith, that *Eurologius* the Rhetorician, professing the Rhetorick of *Cicero* at *Carthage*, he found a difficult and obscure place that was not declared to him; so that waking and sleeping he vexed himself by reason of his ignorance: but, in a certain night, the image of *Aurelius Augustine* appeared to him, and taught him in what maner the dark and difficult place was to be understood.

Poll[ux]. Augustine doth therefore conclude, without doubt, that they are not souls.

Cast[or]. He doth so conclude: and the greater to strengthen such his judgement, he addeth, That if the souls of the dead have any interest or counsel in the affairs of the living, he undoubtedly knew, that his own pious mother did not desert him, not for one night, but when she was living, followed him both by sea and land: neither did he at any time sustain any anguish of heart, but comforted his sorrows. And that this may not seem too hard a speech, the president[136] of Christ teacheth, that they do not erre, who affirm that the good Angels, by the appointment of God, and Divine dispensation, do sometimes come to, and visit men, both living and sleeping, and sometimes to the place where souls endure punishment.[137]

Notwithstanding, it is not unto all, but onely unto those who are so lived, that God shall judge them worthy of this mercy; or unto those upon whom, without any respect unto their deserts, God will be pleased to glorifie his unspeakable mercy; that by the prayers of the living they may obtain pardon of their sins, and deliverance from the prison of torments.

Poll[ux]. I have sometimes read, that the same St. *Augustine* did write, that it is better for a man to doubt of secret things, then to contend about things uncertain.

---

[136] Probably "precedents" is meant here.

[137] SB. Originally a colon here.

Cast[or]. That is certainly true; neither doth he declare himself to be an offence to those who do leave all these things to the unsearchable judgements of God, and labour not to finde our the secrets thereof.

Poll[ux]. Because I have easily understood thy answers hitherto, I will not desist till thou hast fully resolved me concerning this subject. I desire therefore to know whether all Miracles which the devils perform, are done really, or [just] imaginary phantasies.[138]

Cast[or]. That they perform many things really, and many things onely seemingly, we have already manifested out of the Writings of St. *Augustine.* For that great Prelate of the Christian Church, writeth, in the 11th Chapter of his book *de Trinitate,* That *it is a very easie thing for the wicked Spirits, through the aëry substance or their bodies, to perform many things which seem wonderful (to the souls that are oppressed with earthly bodies) to be done.* He also saith, *That earthly bodies may so qualified with art and exercise, that in publike Theaters they may perform such wonderful things, that those who never have seen them will not believe them, but that they were done by the assistance of the devil and his ministers, to make their bodies of such an aëry element, that the flesh wonders at.*

Or else, which is much, he saith also, *That they do contrive with occult inspirations, forms, and fantasies of images, to delude humane sense; wherewith, waking or sleeping, they may be deceived.* Thus far *Augustine.* But, if thou wilt, I will produce also another witness without exception, *Pollux.*

Poll[ux]. I would have thee tell me who that is.

Cast[or]. Abbas Tritemius, in his third Question to St. *Maximus Emilianus,* which is spoken of before, saith thus: *The devils, amongst unfaithful people, do seem to raise up the dead to life, and to shew miracles to curious men, that they might as it were swallow them up with errour in stead of miracles; and are altogether pertinacious and obstinate: but they cannot truly and really raise up the dead, but do variously deceive the senses of men, shewing them feigned resemblances of the dead. For it is certainly manifest, that the devils can do all things, but onely in a false similitude of holy miracles in truth.*[139]

---

[138] Margin note: Whether the devils work Miracles really, or not.

[139] The author here seems to be carping, having admitted that "the devils can

Poll[ux]. Some say that the devils are obedient to wicked men, because of the similitude of their malice. How seemeth that to thee?

Cast[or]. It seemeth to me, that they are obedient to evil men, but not to all men.

Poll[ux]. But to whom?

Cast[or]. To those certainly with whom they have contracted and made compacts and covenants; as those women which they call *Pythonists*[140] are accounted, who have vowed themselves by promise unto him.

Poll[ux]. But although they are compelled to be so serviceable unto them, yet is this service true or feigned?

Cast[or]. It is feigned, certainly: for they are subservient unto men of their own accord, and genuine work, that they may deceive them, and allure them to themselves. Although we do not deny that their service is sometimes true, but onely towards those men, whose faith in the Lord Jesus Christ, by the merit of his holiness, hath caused them to be acceptable, and friends unto him.

And that *Lactantius* also testifies, in these words, in his second book *De origine Erroris*, and 16th Chapter, That the devils do fear the just, that is, those that worship God, in whose Name they are conjured to depart out of bodies, and with whose words they are beaten as it were with scourges: and they do not onely confess that they are devils, but do declare their names: neither can they lye unto the just.[141] And the same *Lactantius* in his fourth book *De vera Sapientia*, Chap. 27. saith, That it is necessary that they who are of the true Christian Religion, should know the course and order of the devils, and understand their subtilty, and restrain their force, and conquer and subdue them with spiritual weapons, and force them to obey him.

---

do all things." Margin note: The devils cannot really raise the dead.
[140] Oracles.

[141] It is interesting that techniques of evocation listed in grimoires always took the view that holy words of power were enough to constrain the spirits, and to force them to admit to their real names, an important point in practical magic.

Poll[ux]. I am now by thee sufficiently informed or all things which I have hitherto desired to know; wherefore I shall not any further trouble thee with my Questions, or rather Riddles, but leave thee to thy own occasions.

Cast[or]. Neither have I counted my self idle in answering thee: but let the use thereof yeeld us each to other an equal recompence. Farewel therefore.

Poll[ux]. And thee also.

אַרְבַעְתָאל

OF THE MAGICK OF THE ANCIENTS, THE GREATEST STUDIE OF WISDOM.

In all things, ask counsel of the Lord;
and do not thou think, speak, or do
any thing, wherein God is not thy counsellor.

Proverbs 11.

He that walketh fraudulently, revealeth secrets:
but he that is of a faithful spirit, concealeth the
matter.

ARBATEL OF MAGICK:

OR,

THE SPIRITUAL WISDOM OF THE ANCIENTS,

AS WELL WISE-MEN OF THE PEOPLE OF GOD,

AS MAGI OF THE GENTILES: FOR THE ILLUSTRATION OF

THE GLORY OF GOD, AND HIS

LOVE TO MANKINDE.

Now first of all produced out of darkness into the light, against all caco-Magicians,[1] and contemners of the gifts of God; for the profit and delectation of all those, who do truely and piously love the creatures of God, and do use them with thanksgiving, to the honour of God, and profit of themselves and their neighbours.

---

[1]   A caller of cacodemons, or evil spirits.

Containing nine Tomes, and seven Septenaries of
APHORISMS.

The first[2] is called *Isagoge*,[3] or, A Book of the Institutions of Magick: or ἡ παιδμαπκῆς , which in fourty and nine Aphorisms[4] comprehendeth, the most general Precepts of the whole Art.

The second is Microcosmical Magick, what *Microcosmus*[5] hath effected Magically, by his Spirit and Genius addicted to him from his Nativity,[6] that is, spiritual wisdom: and how the same is effected.

The third is Olympick Magick, in what maner a man may do and suffer by the spirits of *Olympus*.[7]

The fourth is Hesiodiacal, and Homerical Magick,[8] which teacheth the operations by the Spirits called *Cacodæmones*,[9] as it were not adversaries to mankinde.

---

[2] The titles of all nine Tomes (volumes) are listed on this and the following page, but only the first Tome has been here translated by Robert Turner.

[3] This simply means an introduction.

[4] The seven Septenaries (*septenary*: group of seven) of aphorisms follow. Many of these aphorisms are pompous and moralistic in tone, and the *only* practical magical information given is to be found in the Third Septenary, Aphorisms 15–21.

[5] Man as opposed to the Universe, *Macrocosmus*.

[6] His holy guardian angel. "Addicted" in the sense of staying closely with him.

[7] The Olympic spirits appear in many grimoires, and are Aratron, Bethor, Phaleg, Och, Hagith, Ophiel, and Phul.

[8] So called after Hesiod and Homer, Greek poets, whose works tell of Greek mythology and magic. Hesiod wrote the *Theogony* and Homer is famous for the *Iliad* and the *Odyssey* The Homeric hymns (written by his followers) have been used to invoke the Greek gods.

[9] Evil demons, from the Greek *kakos*, or evil.

The fifth is Romane or Sibylline[10] Magick, which acteth and operates with Tutelar Spirits[11] and Lords, to whom the whole Orb of the earth is distributed.[12] This is *valde insignis Magia*. To this also is the doctrine of the *Druids* referred.

The sixth is Pythagorical[13] Magick, which onely acteth with Spirits to whom is given the doctrine of Arts, as Physick, Medicine, Mathematics, Alchymie, and such kinde of Arts.

The seventh is the Magick of *Apollonius*,[14] and the like, and agreeth with the Romane and Microcosmical Magick: onely it hath this thing peculiar, that it hath power over the hostile spirits of mankinde.

The eighth is Hermetical, that is, ægyptiacal Magick; and differeth not much from Divine Magick.

The ninth is that wisdom which dependeth solely upon the Word of God; and this is called Prophetical Magick.[15]

---

[10] The sibyls were Greek prophetesses.

[11] Guardian or protective spirits.

[12] Each is allocated a geographic area or country to watch over.

[13] Based on the numerical harmonies of Pythagoras.

[14] The great magician and miracle worker Apollonius of Tyana who was a contemporary of Christ.

[15] This ninefold division of magic is of limited value.

The first Tome of the Book of

Arbatel of Magick,

CALLED

ISAGOGE

N THE NAME of the Creator of all things both visible and invisible, who revealeth his Mysteries out of his Treasures to them that call upon him; and fatherly and mercifully bestoweth those his Secrets upon us without measure. May he grant unto us, through his onely-begotten Son Jesus Christ our Lord, his ministring spirits, the revealers of his secrets, that we may write this Book of Arbatel,[1] concerning the greatest Secrets which are lawful for man to know, and to use them without offence unto God. *Amen.*

The first Septenary of Aphorisms.

The first Aphorism.

Whosoever would know Secrets, let him know how to keep secret things secretly; and to reveal those things that are to be revealed, and to seal those things which are to be sealed: and *not to give holy things to dogs, nor cast pearls before swine.* Observe this Law, and the eyes of thy understanding shall be opened, to understand secret things; and thou shalt have whatsoever thy minde desireth to be divinely revealed unto thee. Thou shalt have also the Angels

---

[1] It is not clear if "Arbatel" is a person or a thing. If we look up the Hebrew spelling of Arbatel printed at the beginning of this book, we can see that the "el" at the end could be El, the name of God, which is often applied as a suffix to form angelic names. This leaves ARBAT, which might have "ARB" as its root, which means "to lie in wait" (as an animal in a den). So it could be that Arbatel is the name of a rather interesting angel, fallen or otherwise.

and Spirits of God prompt and ready in their nature to minister unto thee, as much as any humane minde can desire.

Aphor. 2.

In all things, call upon the Name of the Lord: and without prayer unto God through his onely-begotten son, do not thou undertake to do or think any thing. And use the Spirits given and attributed unto thee, as Ministers, without rashness and presumption,[2] as the messengers of God; having a due reverence towards the Lord of Spirits. And the remainder of thy life do thou accomplish, demeaning thy self peaceably, to the honour of God, and the profit of thy self and thy neighbour.

Aphor. 3.

Live to thy self, and the Muses: avoid the friendship of the Multitude: be thou covetous of time, beneficial to all men. Use thy Gifts, be vigilant in thy Calling; and let the Word of God never depart from thy mouth.

Aphor. 4.

Be obedient to good Admonitions: avoid all procrastination: accustom thy self to Constancie and Gravity, both in thy words and deeds. Resist the temptations of the Tempter, by the Word of God. Flee from earthly things; seek after heavenly things. Put no confidence in thy own wisdom; but look unto God in all things, according to that sentence of the Scripture: *When we know not what we shall do, unto thee, O God, do we lift up our eyes, and from thee we expect our help.* For where all humane refuges do forsake us, there will the help of God shine forth, according to the saying of *Philo.*

Aphor. 5.

Thou shalt love the Lord thy God with all thy heart, and with all thy strength, and thy neighbour as thy self: And the Lord will keep thee as the apple of his eye, and will deliver thee from all evil, and will replenish thee with all good; and nothing shall thy soul desire,

---

[2]   In short, treat well any spirits that you bind, or that are given to you.

but thou shalt be fully endued therewith, so that it be contingent to the salvation of thy soul and body.

Aphor. 6.

Whatsoever thou hast learned, frequently repeat, and fix the same in thy minde: and learn much, but not many things, because a humane understanding cannot be alike capable in all things, unless it be such a one that is divinely regenerated; unto him nothing is so difficult or manifold, which he may not be able equally to attain to.

Aphor. 7.

Call upon me in the day of trouble, and I will hear thee, and thou shalt glorifie me, saith the Lord. For all Ignorance is tribulation of the minde; therefore call upon the Lord in thy ignorance, and he will hear thee. And remember that thou give honour unto God, and say with the Psalmist, *Not unto us, Lord, not unto us, but unto thy Name give the glory.*

THE SECOND SEPTENARY.

Aphor. 8.

Even as the Scripture testifies, that God appointeth names to things or persons, and also with them hath distributed certain powers and offices out of his treasures: so the Characters and Names of Stars have not any power by reason of their figure or pronunciation, but by reason of the vertue or office which God hath ordained by nature either to such a Name or Character. For there is no power either in heaven or in earth, or hell, which doth not descend from God; and without his permission, they can neither give or draw forth into any action, any thing they have.

Aphor. 9.

That is the chiefest wisdom, which is from God; and next, that which is in spiritual creatures; afterwards, in corporal creatures;

fourthly, in Nature, and natural things. The Spirits that are apostate,[3] and reserved to the last judgement, do follow these, after a long interval. Sixthly, the ministers of punishments in hell, and the obedient unto God. Seventhly, the Pigmies[4] do not possess the lowest place, and they who inhibit in elements, and elementary things. It is convenient therefore to know and discern all differences of the wisdom of the Creator and the Creatures, that it may be certainly manifest unto us, what we ought to assume to our use of every thing, and that we may know in truth how and in what maner that may be done. For truely every creature is ordained for some profitable end to humane nature, and for the service thereof; as the holy Scriptures, Reason, and Experience, do testifie.

Aphor. 10.

God the Father Almighty, Creator of heaven and earth, and of all things visible and invisible, in the holy Scriptures proposeth himself to have an eye over us; and as a tender father which loveth his children, he teacheth us what is profitable, and what not; what we are to avoid, and what we are to embrace: then he allureth us to obedience with great promises of corporal and eternal benefits, and deterreth us (with threatning of punishments) from those things which are not profitable for us. Turn over therefore with thy hand, both night and day, those holy Writings, that thou mayest be happie in things present, and blessed in all eternity. Do this, and thou shalt live, which the holy Books have taught thee.

Aphor. 11.

A number of Four is *Pythagorical*, and the first Quadrate; therefore here let us place the foundation of all wisdom, after the wisdom of God revealed in the holy Scriptures, and to the considerations proposed in Nature.

Appoint therefore to him who solely dependeth upon God, the wisdom of every creature to serve and obey him, *nolens volens*, willing or unwilling. And in this, the omnipotency of God shineth forth. It consisteth therefore in this, that we will discern the creatures which serve us, from those that are unwilling; and that we may learn how to accommodate the wisdom and offices of every

---

[3]   Fallen spirits, who have rebelled against God.

[4]   Pygmy was originally used to denote an elf, pixie, or Earth elemental.

creature unto our selves. This Art is not delivered, but divinely. Unto whom God will, he revealeth his secrets; but to whom he will not bestow any thing out of his treasuries, that person shall attain to nothing without the will of God.

Therefore we ought truely to desire *τὴν πνεύμα πικὴν σοφίαν* from God alone, which will mercifully impart these things unto us. For he who hath given us his Son, and commanded us to pray for his holy Spirit, How much more will he subject unto us the whole creature, and things visible and invisible? *Whatsoever ye ask, ye shall receive.* Beware that ye do not abuse the gifts of God, and all things shall work together unto you for your salvation. And before all things, be watchful in this, That your names be written in heaven: this is more light, That the spirits be obedient unto you, as Christ admonisheth.

Aphor. 12.

In the *Acts of the Apostles*, the Spirit saith unto *Peter* after the Vision, *Go down, and doubt not but I have sent them,* when he was sent for from *Cornelius* the Centurion. After this maner, in vocal words, are all disciplines delivered, by the holy Angels[5] of God, as it appeareth out of the Monuments of the ægyptians. And these things afterwards were vitiated and corrupted with humane opinions; and by the instigation of evil spirits, who sow tares amongst the children of disobedience, as it is manifest out of *St. Paul*, and *Hermes Trismegistus*. There is no other maner of restoring these Arts, then by the doctrine of the holy Spirits of God; because true *faith cometh by hearing.* But because thou mayst be certain of the truth, and mayst not doubt whether the spirits that speak with thee, do declare things true or false,[6] let it onely depend upon thy faith in God; that thou mayst say with *Paul, I know on whom I trust.* If no sparrow can fall to the ground without the will of the Father which is in heaven, How much more will not God suffer thee to be deceived, O thou of little faith, if thou dependest wholly upon God, and adherest onely to him?

---

[5] The meaning of angel is "messenger."

[6] When questioning spirits or even angels, as John Dee discovered, it is often difficult to tell if they are telling the truth or not.

Aphor. 13.

The Lord liveth; and all things which live, do live in him. And he
is truly יהוה [IHVH], who hath given unto all things, that they
be that which they are: and by his word alone, through his Son,
hath produced all things out of nothing, which are in being. He
calleth all the stars. and all the host of heaven by their names. He
therefore knoweth the true strength and nature of things, the order
and policie of every creature visible and invisible, to whom God
hath revealed the names of his creatures. It remaineth also, that
he receive power from God, to extract the vertues in nature, and
hidden secrets of the creature; and to produce their power into
action, out of darkness into light. Thy scope therefore ought to be,
that thou have the names of the Spirits, that is, their powers and
offices, and how they are subjected and appointed by God to minister unto thee; even as *Raphael* was sent to *Tobias*, that he should
heal[7] his father, and deliver his son from dangers, and bring him
to a wife. So *Michael*, the fortitude of God governeth the people
of God: *Gabriel*, the messenger of God, was sent to *Daniel*, *Mary*,
and *Zachary* the father of *John Baptist*. And he shall be given to
thee that desirest him, who will teach thee whatsoever thy soul
shall desire, in the nature of things. His ministery thou shalt use
with trembling and fear of thy Creator, Redeemer, and Sanctifier,
that is to say, the Father, Son, and holy Ghost: and do not thou
let slip any occasion of learning and be vigilant in thy calling, and
thou shalt want nothing that is necessary for thee.

Aphor. 14.

Thy soul liveth for ever, through him that hath created thee: call
therefore upon the Lord thy God, and him onely shalt thou serve.
This thou shalt do, if thou wilt perform that end for which thou
art ordained of God, and what thou owest to God and to thy neighbour. God requireth of thee a minde, that thou shouldest honour
his Son, and keep the words of his Son in thy heart: if thou honour
him, thou hast done the will of thy Father which is in heaven. To
thy neighbour thou owest offices of humanity, and that thou draw
all men that come to thee, to honour the Son. This is the Law and
the Prophets. In temporal things, thou oughtest to call upon God
as a father, that he would give unto thee all necessaries of this life:

---

[7] Raphael is often called "the Medicine of God."

and thou oughtest to help thy neighbour with the gifts which God bestoweth upon thee, whether they be spiritual or corporal.

Therefore thou shalt pray thus:

> *O Lord of heaven and earth, Creator and Maker of all things visible and invisible; I, though unworthy, by thy assistance call upon thee, through thy onely-begotten Son Jesus Christ our Lord, that thou wilt give unto me thy holy Spirit, to direct me in thy truth unto all good. Amen.*
>
> *Because I earnestly desire perfectly to know the Arts of this life, and such things as are necessary for us, which are so overwhelmed in darkness, and polluted with infinite humane opinions, that I of my own power can attain to no knowledge in them, unless thou teach it me: Grant me therefore one of thy spirits, who may teach me those things which thou wouldest have me to know and learn, to thy praise and glory, and the profit of our neighbour. Give me also an apt and teachable heart, that I may easily understand those things which thou shalt teach me, and may hide them in my understanding, that I may bring them forth as out of thy inexhaustible treasures, to all necessary uses. And give me grace, that I may use such thy gifts humbly, with fear and trembling, through our Lord Jesus Christ, with thy holy Spirit.* Amen

The Third Septenary.

Aphor. 15.

They are called Olympick spirits, which do inhabit in the firmament, and in the stars of the firmament: and the office of these spirits is to declare Destinies, and to administer fatal Charms, so far forth as God pleaseth to permit them: for nothing, neither evil spirit nor evil Destiny, shall be able to hurt him who hath the most High for his refuge. If therefore any of the *Olympick* spirits shall teach or declare that which his star to which he is appointed portendeth, nevertheless he can bring forth nothing into action, unless he be permitted by the Divine power. It is God alone who giveth them power to effect it. Unto God the maker of all things, are obedient all things celestial, sublunary, and infernal. Therefore rest in this: Let God be thy guide in all things which thou undertakest, and all things shall attain to a happie and desired end; even as the history of the whole world testifieth, and daily experience sheweth. There is peace to the godly: *there is no peace to the wicked, saith the Lord.*

Aphor. 16.

There are seven different governments of the Spirits of *Olympus*, by whom God hath appointed the whole frame and universe of this world to be governed: and their visible stars are ARATRON, BETHOR, PHALEG, OCH, HAGITH, OPHIEL, PHUL, after the *Olympick* speech.[8] Every one of these hath under him a mighty *Militia* in the firmament.[9]

ARATHON ruleth visible Provinces XLIX.
BETHOR,   XXXII.[10]
PHALEG,   XXXV.
OCH,   XXVIII.
HAGITH,   XXI.
OPHIEL,   XIIII.
PHUL,   VII.

So that there are 186 *Olympick* Provinces in the whole Universe, wherein the seven Governours do exercise their power: all which are elegantly set forth in Astronomy. But in this place it is to be explained, in what maner these Princes and Powers may he drawn into communication. *Aratron* appeareth in the first hour of *Saturday*, and very truely giveth answers concerning his Provinces and Provincials. So likewise do the rest appear in order in their days and hours. Also every one of them ruleth 490 yeers. The beginning of their simple *Anomaly*, in the 60 yeer before the Nativity of Christ, was the beginning of the administration of *Bethor*, and it lasted until the yeer of our Lord Christ 430. To whom succeeded *Phaleg*, until the 920 yeer. Then began *Och*, and continued until the year 1410, and thenceforth *Hagith* ruleth untill the year 1900.[11]

---

[8] "Olympick speech" refers to the Greek language.

[9] Their rulership is such that each rules 7 of the 49 "provinces." John Dee was very much concerned to find out which parts of the Earth were under the rulership of which spirits.

[10] This is likely a typographical error and should read "XLII."

[11] Trithemius divided history up into periods governed by each of these spirits. The ruler of the current period is Ophiel, who will reign, by this calculation, until the year 2390.

Aphor. 17.

Magically the Princes of the seven Governments are called simply, in that time, day and hour wherein they rule visibly or invisibly, by their Names and Offices which God hath given unto them; and by proposing their Character which they have given or confirmed.

The governor *Aratron* hath in his power those things which he doth naturally, that is, after the same manner and subject as those things which in Astronomy are ascribed to the power of *Saturn*.

Those things which he doth of his own free will, are,

1. That he can convert any thing into a stone in a moment, either animal or plant, retaining the same object to the sight.
2. He converteth treasures into coles, and coles[12] into treasure.
3. He giveth familiars with a definite power.
4. He teacheth *Alchymy*, Magick, and Physick.[13]
5. He reconcileth the subterranean spirits to men;[14] maketh hairy men.
6. He causeth one to bee invisible.
7. The barren he maketh fruitful, and giveth long life.

His character.

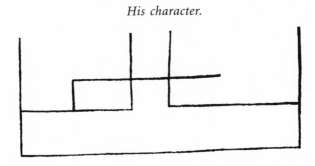

He hath under him 49 Kings, 42 Princes, 35 Presidents, 28 Dukes, 21 Ministers, standing before him; 14 familiars, seven messengers: he commandeth 36000 legions of spirits; the number of a legion is 490.

---

[12] Coal.

[13] Medicine.

[14] Control Earth elementals.

Bether[15] governeth those things which are ascribed to *Jupiter*: he soon cometh being called. He that is dignified with his character, he raiseth to very great dignities,[16] to cast open treasures: he reconcileth the spirits of the aire, that they give true answers: they transport precious stones from place to place, and they make medicines to work miraculously in their effects: he giveth also familiars of the firmament, and prolongeth life to 700 yeares if God will.

His character.

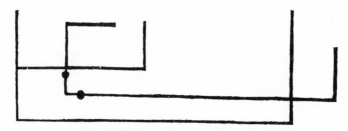

He hath under him 42 Kings, 35 Princes, 28 Dukes, 21 Counsellors, 14 Ministers, 7 Messengers, 29000 legions of Spirits.

Phalec[17] ruleth those things which are attributed to *Mars*, the Prince of peace. He that hath his character, he raiseth to great honours in warlike affaires.

His character.

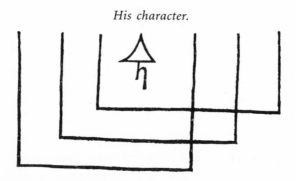

Och governeth solar things; he giveth 600 yeares, with perfect health; he bestoweth great wisdom, giveth the most excellent Spirits,

---

[15] Should be "Bethor."
[16] Provides career advancement.
[17] Should be "Phaleg."

teacheth perfect Medicines: he converteth all things into most pure gold and precious stones: he giveth gold, and a purse springing with gold. He that is dignified with his Character, he maketh him to be worshipped as a Deity, by the Kings of the whole world.

The Character.

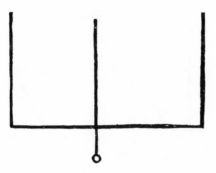

He hath under him 36536[18] Legions: he administreth all things alone: and all his spirits serve him by centuries.[19]

Hagith governeth *Venereous* things.[20] He that is dignified with his Character, he maketh very fair, and to be adorned with all beauty. He converteth copper into gold, in a moment, and gold into copper: he giveth Spirits which do faithfully serve those to whom they are addicted.

His character.

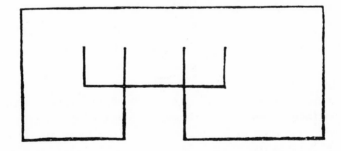

---

[18] As Olympic spirit of the Sun it is appropriate that Och has 100 times 365.36 Legions, symbolic of the number of days in the year.

[19] In groups of 100.

[20] Those things connected with Venus.

He hath 4000 Legions of Spirits, and over every thousand he ordaineth Kings for their appointed seasons.

Ophiel is the governour of such things as are attributed to Mercury: his Character is this.

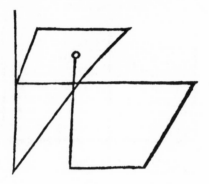

His Spirits are 100000 Legions: he easily giveth Familiar Spirits: he teacheth all Arts: and he that is dignified with his Character, he maketh him to be able in a moment to convert Quicksilver into the Philosophers stone.

Phul[21] *hath this Character.*

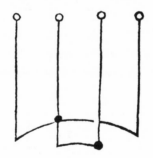

He changeth all metals into silver, in word and deed; governeth Lunary things; healeth the dropsie: he giveth spirits of the water, who do serve men in a corporeal and visible form; and maketh men to live 300 yeers.

---

[21] The spirit of the Moon.

The most general Precepts of this Secret.

1. Every Governour acteth with all his Spirits, either naturally, to wit, always after the same maner; or otherwise of their own free-will, if God hinder them not.

2. Every Governour is able to do all things which are done naturally in a long time, out of matter before prepared; and also to do them suddenly, out of matter not before prepared. As *Och*, the Prince of Solar things, prepareth gold in the mountains in a long time; in a less time, by the Chymical Art; and Magically, in a moment.

3. The true and divine Magician may use all the creatures of God, and offices of the Governours of the world, at his own will, for that the Governours of the world are obedient unto them, and come when they are called, and do execute their commands: but God is the Author thereof: as *Joshua* caused the Sun to stand still in heaven.

   They send some of their Spirits to the mean[22] Magicians, which do obey them onely in some determinate business: but they hear not the false Magicians, but expose them to the deceits of the devils, and cast them into divers dangers, by the Command of God; as the Prophet *Jeremiah* testifieth, in his eighth Chapter, concerning the Jews.

4. In all the elements there are the seven Governours with their hosts, who do move with the equal motion of the firmament; and the inferiours do always depend upon the superiours, as it is taught in Philosophy.

5. A man that is a true Magician, is brought forth a Magician from his mothers womb: others, who do give themselves to this office, are unhappie.[23] This is that which *John* the Baptist speaketh of: *No man can do any thing of himself, except it be given him from above.*

   Every Character given from a Spirit, for what cause soever, hath his efficacie in this business, for which it is given, in the time prefixed: But it is to be used the same day and Planetary hour wherein it is given.

7. God liveth, and thy soul liveth: keep thy Covenant, and thou hast whatsoever the spirit shall reveal unto thee in God, because all things shall be done which the Spirit promiseth unto thee.

---

[22] Average.

[23] The author suggests that true magicians are born, not made.

Aphor. 18.

There are other names of the *Olymick* spirits delivered by others; but they onely are effectual, which are delivered to any one, by the Spirit the revealer, visible or invisible: and they are delivered to every one as they are predestinated: therefore they are called Constellations; and they seldome have any efficacie above 40 yeers.[24] Therefore it is most safe for the young practisers of Art, that they work by the offices[25] of the Spirits alone, without their names; and if they are pre-ordained to attain the Art of Magick, the other parts of the Art will offer themselves unto them of their own accord. [P]ray therefore for a constant faith, and God will bring to pass all things in due season.

Aphor. 19.

Olympus and the inhabitants thereof, do of their own accord offer themselves to men in the forms of Spirits, and are ready to perform their Offices for them, whether they will or not: by how much the rather will they attend you, if they are desired? But there do appear also evil Spirits, and destroyers, which is caused by the envy and malice of the devil; and because men do allure and draw them unto themselves with their sins, as a punishment due to sinners. Whosoever therefore desireth familiarly to have a conversation with Spirits, let him keep himself from enormious[26] sins, and diligently pray to the most High to be his keeper; and he shall break through all the snares and impediments of the devil: and let him apply himself to the service of God, and he will give him an increase in wisdom.

Aphor. 20.

All things are possible to them that believe them, and are willing to receive them; but to the incredulous and unwilling, all things are unpossible: there is no greater hinderance then a wavering

---

[24] If this statement is true, then the spirit characters given in this book are no longer of any use.

[25] The author here suggests that you simply use the function "spirit of x" rather than the name, with the proviso that the spirit, when called, will later give to you its real name (or at least the one by which you can call it again at a later date).

[26] Enormous.

minde, levity, unconstancy, foolish babbling, drunkenness, lusts, and disobedience to the word of God. A Magician therefore ought to be a man that is godly, honest, constant in his words and deeds, having a firm faith toward God, prudent, and covetous of nothing but of wisdom about divine things.

Aphor. 21.

When you would call any of the *Olympick* Spirits, observe the rising of the Sun that day, and of what nature the Spirit is which you desire; and saying the prayer following, your desires shall he perfected.

> *Omnipotent and eternal God, who hast ordained the whole creation for thy praise and glory, and for the salvation of man, I beseech thee that thou wouldst send thy Spirit N.N. of the solar order,[27] who shall inform and teach me those things which I shall ask of him; or, that he may bring me medicine against the dropsie,[28] &c. Nevertheless not my will be done, but thine, through Jesus Christ thy onely begotten Son, our Lord. Amen.*

But thou shalt not detain the Spirit above a full hour, unless he be familiarly addicted unto thee.

> *Forasmuch as thou camest in peace, and quietly, and hast answered unto my petitions; I give thanks unto God, in whose Name thou camest: and now thou mayest depart in peace unto thy orders; and return to me again when[29] I shall call thee by thy name, or by thy order, or by thy office, which is granted from the Creator. Amen.[30]*

Ecclesiast. Chap. 5. *Be not rash with thy mouth, neither let thy heart be hasty to utter any thing before God; for God is in Heaven, and thou in earth: Therefore let thy words be few; for a dream cometh through the multitude of business.*

---

[27] "N.N." stands for the name of the spirit you wish to call. In this example, the spirit is a solar one, but you should change this word according to the planet that is associated with the spirit being called.

[28] Or whatever is the purpose of the invocation.

[29] Duplicate word "when" in original text deleted here.

[30] The Licence to Depart is the most necessary ending to the ritual, without which the operator should not leave the circle.

THE THIRD[31] SEPTENARY.

Aphor. 22.

We call that a secret, which no man can attain unto by humane industry without revelation; which Science lieth obscured, hidden by God in the creature; which nevertheless he doth permit to be revealed by Spirits, to a due use of the thing it self. And these secrets are either concerning things divine, natural or humane. But thou mayst examine a few, and the most select, which thou wilt commend with many more.

Aphor. 23.

Make a beginning of the nature of the secret, either by a Spirit in the form of a person, or by vertues separate, either in humane Organs, or by what manner soever the same may be effected; and this being known, require of a Spirit which knoweth that art, that he would briefly declare unto thee whatsoever that secret is: and pray unto God, that he would inspire thee with his grace, whereby thou maist bring the secret to the end thou desireth, for the praise and glory of God, and the profit of thy neighbour.

Aphor. 24.

The greatest secrets are in number seven.

1. The first is the curing of all diseases in the space of seven dayes, either by character, or by natural things, or by the superior Spirits with the divine assistance.
2. The second is, to be able to prolong life to whatsoever age we please: I say, a corporal and natural life.
3. The third is, to have the obedience of the creatures in the elements which are in the forms of personal Spirits; also of Pigmies,[32] Sagani, Nymphes, Dryades, and Spirits of the woods.
4. The fourth is, to be able to discourse with knowledge and understanding of all things visible and invisible, and

---

[31] This should read "the Fourth Septenary."

[32] Margin note: Spirits of the four elements. Paracels[us].

to understand the power of every thing, and to what it
belongeth.

5. The fifth is, that a man be able to govern himself according
to that end for which God hath appointed him.

6. The sixth is, to know God, and Christ, and his holy Spirit:
this is the perfection of the *Microcosmus*.

7. The seventh, to be regenerate, as *Henochius*[33] the King of
the inferiour world.

These seven secrets a man of an honest and constant minde may
learn of the Spirits, without any offence unto God.

The mean[34] Secrets are likewise seven in number.

1. The first is, the transmutation of Metals, which is vulgarly
called *Alchymy*; which certainly is given to very few, and not
but of special grace.

2. The second is, the curing of diseases with Metals, either by
the magnetick vertues of precious stones, or by the use of
the Philosophers stone, and the like.

3. The third is, to be able to perform Astronomical and
Mathematical miracles, such as are *Hydraulick*-engines, to
administer business by the influence of Heaven, and things
which are of the like sort.

4. The fourth is, to perform the works of natural Magick, of
what sort soever they be.

5. The fifth is, to know all Physical secrets.

6. The sixth is, to know the foundation of all Arts which are
exercised with the hands and offices of the body.

7. The seventh is, to know the foundation of all Arts which
are exercised by the angelical nature of man.

The lesser secrets are seven.

1. The first is, to do a thing diligently, and to gather together
much money.

2. The second is, to ascend from a mean state to dignities and
honours, and to establish a newer family, which may be
illustrious and do great things.

---

[33] This may be a reference to Enoch.

[34] The middle secrets.

3. The third is, to excel in military affairs, and happily to achieve to great things, and to be an head of the head of Kings and Princes.
4. To be a good house-keeper both in the Country and City.
5. The fifth is, to be an industrious and fortunate Merchant.
6. To be a Philosopher, Mathematician, and Physician, according to *Aristotle, Plato, Ptolomy, Euclides, Hippocrates,* and *Galen.*
7. To be a Divine according to the Bible and Schooles,[35] which all writers of divinity both old and new have taught.

Aphor. 25.

We have already declared what a secret is, the kindes and species thereof: it remaineth now to shew how we may attain to know those things which we desire.

The true and onely way to all secrets, is to have recourse unto God the Author of all good; and as Christ teacheth,

[1.] *In the first place seek ye the kingdom of God and his righteousness, and all these things shall be added unto you.*
2. *Also see that your hearts be not burthened with surfeting, and drunkenness, and the cares of this life.*
3. *Also commit your cares unto the Lord, and he will do it.*
4. *Also I the Lord thy God do teach thee, what things are profitable for thee, and do guide thee in the way wherein thou walkest.*
5. *And I will give thee understanding, and will teach thee in the way wherein thou shalt go, and I will guide thee with my eye.*
6. *Also if you which are evil, know how to give good things to your children, how much more shall your Father which is in heaven give his holy Spirit to them that ask him?*
7. *If you will do the will of my Father which is in heaven, ye are truly my disciples, and we will come unto you, and make our abode with you.*

If you draw these seven places of Scripture from the letter unto the Spirit, or into action, thou canst not erre, but shalt attain to the desired bound; thou shalt not erre from the mark, and God himself

---

[35] Schools of Divinity.

by his holy Spirit will teach thee true and profitable things: he will give also his ministring Angels unto thee, to be thy companions, helpers, and teachers of all the secrets of the world, and he will command every creature to be obedient unto thee, so that cheerfully rejoycing thou maist say with the Apostles, That the Spirits are obedient unto thee; so that at length thou shalt be certain of the greatest thing of all, That thy name is written in Heaven.

Aphor. 26.

There is another way which is more common, that secrets may be revealed unto thee also, when thou art unwitting thereof, either by God, or by Spirits which have secrets in their power; or by dreams, or by strong imaginations and impressions, or by the constellation of a nativity by celestial knowledge. After this manner are made heroick men, such as there are very many, and all learned men in the world, *Plato, Aristotle, Hippocrates, Galen, Euclides, Archimedes, Hermes Trismegistus* the father of secrets, with *Theophrastus, Paracelsus*; all which men had in themselves all the vertues of secrets. Hitherto also are referred, *Homer, Hesiod, Orpheus, Pytagoras*; but these had not such gifts of secrets as the former. To this are referred, the Nymphes, and sons of *Melusina*, and Gods of the Gentiles, *Achilles, æneas, Hercules*: also, *Cyrus, Alexander* the great, *Julius Cæsar, Lucullus, Sylla, Marius*.

It is a canon, That every one know his own Angel. and that he obey him according to the word of God; and let him beware of the snares of the evil Angel, lest he be involved in the calamities of *Brute* and *Marcus Antonius*. To this refer the book of *Jovianus Pontanus*[36] of Fortune, and his *Eutichus*.

The third way is, diligent and hard labor, without which no great thing can be obtained from the divine Deity worthy admiration, as it is said,

Tu nihil invita dices facie sue Minerva.
Nothing canst thou do or say against *Minerva's* will.

We do detest all evil Magicians, who make themselves associates with the devils with their unlawful superstitions, and do obtain and effect some things which God permitteth to be done, instead

---

[36] A fifteenth-century Italian writer on love, astronomy and agriculture.

of the punishment of the devils. So also they do other evil acts, the devil being the author, as the Scripture testifie of *Judas*. To these are referred all idolaters of old, and of our age, and abusers of Fortune,[37] such as the heathens are full of. And to these do appertain all Charontick[38] evocation of Spirits, the works of *Saul* with the woman,[39] and *Lucanus* prophesie of the deceased souldier, concerning the event of the Pharsalian war, and the like.

Aphor. 27.

Make a Circle with a center A, which is B. C. D. E. At the East let there be B.C. a square. At the North, C.D. At the West, D.E. And at the South, E.D. Divide the several quadrants into seven parts, that there may be in the whole 28 parts: and let them be again divided into four parts, that there may be 112 parts of the Circle: and so many are the true secrets to revealed. And this Circle in this manner divided, is the seal of the secrets of the world, which they draw from the onely center A, that is, from the invisible God, unto the whole creature.[40]

The Prince of the Oriental secrets is resident in the middle, and hath three Nobles on either side, every one whereof hath four under him, and the Prince himself hath four appertaining unto him. And in this manner the other Princes and Nobles have their quadrants of secrets, with their four secrets. But the Oriental secret is the study of all wisdom; The West, of strength; The South, of tillage; The North, of more rigid life. So that the Eastern secrets are commended to be the best; the Meridian to be mean; and the East and North to be lesser. The use of this seal of secrets is, that thereby thou maist know whence the Spirits or Angels are produced,[41] which may teach the secrets delivered unto them from God. But they have names taken from their offices and powers, according to the gift which God hath severally distributed to every one of them.

---

[37] Fortunetellers.

[38] Necromancy, from Charon the ferryman who takes dead souls to Hades.

[39] The witch of Endor who performed necromancy for Saul.

[40] This does not make a lot of sense as straight geometry. It does not even have the ingenuity of Dee's *Hieroglyphic Monad*, which uses similar "mystical geometry."

[41] Traditionally, individual angels or spirits come from specific directions.

One hath the power of the sword; another, of the pestilence; and another, of inflicting famine upon the people, as it is ordained by God. Some are destroyers of Cities, as those two were, who were sent to overthrow *Sodom* and *Gomorrha*, and the places adjacent, examples whereof the holy Scripture witnesseth. Some are the watch-men over Kingdoms; others, the keepers of private persons;[42] and from thence, anyone may easily form their names in his own language: so that he which will, may ask a physical Angel, mathematical, or philosophical, or an Angel of civil wisdom, or of supernatural or natural wisdom, or for any thing whatsoever.[43] And let him ask seriously, with a great desire of his minde, and with faith and constancy; and without doubt, that which he asketh he shall receive from the Father and God of all Spirits.

This faith surmounteth all seals, and bringeth them into subjection to the will of man. The Characteristical maner of calling Angels succeedeth this faith, which dependeth onely on divine revelation; But without the said faith preceding it, it lieth in obscurity. Nevertheless, if any one will use them[44] for a memorial, and no[t] otherwise, and as a thing simply created by God to his purpose, to which such a spiritual power or essence is bound; he may use them without any offence unto God. But let him beware, lest that he fall into idolatry, and the snares of the devil, who with his cunning sorceries, easily deceiveth the unwary. And he is not taken but onely by the finger of God, and is appointed to the service of man; so that they unwillingly serve the godly; but not without temptations and tribulations, because the commandment hath it, That he shall bruise the heel of Christ, the seed of the woman. We are therefore to exercise our selves about spiritual things, with fear and trembling, and with great reverence towards God, and to be conversant in spiritual essences with gravity and justice. And he which medleth with such things, let him beware of all levity, pride, covetousness, vanity, envy and ungodliness, unless he wil miserably perish.

---

[42] Guardian angels.

[43] The doctrine that the names of angels and spirits can be formed by manipulating the letters of the words that describe their qualities or "offices." New sentence break introduced here.

[44] Angels.

Aphor. 28.

Because all good is from God, who is onely good, those things which we would obtain of him, we ought to seek them by prayer in Spirit and Truth, and a simple heart. The conclusion of the secret of secrets is, That every one exercise himself in prayer, for those things which he desires, and he shall not suffer a repulse. Let not any one despise prayer; for by whom God is prayed unto, to him he both can and will give. Now let us acknowledge him the Author, from whom let us humbly seek for our desires. A merciful & good Father, loveth the sons of desires, as *Daniel*; and sooner heareth us, then we are able to overcome the hardness of our hearts to pray. But he will not that we give holy things to dogs, nor despise and condemn the gifts of his treasury. Therefore diligently and often read over and over the first Septenary of secrets, and guide and direct thy life and all thy thoughts according to those precepts; and all things shall yield to the desires of thy minde in the Lord, to whom thou trustest.

THE FIFTH SEPTENARY

Aphor. 29.

As our study of Magick proceedeth in order from general Rules premised, let us now come to a particular explication thereof. Spirits either are divine ministers of the word, and of the Church, and the members thereof; or else they are servient to the Creatures in corporal things, partly for the salvation of the soul and body, and partly for its destruction. And there is nothing done, whether good or evil, without a certain and determinate order and government. He that seeketh after a good end, let him follow it; and he that desires an evil end, pursueth that also, and that earnestly, from divine punishment, and turning away from the divine will. Therefore let every one compare his ends with the word of God, and as a touchstone that will judge between good and evil; and let him propose unto himself what is to be avoided, and what is to be sought after; and that which he constituteth and determineth unto himself, let him follow diligently, not procrastinating or delaying, until he attain to his appointed bound.

Aphor. 30.

They which desire riches, glory of this world, Magistracy, honours, dignities, tyrannies, (and that magically) if they endeavour diligently after them, they shall obtain them, every one according to his destiny, industry, and magical Sciences, as the History of *Melesina* witnesseth, and the Magicians thereof, who ordained, That none of the Italian nation should for ever obtain the Rule or Kingdom of *Naples*; and brought it to pass, that he who reigned in his age, to be thrown down from his seat: so great is the power of the guardian or tutelar Angels of the Kingdoms of the world.

Aphor. 31.

Call the Prince of the Kingdom, and lay a command upon him, and command what thou wilt, and it shall be done, if that Prince be not again absolved from his obedience by a succeeding Magician. Therefore the Kingdom of *Naples* may be again restored to the Italians, if any Magician shall call him who instituted this order, and compel him to recal his deed; he may be compelled also, to restore the secret powers taken from the treasury of Magick; A Book, a Gemme, and magical Horn, which being had, any one may easily, if he will, make himself the Monarch of the world. But *Judæus* chused rather to live among Gods, until the judgement, before the transitory good of this world; and his heart is so blinde, that he understandeth nothing of the God of heaven and earth, or thinketh more, but enjoyeth the delights of things immortal, to his own eternal destruction. And he may be easier called up, then the Angel of *Plotinus* in the Temple of *Isis*.

Aphor. 32.

In like manner also, the Romans were taught by the Sibyls books; and by that means made themselves the Lords of the world, as Histories witness. But the Lords of the Prince of a Kingdom do bestow the lesser Magistracies. He therefore that desireth to have a lesser office, or dignity, let him magically call a Noble of the Prince, and his desire shall be fulfilled.

Aphor. 33.

But he who coveteth contemptible dignities, as riches alone, let him call the Prince of riches, or one of his Lords, and he shall obtain his desire in that kinde, whereby he would grow rich, either in earthly goods, or merchandize, or with the gifts of Princes, or by the study of Metals, or Chymistry: as he produceth any president of growing rich by these means, he shall obtain his desire therein.

Aphor. 34.

All manner of evocation is of the same kinde and form, and this way was familiar of old time to the Sibyls and chief Priests. This in our time, through ignorance and impiety, is totally lost; and that which remaineth, is depraved with infinite lyes and superstitions.

Aphor. 35.

The humane understanding is the onely effecter of all wonderful works, so that it be joyned to any Spirit; and being joyned, she produceth what she will. Therefore we are carefully to proceed in Magick, lest that Syrens and other monsters deceive us, which likewise do desire the society of the humane soul. Let the Magician carefully hide himself alwaies under the wings of the most High, lest he offer himself to be devoured of the roaring Lion; for they who desire earthly things, do very hardly escape the snares of the devil.

THE SIXTH SEPTENARY.

Aphor. 36.

Care is to be taken, that experiments be not mixed with experiments; but that every one be onely simple and several: for God and Nature have ordained all things to a certain and appointed end: so that for examples sake, they who perform cures with the most simple herbs and roots, do cure the most happily of all. And in this manner, in Constellations, Words and Characters, Stones, and such like, do lie hid the greatest influences or vertues in deed, which are in stead of a miracle.

So also are words, which being pronounced, do forthwith cause creatures both visible and invisible to yield obedience, as wel[l] creatures of this our world, as of the watry, aëry, subterranean, and Olympick, supercelestial and infernal, and also the divine.

Therefore simplicity is chiefly to be studied, and the knowledge of such simples is to be sought for from God; otherwise by no other means or experience they can be found out.

Aphor. 37.

And let all lots have their place decently: Order, Reason and Means, are the three things which do easily render all learning aswell of the visible as invisible creatures. This is the course of Order, That some creatures are creatures of the light; others, of darkness: these are subject to vanity, because they run headlong into darkness, and inthral themselves in eternal punishments for their rebellion. Their Kingdom is partly very beautiful in transitory and corruptible things on the one part, because it cannot consist without some vertue and great gifts of God; and partly most filthy and horrid to be spoken of, because it aboundeth with all wickedness and sin, idolatry, contempt of God, blasphemies against the true God and his works, worshipping of devils, disobedience towards Magistrates, seditions, homicides, robberies, tyranny, adulteries, wicked lusts, rapes, thefts, lyes, perjuries, pride, and a covetous desire of rule; in this mixture consisteth the kingdom of darkness: but the creatures of the light are filled with eternal truth, and with the grace of God, and are Lords of the whole world, and do reign over the Lords of darkness, as the members of Christ. Between these and the other, there is a continual war, until God shall put an end to their strife, by his last judgement.

Aphor. 38.

Therefore Magick is twofold in its first division; the one is of God, which he bestoweth on the creatures of light; the other also is of God, but it is the gift which he giveth unto the creatures of darkness: and this is also two-fold: the one is to a good end, as when the Princes of darkness are compelled to do good unto the creatures, God enforcing them; the other is for an evil end, when God permitteth such to punish evil persons, that magically they are deceived to destruction; or, also he commandeth such to be cast out into destruction.

The second division[45] of Magick is, that it bringeth to pass some works with visible instruments, through visible things; and it effecteth other works with invisible instruments by invisible things; and it acteth other things, as wel[l] with mixed means, as instruments and effects.

The third division is, There are some things which are brought to pass by invocation of God alone: this is partly Prophetical, and Philosophical; and partly, as it were Theophrastical.[46]

Other things there are, which by reason of the ignorance of the true God, are done with the Princes of Spirits, that his desires may be fulfilled; such is the work of the Mercurialists.

The fourth division is, That some exercise their Magick with the good Angels in stead of God, as it were descending down from the most high God: such was the Magick of *Baalim*.

Another Magick is, that which exerciseth their actions with the chief of the evil Spirits; such were they who wrought by the minor Gods of the heathens.

The fifth division is, That some do act with Spirits openly, and face to face; which is given to few: others do work by dreams and other signs; which the ancients took from their auguries and sacrifices.

The sixth division is, That some work by immortal creatures, others by mortal Creatures, as Nymphs, Satyrs, and such-like inhabitants of other elements, Pigmies, &c.

The seventh division is, That the Spirits do serve some of their own accord, without art; others they will scarce attend, being called by art. Among these species of Magick, that is the most excellent of all, which dependeth upon God alone. The second, Them whom the Spirits do serve faithfully of their own accord. The third is, that which is the property of Christians, which dependeth on the power of Christ which he hath in heaven and earth.

---

[45] Here the author again tries to divide magic into 7 categories, but a different set of categories to those he used in the preface to the *Arbatel*.

[46] After Theophrastus, the Greek philosopher who inherited Aristotle's library, and wrote about the virtues of plants and stones.

Aphor. 39.

There is a seven-fold preparation to learn the Magick Art.

The first is, to meditate day and night how to attain to the true knowledge of God, both by his word revealed from the foundation of the world; as also by the seal of the creation, and of the creatures; and by the wonderful effects which the visible and invisible creatures of God do shew forth.

Secondly it is requisite, that a man descend down into himself, and chiefly study to know himself; what mortal part he hath in him, and what immortal; and what part is proper to himself, and what diverse.

Thirdly, That he learn by the immortal part of himself, to worship, love and fear the eternal God, and to adore him in Spirit and Truth; and with his mortal part, to do those things which he knoweth to be acceptable to God, and profitable to his neighbours.

These are the three first and chiefest precepts of Magick, wherewith let every one prepare himself that covets to obtain true Magick or divine wisdom, that he may be accounted worthy thereof, and one to whom the Angelical creatures willingly do service, not occultly onely, but also manifestly, and as it were face to face.

Fourthly, Whereas every man is to be vigilant to see to what kinde life he shall be called from his mothers wombe, that every one may know whether he be born to Magick, and to what species thereof, which every one may perceive easily that readeth these things, and by experience may have success therein; for such things and such gifts are not given but onely to the low and humble.

In the fifth place we are to take care, that we understand when the Spirits are assisting us, in undertaking the greatest business; and he that understands this, it is manifest, that he shall be made a Magician of the ordination of God; that is, such a person who useth the ministery of the Spirits to bring excellent things to pass. Here, as for the most part, they sin, either through negligence, ignorance, or contempt, or by too much superstition; they offend also by ingratitude towards God, whereby many famous men have afterwards drawn upon themselves destruction: they sin also by rashness and obstinacy; and also when they do not use their gifts for that honor of God which is required, and do prefer πάριργα ἔρρτοις.

Sixthly, The Magitian hath need of faith and taciturnity, especially, that he disclose no secret which the Spirit hath forbid him, as he commanded *Daniel* to seal some things, that is, not to declare them in publick; so as it was not lawful for *Paul* to speak openly of all things which he saw in a vision. No man will believe how much is contained in this one precept.

Seventhly, In him that would be a Magician, there is required the greatest justice, that he undertake nothing that is ungodly, wicked or unjust, nor to let it once come in his minde; and so he shall be divinely defended from all evil.

Aphor. 40.

When the Magician determineth with himself to do any incorporeal thing either with any exteriour or interiour sense, then let him govern himself according to these seven subsequent laws, to accomplish his Magical end.

The first Law is this, That he know that such a Spirit is ordained unto him from God; and let him meditate that God is the beholder of all his thoughts and actions; therefore let him direct all the course of his life according to the rule prescribed in the word of God.

Secondly, Alwaies pray with *David, Take not thy holy Spirit from me; and strengthen me with thy free Spirit; and lead us not into temptation, but deliver us from evil: I beseech thee, O heavenly Father, do not give power unto any lying Spirit, as thou didst over* Ahab *that he perished; but keep me in thy truth.* Amen.

Thirdly, Let him accustome himself to try the Spirits,[47] as the Scripture admonisheth; for grapes cannot be gathered of thorns: let us try all things, and hold fast that which is good and laudable, that we may avoid every thing that is repugnant to the divine power.

The fourth is, To be remote and cleer from all manner of superstition; for this is superstition, to attribute divinity in this place to things, wherein there is nothing at all divine; or to chuse or frame to our selves, to worship God with some kinde of worship which he hath not commanded: such are the Magical ceremonies of Satan, whereby he impudently offereth himself to be worshipped as God.

The fifth thing to be eschewed, is all worship of Idols, which bindeth any divine power to idols or other things of their own proper motion, where they are not placed by the Creator, or by the order of Nature: which things many false and wicked Magitians faign.

---

[47] To carefully cross-examine the spirits to determine exactly what has been called, and its veracity.

Sixthly, All the deceitful imitations and affections of the devil are also to be avoided, whereby he imitateth the power of the creation, and of the Creator, that he may so produ[c]e things with a word, that they may not be what they are. Which belongeth onely to the Omnipotency of God, and is not communicable to the creature.

Seventhly, Let us cleave fast to the gifts of God, and of his holy Spirit, that we may know them, and diligently embrace them with our whole heart, and all our strength.

Aphor. 41.

We come now to the nine last Aphorismes of this whole Tome; wherewith we will, the divine mercy assisting us, conclude this whole Magical *Isagoge*.[48]

Therefore in the first place it is to be observed, what we understand by Magitian in this work.

Him then we count to be a Magitian, to whom by the grace of God, the spiritual essences do serve to manifest the knowledge of the whole universe, & of the secrets of Nature contained therein, whether they are visible or invisible. This description of a Magitian plainly appeareth, and is universal.

An evil Magician is he, whom by the divine permission the evil Spirits do serve, to his temporal and eternal destruction and perdition, to deceive men, and draw them away from God; such was *Simon Magus*, of whom mention is made in the *Acts of the Apostles*, and in *Clemens;* whom Saint *Peter* commanded to be thrown down upon the earth, when as he had commanded himself, as it were a God, to be raised up into the air by the unclean Spirits.

Unto this order are also to be referred all those who are noted in the two Tables of the Law; and are set forth with their evil deeds.

The subdivisions and species of both kindes of Magick, we will note in the Tomes following.[49] In this place it shall suffice, that we distinguish the Sciences, which is good, and which is evil: Whereas man sought to obtain them both at first, to his own ruine and destruction, as *Moses* and *Hermes* do demonstrate.

---

[48] Introduction.

[49] These do not appear to have survived.

Aphor. 42.

Secondly, we are to know, That a Magitian is a person predestinated to this work from his mothers wombe; neither let him assume any such great things to himself, unless he be called divinely by grace hereunto, for some good end; to a bad end is, that the Scripture might be fulfilled, *It must be that offences will come; but wo[e] be to that man through whom they come.* Therefore, as we have before oftentimes admonished, With fear and trembling we must live in this world.

Notwithstanding I will not deny, but that some men may with study and diligence obtain some species of both kindes of Magick, if it may be admitted. But he shall never aspire to the highest kindes thereof; yet if he covet to assail them, he shall doubtless offend both in soul and body. Such are they, who by the operations of false Magicians, are sometimes carried to Mount *Horeb*, or in some wilderness, or desarts;[50] or they are maimed in some member, or are simply torn in pieces, or are deprived of their understanding; even as many such things happen by the use thereof, where men are forsaken by God, and delivered to the power of Satan.

THE SEVENTH SEPTENARY.

Aphor. 43.

The Lord liveth, and the works of God do live in him by his appointment, whereby he willeth them to be; for he will have them to use their liberty in obedience to his commands, or disobedience thereof. To the obedient, he hath proposed their rewards; to the disobedient he hath propounded their deserved punishment. Therefore these Spirits of their freewil, through their pride and contempt of the Son of God, have revolted from God their Creator, and are reserved unto the day of wrath; and there is left in them a very great power in the creation; but notwithstanding it is limited, and they are confined to their bounds with the bridle of God. Therefore the Magitian of God, which signifies a wise man of God, or one informed of God, is led forth by the hand of God unto all everlasting good, both mean things, and also the chiefest corporal things.

---

[50] Deserts.

Great is the power of Satan, by reason of the great sins of men. Therefore also the Magitians of Satan do perform great things, and greater then any man would believe: although they do subsist in their own limits, nevertheless they are above all humane apprehension, as to the corporal and transitory things of this life; which many ancient Histories, and daily Examples do testifie. Both kindes of Magick are different one from the other in their ends: the one leadeth to eternal good, and useth temporal things with thanksgiving; the other is a little sollicitous about eternal things; but wholly exerciseth himself about corporal things, that he may freely enjoy all his lusts and delights in contempt of God and his anger.

Aphor. 44.

The passage from the common life of man unto a Magical life, is no other but a sleep, from that life; and an awaking to this life; for those things which happen to ignorant and unwise men in their common life, the same things happen to the willing and knowing Magitian.

The Magitian understandeth when the minde doth meditate of himself; he deliberateth, reasoneth, constituteth and determineth what is to be done; he observeth when his cogititions do proceed from a divine separate essence, and he proveth of what order that divine separate essence is.

But the man that is ignorant of Magick, is carried to and fro, as it were in war with his affections; he knoweth not when they issue out of his own minde, or are impressed by the assisting essence; and he knoweth not how to overthrow the counsels of his enemies by the word of God, or to keep himself from the snares and deceits of the tempter.

Aphor. 45.

The greatest precept of Magic is, to know what every man ought to receive for his use from the assisting Spirit, and what to refuse: which he may learn of the Psalmist, saying, *Wherewith shall a yo[u]ng man cleanse his way? in keeping thy word, Oh Lord.* To keep the word of God, so that the evil one snatch it not out of the heart, is the chiefest precept of wisdom. It is lawful to admit of, and exercise other suggestions which are not contrary to the glory of God, and charity towards our neighbours, not inquiring from what Spirit such suggestions proceed: But we ought to take heed, that we are not too much busied with unnecessary things according to the admonition of Christ; *Martha, Martha, thou art troubled about many things; but Mary hath chosen the better part, which shall not be taken from her.* Therefore let us alwaies have regard unto the saying of Christ, *Seek ye first the kingdom of God and his righteousness, and all these things shall be added unto you.* All other things, that is, all things which are due to the mortal Microcosme, as food, raiment, and the necessary arts of this life.

Aphor. 46.

There is nothing so much becometh a man, as constancy in his words and deeds, and when the like rejoyceth in his like; there are none more happy then such, because the holy Angels are conversant about such, and possess the custody of them: on the contrary, men that are unconstant are lighter then nothing, and rotten leaves. We chuse the 46 Aphorisme from these. Even as every one governeth himself, so he allureth unto himself Spirits of his nature and condition; but one very truely adviseth, that no man should carry himself beyond his own calling, lest that he draw unto himself some malignant Spirit from the uttermost parts of the earth, by whom either he shall be infatuated and deceived, or brought to final destruction. This precept appeareth most plainly: for *Midas*, when he would convert all things into gold, drew up such a Spirit unto himself, which was able to perform this; and being deceived by him, he had been brought to death by famine, if his foolishness had not been corrected by the mercy of God. The same thing happened to a certain woman about *Franckford* at *Odera*, in our times, who would scrape together & devour mony of any thing. Would that men would diligently weigh this precept, and not account the Histories of *Midas*, and the like, for fables; they would be much more diligent in moderating their thoughts and affections, neither would they be so perpetually vexed with the Spirits of the golden mountains of *Utopia*. Therefore we ought most diligently to observe, that such presumptions should be cast out of the minde, by the word, while they are new; neither let them have any habit in the idle minde, that is empty of the divine word.

Aphor. 47.

He that is faithfully conversant in his vocation, shall have also the Spirits constant companions of his desires, who will successively supply him in all things. But if he have any knowledge in Magick, they will not be unwilling to shew him, and familiarly to converse with him, and to serve him in those several ministeries, unto which they are addicted; the good Spirits in good things, unto salvation; the evil Spirits in every evil thing, to destruction. Examples are not wanting in the Histories of the whole World; and do daily happen in the world. *Theodosius* before the victory of *Arbogastus*, is an example of the good; *Brute*[51] before he was slain, was an example of the evil Spirits, when he was persecuted of the Spirit of *Cæsar*, and exposed to punishment, that he slew himself, who had slain his own Father, and the Father of his Country.

Aphor. 48.

All Magick is a revelation of Spirits of that kinde, of which sort the Magick is; so that the nine Muses are called, in *Hesiod*, the ninth Magick, as he manifestly testifies of himself in *Theogony*. In *Homer*, the genius of *Ulysses* in *Psigiogagia*. *Hermes*, the Spirits of the more sublime parts of the minde. God revealed himself to *Moses* in the bush. The three wise men who came to seek Christ at *Jerusalem*, the Angel of the Lord was their leader. The Angels of the Lord directed *Daniel*. Therefore there is nothing whereof any one may glory; *For it is not unto him that willeth, nor unto him that runneth; but to whom God will have mercy*, or of some other spiritual fate. From hence springeth all Magick, and thither again it will revolve, whether it be good or evil. In this manner *Tages* the first teacher of the Magick of the Romanes, gushed out of the earth. *Diana* of the Ephesians shewed her worship, as if it had been sent from heaven. So also *Apollo*. And all the Religion of the Heathens is taken from the same Spirits; neither are the opinions of the Sadduces, humane inventions.

Aphor. 49.

The conclusion therefore of this *Isagoge* is the same which we have above already spoken of, That even as there is one God, from whence is all good; and one sin, to wit, disobedience, against the will of the commanding God, from whence comes all evil; so that *the fear of God is the beginning of all wisdom*, and the profit of all Magick; for obedience to the will of God, followeth the fear of

---

[51] Brutus.

God;[52] and after this, do follow the presence of God and of the holy Spirit, and the ministery of the holy Angels, and all good things out of the inexhaustible treasures of God.

But unprofitable and damnable Magick ariseth from this; where we lose the fear of God out of our hearts, and suffer sin to reign in us, there the Prince of this world, the God of this world beginneth, and setteth up his kingdom in stead of holy things, in such as he findeth profitable for his kingdom; there, even as the spider taketh the flye which falleth into his web, so Satan spreadeth abroad his nets, and taketh men with the snares of covetousness, until he sucketh him, and draweth him to eternal fire: these he cherisheth and advanceth on high, that their fall may be the greater.

Courteous Reader, apply thy eyes and minde to the sacred and profane Histories, & to those things which thou seest daily to be done in the world, and thou shalt finde all things full of Magick, according to a two-fold Science, good and evil, which that they may be the better discerned, we will put here their division and subdivision, for the conclusion of these *Isagoges*; wherein every one may contemplate, what is to be followed, and which to be avoided, and how far it is to be labored for by every one, to a competent end of life and living.

---

[52] A religion based on fear is not a good starting point for a magician who needs certainty in his workings.

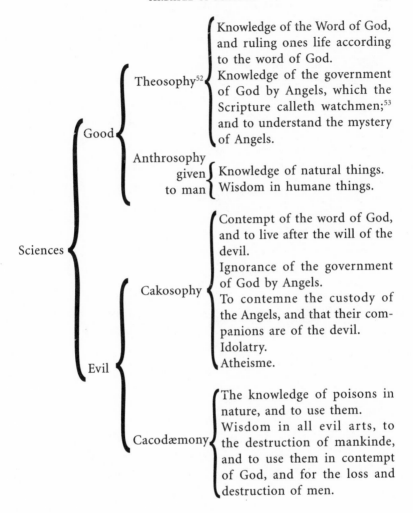

Sciences
- Good
  - Theosophy[52]
    - Knowledge of the Word of God, and ruling ones life according to the word of God.
    - Knowledge of the government of God by Angels, which the Scripture calleth watchmen;[53] and to understand the mystery of Angels.
  - Anthrosophy given to man
    - Knowledge of natural things.
    - Wisdom in humane things.
- Evil
  - Cakosophy
    - Contempt of the word of God, and to live after the will of the devil.
    - Ignorance of the government of God by Angels.
    - To contemne the custody of the Angels, and that their companions are of the devil.
    - Idolatry.
    - Atheisme.
  - Cacodæmony
    - The knowledge of poisons in nature, and to use them.
    - Wisdom in all evil arts, to the destruction of mankinde, and to use them in contempt of God, and for the loss and destruction of men.

FINIS.

---

[52] Not in the modern sense (a philosophy founded by H. P. Blavatsky) but in the old sense of a knowledge of God.

[53] A reference to the Watchers or Nephilim.

PART II
GEOMANCY

Henry Cornelius Agrippa

Of Geomancy

[Introduction]

*EOMANCY*[1] *IS AN ART* of Divination, wherby the judgement may be rendred by lot,[2] or destiny, to every question of every thing whatsoever, but the Art hereof consisteth especially in certain points where of certain figures are deducted according to the reason or rule of equality of inequality, likenesse or unlikenesse; which Figures are also reduced to the Coelestiall[3] Figures, assuming their natures and proprieties, according to the course and forms of the Signes and Planets.[4] Notwithstanding this in the first place we are to consider, that whereas this kinde of Art can declare or shew forth nothing of verity, unless it shall be radicall in some sublime verture.[5] And this [virtue] the Authours of this Science have demonstrated to be two-fold: the one whereof consists in Religion and Ceremonies; and therefore they will have the Projectings of the points of this Art to bee made with signes in the Earth, wherefore this Art is appropriated to this Element of Earth, even as Pyromancy to the fire, and Hydromancy to the Element of Water: Then whereas they judged the hand of the Projector[6] or Worker to be most powerfully moved, and directed to the terrestriall spirits; and therefore they first used certaine holy

---

[1] There is no doubt that this text is by Henry Cornelius Agrippa. It was written before 1526 and appears in his Latin *Opera*, from which the present text is translated.

[2] A method of divining the future by chance selection.

[3] Celestial figures or stars.

[4] SB. A semicolon occurs here in the original text.

[5] Rooted in some sublime virtue. SB. A comma occurs here in the original.

[6] The person doing the divination.

incantations and deprecations, with other rites and observations, provoking and alluring spirits of this nature[7] hereunto.

Another power there is that doth direct and rule this Lot or Fortune, which is in the very soule it selfe of the Projector,[8] when he is carried to this work with some great egresse of his owne desire, for this Art hath a natural obedience to the soule it selfe, and of necessity hath efficacy and is moved to that which the soule it self desires, and this way is by far more true and pure; neither matters it where or how these points are projected.[9] Therefore this Art hath the same Radix with the Art of Astrologicall Questions:[10] which also can no otherwise bee verified, unlesse with a constant and excessive affection of the Querent himselfe.[11]

Now then that wee may proceed to the Praxis[12] of this Art; first it is to be knowne, that all Figures upon which this whole Art is founded are onely sixteen, as in this following Table you shall see noted, with their names [see page 179].

[Planets and the Geomantic Figures]

Now we proceed to declare with what Planets these Figures are distributed; for hereupon all the propriety and nature of Figures and the judgement of the whole Art dependeth.[13]

Therefore the greater and lesser Fortune are ascribed to the Sun; but the first or greater Fortune is when the Sun is diurnall,[14] and posited in his dignities; the other, or lesser Fortune is when the Sun is nocturnall, or placed in lesse dignities.[15]

---

[7]   Earth spirits.

[8]   The second explanation of how geomancy works (apart from with the help of Earth or terrestrial spirits) is that it is driven by the strong desire of the operator or querent's soul.

[9]   SB. A semicolon occurs here in the original text.

[10]   Geomancy has the same roots as astrology.

[11]   SB. A colon occurs here in the original text.

[12]   Practice.

[13]   SB; originally a colon here. There is no disagreement among practitioners as to the attribution of planets to figures.

[14]   During the day time.

[15]   SB. Originally a colon here.

The Greater Fortune.	The Lesser Fortune.	Solis.
* * * * * *	* * * * * *	◯
Via. * * * *	**Populus.** * * * * * * * *	**Lunæ.** ☽
Acquisitio. * * * * * *	**Lætitia.** * * * * * * *	**Jovis.** ♃
Puella. * * * * *	**Amissio.** * * * * * *	**Veneris.** ♀
Conjunctio. * * * * * *	**Albus.** * * * * * * *	**Mercurii.** ☿
Puer. * * * * *	**Rubeus.** * * * * * * *	**Martis.** ♂
Carcer. * * * * * *	**Tristitia.** * * * * * * *	**Saturni.** ♄
☊ **Dragons head.** * * * * *	☋ **Dragons taile.** * * * * *	

[The 16 Figures of Geomancy with the Corresponding Latin Names
of the Planets]

Via, and *Populus* (that is, the Way, and People) are referred to the Moone; the first from her beginning and encreasing, the second from her full light and quarter decreasing.[16]

Acquisitio, and *Laetitia* (which is Gaine, Profit; [and] Joy and Gladness) are of *Jupiter*: But the first hath *Jupiter* the greater Fortune, the second the lesse, but without detriment.[17]

Puella, and *Amissio* are of *Venus*; the first fortunate, the other (as it were) retrograde, or combust.[18]

Conjunctio and *Albus* are both Figures of *Mercury*, and are both good; but the first [is] the more Fortunate.[19]

Puer and *Rubeus* are Figures ascribed to *Mars*; the first whereof hath *Mars* benevolent, the second malevolent.[20]

Carcer, and *Tristitia* are both Figures of *Saturn*, and both evill; but the first of the greater detriment.[21]

The Dragons head, and Dragons tayle doe follow their owne natures.[22]

[ZODIACAL SIGNS AND THE FIGURES]

And these are the infallible comparisons of the Figures, and from these wee may easily discerne the equality of their signes.[23]

---

[16] SB; originally a semicolon. Waxing and waning moon respectively.

[17] SB. Originally a colon.

[18] SB. Originally a colon.

[19] SB. Originally a colon.

[20] SB. Originally a colon.

[21] SB. Originally a colon.

[22] The Dragon's Head (*Caput Draconis*) and the Dragon's Tail (*Cauda Draconis*) are nodes of the Moon, where the Moon's path crosses the ecliptic or path of the Sun. These points are not fixed but move around the zodiac, and were given much more attention by 17th-century astrologers than they are today.

[23] SB; originally a semicolon. There is considerable diversity in the attribution of the zodiacal signs to geomantic figures. A table of the main differences, and a history of the subject, is to be found in my book *Terrestrial Astrology: Divination by Geomancy*, 1980, page 233. In fact, there are at least six methods of attributing the signs, three of which are given by Agrippa, and one by Gerard of Cremona (see his text later in this present book). The Golden Dawn partially follows Agrippa, with Populus and Via = Cancer; Conjunction = Virgo; Carcer = Capricorn; Fortuna Major and Minor = Leo; Acquisition = Sagittarius; Amissio = Taurus; Tristitia = Aquarius; Laetitia = Pisces; Rubeus = Scorpio; Albus = Gemini; Puella = Libra; Puer = Aries.

Therefore the greater and lesser Fortunes have the signes of *Leo*, which is the House of the Sun.[24]

Via and *Populus* have the signe of *Cancer*, which is the House of the Moone.[25]

Acquisitio hath for his signe *Pisces*; and *Laetitia* [has] *Sagitary*,[26] which are both the Houses of *Jupiter*[27]

Puella hath the signe of *Taurus*, and *Amissio* of *Libra*, which are the Houses of *Venus*.[28]

Conjunctio hath for its signe *Virgo*, and *Albus* the signe *Gemini*, the Houses of *Mercury*.[29]

Puella and *Rubeus* have for their signe *Scorpio*, the House of *Mars*.[30]

Carcer hath the signe *Capricorne*, and *Tristitia* [has] *Aquary*,[31] the Houses of *Saturne*.[32]

The Dragons head and taile are thus divided, the head to Capricorne, and the Dragons taile adhereth to Scorpio.[33]

[ASTROLOGICAL TRIPLICITIES AND THE FIGURES]

And from hence you may easily obtaine the triplicities of these signs after the manner of the triplicities of the signes of the Zodiack: *Puer* therefore, both Fortunes, and *Laetitia* do govern the fiery triplicity; *Puella, Conjunctio, Carcer*, and the Dragons head the earthly triplicity; *Albus, Amitia*,[34] and *Tristitia*, doe make the Airy triplicity; and *Via, Populus*, and *Rubeus*, with the Dragons taile, and *Acquisitio* do rule the watry triplicity, and this order is taken according to the course or manner of the signes.

---

[24] SB. Originally a colon.

[25] SB. Originally a colon.

[26] Sagittarius.

[27] SB; originally a colon. These attributions were switched by the Golden Dawn.

[28] SB; originally a colon. These attributions were switched by the Golden Dawn.

[29] SB. Originally a colon.

[30] SB; orignally a colon. Turner should have translated Agrippa to say: *Puer* (not *Puella*) has for its sign *Aries*, the House of *Mars*.

[31] Aquarius.

[32] SB. Originally a colon.

[33] SB. Originally a semicolon.

[34] Amissio.

But if any one will constitute these triplicities according to the nature of the Planets, and Figures themselves, let him observe this Rule, that *Fortuna major, Rubeus, Puer,* and *Amissio* doe make the fiery triplicity: *Fortuna minor, Puella, Laetitia* and *Conjunctio* [govern the] triplicity of the Ayre:[35] *Acquisitio,* the Dragons taile, *Via,* and *Populus* doe governe the watry triplicity; and the earthly triplicity is ruled by *Carcer, Tristitia, Albus,* and the Dragons head. And this way is rather to be observed then the first which we have set forth; because it is constituted according to the Rule and manner of the signes.[36]

This order is also far more true and rationall then that which vulgarly is used, which is described after this manner: of the Fiery triplicity are, *Cauda, Fortuna minor, Amissio,* and *Rubeus*: of the Airy triplicity are, *Acquisitio, Laetitia, Puer,* and *Conjunctio*: of the watry triplicity are, *Populus, Via, Albus,* and *Puella*: And *Caput, Fortuna major, Carcer,* and *Tristitia* are of the earthly triplicity.

They doe likewise distribute these Figures to the twelve signes of the Zodiack, after this manner, *Acquisitio* is given to *Aries*; *Fortuna,* both major and minor to *Taurus*; *Laetitia* to the signe *Gemini*; *Puella* and *Rubeus* to *Cancer*; *Albus* is assigned to *Leo, Via* to *Virgo*; the Dragons head, and *Conjunctio* to *Libra*; *Puer* is submitted to *Scorpio*; *Tristitia* and *Amissio* are assigned to *Sagitary*; the Dragons taile to *Capricorne*; *Populus* to *Aquarius*; and *Carcer* is assigned the signe *Pisces*.[37]

[THE COMMON TECHNIQUE FOR GENERATING OR PROJECTING THE FIGURES]

And now we come to speake of the manner of projecting or setting downe these Figures, which is thus; that we set downe the points according to their course in four lines, from the right hand towards the left, and this in foure courses.[38] There will therefore result unto

---

[35] Air.

[36] Agrippa suggests that you use the second set of ascriptions. It seems as if Agrippa changed his views on geomancy but felt obliged to list the common (or vulgar) usage for the sake of completeness.

[37] In my *Terrestrial Astrology: Divination by Geomancy,* 1980, I have referred to this as "Agrippa's Esoteric attribution."

[38] SB; originally a colon. Four figures made of four rows of dots, one layer or course upon another. A total of 4 x 4 = 16 rows of dots are used.

us foure Figures made in foure severall[39] lines, according to the even or uneven marking, every severall line.[40] Which [these] foure Figures are wont to be called *Matres*:[41] which doe bring forth the rest [of the Figures], filling up and compleating the whole Figure of Judgement, an example whereof you may see heere following.

* * * * * * *	- -

*
      *
   *   *
      *
	- - - - -
	- - - - -
	- - - -
	- - - - -

* * * * * * *	- -

*
      *
      *
      *
	- - - - -
	- - - - -
	- - - - -
	- - -

Of these foure *Matres* are also produced foure other secondary Figures, which they call *Filiae*,[42] or Succedents, which are gathered together after this manner; that is to say, by making the foure *Matres* according to their order, placing them by course one after another. **[43]

Then that which shall result [by combining the figures] out of every line, maketh the Figure[s] of [four] *Filiae*, the order whereof is [made] by discending from the superior points through both *mediums*[44] to the lowest: as in this example [on page 184].

---

[39] Severall = "different."

[40] SB. Originally a semicolon.

[41] Latin for "Mothers."

[42] Latin for "Daughters."

[43] SB; originally a colon. The double asterisk has no apparent use.

[44] The middle lines.

Matres			

* *
* *
   *
* *
	*
	*
	* *
	*
		* *
		* *
		* *
		   *
			*
			*
			*
			*

Filiæ produced			

* *
   *
* *
   *
	* *
	   *
	* *
	   *
		*
		* *
		* *
		   *
			* *
			   *
			   *
			   *

And these 8 Figures do make 8 Houses of Heaven, after this manner, by placing the Figures from the left hand towards the right: as the foure *Matres* do make the foure first Houses, so the foure *Filiae* doe make the foure following Houses, which are the fift[h], sixt[h], seaventh, and eighth.[45]

And the rest of the Houses are found after this manner; that is to say, out of the first and second [Figure] is derived the ninth [Figure]; out of the third [Figure] and fourth [Figure, is derived] the tenth [Figure]; out of the fifth and sixth [Figure, is derived] the eleventh [Figure]; and out of the seventh and eighth [Figure, is derived] the twelfth [Figure.][46]

[This is done] by the combination or joyning together of two Figures according to the rule of the even or uneven number in the remaining points of each Figure.[47] After the same manner [by combination] there are produced out of the last foure Figures; that is to say, of the ninth, tenth, eleventh, and twelfth [Figures], two Figures which they call *Coadjutrices*, or *Testes*.[48] Out of which two [Testes] is also one constituted, which is called the Index[49] of the whole Figure, or thing Quesited:[50] as appeareth in this example following.

---

[45] SB. Originally a colon.

[46] SB. Originally a colon.

[47] Add two figures together by taking each of the four levels, and adding the points from both figures. If the result is an even number of points, then the resultant figure should have two points. If the answer is an odd number of points, then the resultant figure should have one point.

[48] Witnesses. SB; originally a semicolon.

[49] Also called the Judge or *Judex*.

[50] The thing asked.

A Theme [Chart] of Geomancy.

Filiæ				Matres			
VIII	VII	VI	V	IV	III	II	I
* *	*	* *	* *	*	* *	*	* *
*	* *	* *	*	*	* *	*	* *
*	* *	* *	* *	*	* *	* *	*
*	*	*	*	*	*	*	* *

Nepotes			
XII	XI	X	IX
*	* *	*	*
*	* *	*	*
*	* *	*	*
* *	* *	* *	*

Coadjutrices or Testes	
XIV	XIII
*	* *
*	* *
*	* *
* *	*

Index
XV
*
*
*
*

And this which we have declared is the common manner observed by Geomancers, which we do not altogether reject neither extoll; therefore this is also to be considered in our judgements:[51] Now therefore I shall give unto you the true Figure of Geomancy, according to the right constitution of Astrologicall reason, which is thus.

[TECHNIQUE FOR GENERATING AN ASTROLOGICAL GEOMANTIC FIGURE][52]

As the former *Matres* doe make the foure Angles of an House, the first [Figure] maketh the first Angle,[53] the second [Figure makes] the second Angle, the third maketh the third Angle, and the fourth

---

[51] Effectively the previous section was Agrippa's re-cap on the common method. He now proposes to demonstrate what he suggests is the correct method. If differs considerably from Gerard of Cremona's method.

[52] Gerard of Cremona has a more elegant method for this, see page 209.

[53] Angular house. The angular houses are houses I, X, VII and IV.

the fourth Angle.[54] So the four *Filiae* arising from the *Matres*, doe constitute the foure succedent Houses;[55] the first [*Filiae*] maketh the second House, the second [*Filiae* makes] the eleventh, the third the eighth, and the fourth maketh the first House.[56]

The rest of the Houses, which are Cadents[57] are to be calculated according to the Rule of their triplicity; that is to say, by making the ninth [House] out of the fourth and fifth [Houses], and the [Figure for the] sixth [House] out of the tenth and second [Figures], of the seventh, and eleventh [making] the third [House], and of the fourth and eighth [making] the twelfth [House].[58]

And now you have the whole Figure of true judgement constituted according to true and efficatious reasons, whereby I shal shew [you] how you shall compleat it.[59] The Figure which shall bee in the first House shall give you the signe ascending,[60] which the first Figure sheweth.[61] Which being done, you shall [then] attribute their signes to the rest of their Houses, according to the order of the signes.[62]

Then in every House you shall note the Planets according to the nature of the Figure: then from all these you shall build your judgement according to the signification of the Planets in the signes and Houses wherein they shall be found, and according to their aspects among themselves, and to the place of the querent [in the chart] and thing quosited.[63] And you shall judge according to the natures of the signes ascending in their Houses, and according to the natures and proprieties of the Figures which they have placed in the severall Houses, and according to the commisture[64] of other Figures aspecting them.[65] [I will show you] the Index of the Figure which the Geomancers for the most part have made, [and] how it is found in the former Figure.

---

[54] SB.

[55] The succedent houses are houses II, XI, VIII, and V.

[56] Should be the fifth house. SB; originally a colon.

[57] The cadent houses are houses III, XII, IX, and VI.

[58] To clarify: the Figures in Houses 1 and 5 generate that in House 9; 10 + 2 generate 6; 7 + 11 generate 3; 4 + 8 generate 12.

[59] SB. Originally a semicolon.

[60] The ascendant.

[61] SB. Originally a semicolon.

[62] SB. Originally a colon.

[63] The thing asked. SB; originally a semicolon.

[64] Mixture.

[65] SB. Originally a colon.

[DETERMINING THE INDEX]

But here we shal give you the secret of the whole Art, to find out the Index in the subsequent Figure, which is thus: that you number all the points which are contained in the [original] lines of the projections [the dots], and this you shall divide [this number] by twelve.[66] And that which remaineth project from the Ascendent[67] by the several Houses, and upon which House there falleth a final unity, that Figure giveth you a competent Judgement of the thing quesited; and this together with the significations of the Judgements aforesaid. But if on either part they shall be equal, or ambiguous, then the Index alone shall certified you[68] of the thing quesited. The Example of this Figure is here placed.

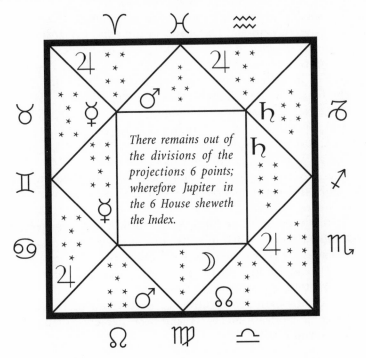

There remains out of the divisions of the projections 6 points; wherefore Jupiter in the 6 House sheweth the Index.

---

[66] SB. Originally a colon.

[67] Count around from the ascendant (House I). Remember when counting, count the ascendant house as "one," the following house as "two" and so on. This is not the same way as we count today, where we would count "one" as we indicate the second house.

[68] Make you certain.

It remaineth now, that we declare, of what thing and to what House a Question doth appertain. Then, what every Figure doth shew or signifie concerning all Questions in every House.

First therefore we shall handle the significations of the Houses; which are these.

[THE SIGNIFICANCE OF THE HOUSES]

The first House sheweth the person of the Querent,[69] as often as a Question shall be proposed concerning himself of his own matters, or any thing appertaining to him. And this House declareth the Judgement of the life, form, state, condition, habit, disposition, form and figure, and of the colour of men.[70]

The second House containeth the Judgement of substance, riches, poverty, gain and loss, good fortune and evil fortune: and of accidents in substance,[71] as theft, loss or negligence.

The third House signifieth brethren, sisters, and Collaterals in blood:[72] It judgeth of small journeys, and [the] fidelities of men.

The fourth House signifies fathers and grandfathers, patrimony and inheritance, possessions, buildings, fields, treasure, and things hidden: It giveth also the description of those who want[73] any thing by theft, losing, or negligence.

The fifth House giveth judgement of Legats,[74] Messengers, Rumours, News; of Honour, and of accidents after death: and of Questions that may be propounded concerning women with childe, or creatures pregnant.

The sixth House giveth Judgement of infirmities, and medicines; of familiars and servants; of cattel and domestick animals.

The seventh House signifies wedlock, whoredom, and fornication; [it] rendreth Judgement of friends, strifes, and controversies; and of matters acted before Judges.

The eighth hath signification of death, and of those things which come by death of Legats, and hereditaments; of the dowry or portion of a wife.

---

[69] The person asking the question.

[70] This house was also thought to be able to describe the physical features of the querent.

[71] Property.

[72] Relatives.

[73] Loose.

[74] This relates to legacies or inheritance.

The ninth House sheweth journeys, faith, and constancie; dreams, divine Sciences, and Religion.

The tenth House hath signification of Honours, and of Magisterial Offices.

The eleventh House signifies friends, and the substance of Princes.

The twelfth House signifies enemies, servants, imprisonment, and misfortune, and whatsoever evil can happen besides death and sickness, the Judgements whereof are [also] to be required in the sixth House, and in the eighth [House].

It rests now, that we shew you what every Figure before spoken of signifieth in these [House] places; which we shall now unfold.

THE GREATER FORTUNE

Fortuna major[75] being found in the first House, giveth long life, and freeth from the molestation of Diseases: it demonstrateth a man to be noble, magnanimous, of good manners, mean of stature, complexion ruddy, hair curling, and his superiour members greater then his inferiour. In the second House, he[76] signifies manifest riches and manifest gain, good fortune, and the gaining of any thing lost or mis-laid; the taking of a thief, and recovery of things stollen. In the third House, he signifies brethren and kinsmen, Nobles, and persons of good conversation; journeys to be prosperous and gainful with honour: it demonstrateth men to be faithful, and their friendship to be unfeigned. In the fourth House, he represents a father to be noble, and of good reputation, and known by many people: He enlargeth possessions in Cities, increaseth Patrimonies, and discovereth hidden treasures. In this place he likewise signifies theft, and recovers everything lost. In the fifth House, he giveth joy by children, and causeth them to attain to great Honours: Embassages he rendereth prosperous; but they are purchased with pains, and prayers: He noteth rumours to be true: he bestoweth publike Honours, and causeth a man to be very famous after death: foresheweth[77] a woman with childe to bring forth a man-childe.

---

[75] Agrippa now examines the meaning of each figure in each of the 12 houses. The names of the 16 figures are printed as marginalia in the original text, but have here been converted to sub-headings for ease of reading.

[76] Fortuna Major.

[77] The Figure shows.

In the sixth House, he freeth from diseases; sheweth those that have infirmities shall in a short time recover; signifieth a Physitian to be faithful and honest to administer good Physick,[78] of which there ought to be had no suspicion; houshold-servants and ministers to be faithful: and of animals, he chiefly signifies Horses. In the seventh House, he giveth a wife rich, honest, and of good manners; loving and pleasant: he overcometh strifes and contentions. But if the Question be concerning them, he signifieth the adversaries to be very potent, and great favourites. In the eighth House, if a Question be proposed of the death of any one, it signifies he shall live: the kinde of death he sheweth to be good and natural; an honest burial, and honourable Funerals: He foresheweth a wife to have a rich dowry, legacies and inheritance. In the ninth House, he signifies journeys to be prosperous; and by land on horseback, rather than on foot, to be long, and not soon accomplished: He sheweth the return of those that are absent; signifies men to be of good faith, and constant in their intentions; and religious; and that never change or alter their faith; Dreams he presageth[79] to be true; signifieth true and perfect Sciences. In the tenth House, he foresheweth great Honours, bestoweth publike Offices, Magistracie, and Judgements; and honours in the Courts of Princes: signifieth Judges to be just, and not corrupted with gifts: bringeth a Cause to be easily and soon expedited: sheweth Kings to be potent, fortunate, and victorious: denoteth Victory to be certain: signifieth a mother to be noble, and of long life. In the eleventh house, he signifies true friends, and profitable; a Prince rich and liberal; maketh a man fortunate, and beloved of his Prince. In the twelfth House, if a Question be proposed of the quality of enemies, it demonstrateth them to be potent and noble, and hardly to be resisted: But if a Question shall be concerning any other condition or respect to the enemies, he will deliver from their treacheries. It signifieth faithful servants; reduceth fugitives; hath signification of animals, as horses, lions, and bulls; freeth from imprisonments; and eminent dangers he either mitigateth or taketh away.

THE LESSER FORTUNE

Fortuna minor in the first house, giveth long life, but incumbred with divers molestations and sicknesses: it signifieth a person of

[78] Medicine.
[79] Predicts.

short stature, a lean body, having a mold or mark in his forehead
or right eye. In the second House, he signifies substance, and that
to be consumed with too much prodigality: hideth a thief; and a
thing stoln is scarcely to be recovered, but with great labour. In the
third House, he causeth discord amongst brethren and kinsfolks;
threatneth danger to be in a journey, but escapeth it: rendreth
men to be of good faith, but of close and hidden mindes. In the
fourth House, he prejudiceth Patrimonies and Inheritances; concealeth treasuries; and things lost cannot be regained, but with
great difficulty: He signifieth a father to be honest, but a spender
of his estate through prodigality, leaving small portions to his
children. *Fortuna minor* in the fifth House giveth few children; a
woman with childe he signifies shall have a woman-childe; signifies
Embassages to be honourable, but little profitable; raiseth to mean[80]
honours; giveth a good fame after death, but not much divulged;
nor of lasting memory.

In the sixth House, he signifies diseases, both Sanguine and
Cholerick;[81] sheweth the sick person to be in great danger, but shall
recover: signifies faithful servants, but slothful and unprofitable:
And the same of other animals. In the seventh House, he giveth
a wife of a good progenie descended;[82] but you shall be incumbred with many troubles with her: causeth love to be anxious &
unconstant: prolongeth contentions, and maketh ones adversary to
circumvent him with many cavillations;[83] but in process of time he
giveth victory. In the eighth House, he sheweth the kind of death to
be good and honest; but obscure, or in a strange place, or [whilst
on a] pilgrimage: discovereth Legacies and Possessions; but to be
obtained with [legal] suit and difficulty: denoteth Funerals and
Buryings to be obscure; the [dowry] portion of a wife to be hardly
gotten, but easily spent. In the ninth House, he maketh journeys
to be dangerous; and a party absent slowly to return: causeth men
to be occupied in offices of Religion: sheweth Sciences to be unac-
complished; but keepeth constancy in faith and Religion. In the
tenth House, he signifieth Kings and Princes to be potent; but to
gain their power with war and violence: banished men he sheweth
shall soon return: it likewise discovereth Honors, great Offices and
benefits; but for which you shall continually labour and strive, and

---

[80] Middling honors.

[81] Two of the four medical "humours," respectively bloody and heated.

[82] A wife from a good family.

[83] Frivolous objections.

wherein you shall have no stable continuance: A Judge shall not favour you: [legal] Suits and contentions he prolongeth: A father and mother he sheweth shall soon die, and always to be affected with many diseases. In the eleventh House, he maketh many friends; but such as are poor and unprofitable, and not able to relieve thy necessities: it ingratiates you with Princes, and giveth great hopes, but small gains; neither long to continue in any benefice or offices bestowed by a Prince. In the twelfth House, he sheweth enemies to be crafty, subtil, and fraudulent, and studying to circumvent you with many secret factions: signifies one in prison to be long detained, but at length to be delivered: Animals he sheweth to be unfruitful, and servants unprofitable; and the changes of fortune to be frequent, from good to evil, and from bad to good.

Way.

Via in the first House, bestoweth a long and prosperous life; giveth signification of a stranger; lean of body, and tall of stature; fair of complexion, having a small beard: a person liberal and pleasant; but slowe, and little addicted to labour. In the second, he increaseth substance and riches; recovereth any thing that is stolen or lost; but signifies the thief to be departed without the City.[84] In the third, he multiplies brethren and kinsfolks; signifies continual journeys, and prosperous; men that are publikely known, honest, and of good conversation. *Via* in the fourth House, signifies the father to be honest; increaseth the Patrimony and Inheritance; produceth wealthy fields; sheweth treasure to be in the place enquired after; recovereth any thing lost. In the fifth, he increaseth the company of male-children; sheweth a woman with childe to bring forth a male-childe; sendeth Embassages to strange and remote parts; increaseth publike honours; signifieth an honest kinde of death, and to be known thorow[85] many Provinces.

In the sixth House, *Via* preserveth from sickness; signifies the diseased speedily to recover; giveth profitable servants, and animals fruitful and profitable. In the seventh House, he bestoweth a wife fair and pleasant, with whom you shall enjoy perpetual felicity: causeth strifes and controversies most speedily to be determined; adversaries to be easily overcome, and that shall willingly sub-

---

[84] Departed beyond the city.
[85] Through.

mit their controversies to the Arbitration of good men. In the eighth House, he sheweth the kinde of death to proceed from Phlegmatick diseases; to be honest, and of good report; discovereth great Legacies, and rich Inheritances to be obtained by the dead: And if any one hath been reported to be dead, it sheweth him to be alive. In the ninth House, *Via* causeth long journeys by water, especially by Sea, and portendeth very great gains to be acquired thereby: he denoteth Priesthoods, and profits from Ecclesiastical employments; maketh men of good Religion, upright, and constant of faith: sheweth dreams to be true, whose signification shall suddenly appear: increaseth Philosophical and Grammatical Sciences, and those things which appertain to the instruction and bringing up of children. In the tenth House if *Via* be found, he maketh Kings and Princes happie and fortunate, and such as shall maintain continual peace with their Allies; and that they shall require amity and friendship amongst many Princes by their several Embassages: promoteth publike Honours, Offices, and Magistracie amongst the vulgar and common people; or about things pertaining to the water, journeys, or about gathering Taxes and Assessments: sheweth Judges to be just and merciful, and that shall quickly dispatch Causes[86] depending before them: and denotes a mother to be of good repute, healthy, and of long life. In the eleventh House, he raiseth many wealthy friends, and acquireth faithful friends in forraign Provinces and Countries, and that shall willingly relieve him that requires them, with all help and diligence.[87] It ingratiates persons with profit and trust amongst Princes, employing him in such Offices, as he shall be incumbred with continual travels. *Via* in the twelfth House, causeth many enemies, but such as of whom little hurt or danger is to be feared: signifies servants and animals to be profitable: whosoever is in prison, to be escaped, or speedily to be delivered from thence: and preserveth a man from the evil accidents of Fortune.

PEOPLE.

Populus being found in the first House, if a Question be propounded concerning that House, sheweth a mean[88] life, of a middle age, but inconstant, with divers sicknesses, and various successes of

---

[86] Legal cases.

[87] SB. Originally a colon.

[88] An average life.

Fortune: signifies a man of middle stature, a gross body, well set in his members; perhaps some mold or mark about his left eye. But if a Question shall be propounded concerning the figure of a man, and to this figure if there be joyned any of the figures of *Saturn* or *Rubeus*, it sheweth the man to be monstrously deformed; and that deformity he signifies to proceed from his birth: but if in the fifth House, if he be encompassed with malevolent Aspects, then that monstrousness is to come. In the second House, *Populus* sheweth a mean substance,[89] and that to be gotten with great difficulty: maketh a man also always sensible of laborious toyl:[90] things stoln are never regained: what is lost shall never be wholly recovered: that which is hidden shall not be found. But if the Question be of a thief, it declareth him not yet to be fled away, but to lie lurking within the City. In the third House, *Populus* raiseth few friends, either of brethren or kindred: forsheweth journeys, but with labour and trouble; notwithstanding some profit may accrue by them: denotes a man unstable in his faith, and causeth a man often to be deceived by his companions. In the fourth House, it signifies a father to be sickly, and of a laborious life, and his earthly posses-sions and inheritances to be taken away: sheweth profit to be gained by water: sheweth treasure not to be hid; or if there be any hidden, that it shall not be found: A patrimony[91] to be preserved with great labour. In the fifth House, he sheweth no honest Messages, but either maketh the messengers to be Porters, or publike Carryers: he divulgeth false rumours, which notwithstanding have the likeness of some truth, and seem to have their original from truth, which is not reported as it is done: It signifies a woman to be barren, and causeth such as are great with childe to be abortives: appointeth an inglorious Funeral, and ill report after death.

In the sixth House, *Populus* sheweth cold sicknesses; and chiefly affecteth the lower parts of the body: A Physician is declared to be careless and negligent in administring Physick to the sick, and signifies those that are affected with sickness to be in danger of death, and scarcely recover at all: it notes the decitfulness of ser-vants, and detriment of cattel. In the seventh House, it sheweth a wife to be fair and pleasant, but one that shall be sollicited with the love of many wooers: signifies her loves to be feigned and dis-

---

[89] Average income.

[90] Toil.

[91] Inheritance.

sembling: maketh weak and impotent adversaries soon to desert prosecuting. In the eighth House, it denotes sudden death without any long sickness or anguish, and oftentimes sheweth death by the water; giveth no inheritance, possession or legacy from the dead; and if any be, they shall be lost by some intervening contention, or other discord: he signifies the dowry of a wife to be little or none. *Populus* in the ninth House, sheweth false dreams, personates a man of rude wit, without any learning or science; In religion he signifies inferiour Offices, such as serve either to cleanse the Church, or ring the bells; and he signifies a man little curious or studious in religion, neither one that is troubled with much conscience. In the tenth House he signifies such Kings and Princes, as for the most part are expulsed out of their Rule and Dominions, or either suffer continual trouble and detriment about them: he signifies Offices and Magistracy, which appertain to matters concerning the waters, as about the Navy, bridges, fishings, shores, meadows, & things of the like sort; maketh Judges to be variable and slowe in expediting of Causes before them; declareth a Mother to be sickly, and of a short life. In the eleventh House he giveth few friends, and many flatterers; and with Princes giveth neither favour nor fortune. In the twelfth House he sheweth weak and ignoble enemies; declareth one in prison not to be delivered, discovereth dangers in waters, and watry places.

GAIN.

Acquisitio found in the first House, giveth a long life and prosperous old age; signifies a man of middle stature, and a great head, a countenance very well to be distinguished or known, a long nose, much beard, hair curling, and fair eyes, free of his meat and drink, but in all things else sparing and not liberal. In the second House, he signifies very great riches, apprehendeth all theeves, and causeth whatsoever is lost to be recovered. In the third House, many brethren, and they to be wealthy; many gainful journies; signifies a man of good faith. In the fourth is signified a Patrimony of much riches, many possessions of copious fruits; he signifieth that treasure hid in any place shall be found; and sheweth a Father to be rich, but covetous. In the fifth House, *Acquisitio* signifies many children of both Sexes, but more Males then Females; sheweth a woman to be with child, and that she shall be delivered without danger: and if a question be propounded concerning any Sex, he signifies it to be Masculine; encreaseth gainful profitable Embassages and Messages, but extendeth fame not far after death, yet causeth a man to be inherited of his own, and signifieth rumours to be true.

In the sixth House he signifies many and grievous sicknesses, and long to continue, maketh the sick to be in danger of death, and often to die: yet he declareth a Physitian to be learned and honest; giveth many servants and chattel,[92] and gains to be acquired from them. In the seventh House he signifies a wife to be rich, but either a widow, or a woman of a well-grown age; signifies [legal] suits and contentions to be great and durable, and that love and wedlock shall be effected by lot. In the eighth House, if a man be enquired after, it sheweth him to be dead, signifieth the kind of death to be short, and sickness to last but a few dayes; discovereth very profitable legacies and inheritances, and signifieth a wife to have a rich dowry. In the ninth House he signifies long and profitable journeys; sheweth if any one be absent he shall soon return; causeth gain to be obtained from Religious and Ecclesiastical Persons or Scholars, and signifies a man of a true and perfect Science. In the tenth House, he maketh Princes to inlarge their Dominions; a Judge favourable, but one that must be continually presented with gifts; causeth Offices and Magistracy to be very gainful; signifieth a Mother rich and happy. In the eleventh House, *Acquisitio* multiplieth friends, and bringeth profit from them, and increaseth favour with Princes. In the twelfth House he signifieth a man shall have many powerful or potent enemies; reduceth and bringeth home servants fled away, and cattel strayed; and signifies he that is in prison shall not be delivered.

JOY.

Laetitia in the first House signifies long life with prosperity, and much joy and gladness, and causeth a man to out-live and be more victorious than all his brethren; signifies a man of a tall stature, fair members, a broad forehead, having great and broad teeth; and that hath a face comely and well coloured. In the second House it signifies riches and many gains, but great expences and various mutations of ones state and condition; theft and any thing lost is recovered and returned: but if the Question be of a theef, it declareth him to be fled away. In the third House *Laetitia* sheweth brethren to be of a good conversation, but of short life; journeys pleasant and comfortable; men of good credit and faith. In the

---

[92] Possessions.

fourth he signifies happy Patrimonies and possessions, a Father to
be noble, and honoured with the dignity of some princely office;
sheweth treasure to be in the place enquired after, but of less worth
and value then is supposed, and causeth it to be found. In the fifth
House he giveth obedient children, endued with good manners,
and in whom shall be had the greatest joy and comfort of old age;
signifies a woman with child to bring forth a daughter; sheweth
honourable Embassages, and declares rumours and news to be
altogether true, and leaveth a good and ample fame after death.

In the sixth House it sheweth the sick shall recover, denoteth
good servants, good and profitable cattel and animals. In the seventh House *Laetitia* giveth a wife fair, beautiful and young; overcometh strifes and contentions, and rendereth the success thereof
to be love. *Laetitia* in the eighth House giveth Legacies and possessions, and a commendable portion with a wife: if a Question be
proposed concerning the condition of any man, it signifies him to
be alive, and declares an honest, quiet, and meek kinde of death. In
the ninth House *Laetitia* signifies very few journies, and those that
do apply themselves to travail,[93] their journeyes either are about
the Messages and Embassages of Princes, or Pilgrimages to fulfil
holy vows; sheweth a man to be of a good religion, of indifferent
knowledge, and who easily apprehendeth all things with natural
ingenuity. In the tenth House, it raiseth Kings and Princes to honour and great renown; maketh them famous by maintaining peace
during their times; signifies Judges to be cruel & severe; honest
Offices and Magistracy; signifies those things which are exercised
either about Ecclesiastical affairs, schools, or the administration of
justice; sheweth a mother if she be a widow, that she shall be mar-
ried again. In the eleventh House *Laetitia* increaseth favour with
Princes, and multiplies friends. And in the twelfth House *Laetitia*
giveth the victory over enemies; causeth good servants and families,
delivereth from imprisonment, and preserveth from future evils.

MAID

Puella in the first House signifies a person of a short life, weak
constitution of body, middle stature, little fat, but fair, effeminate
and luxurious, and one who will incur many troubles and dangers
in his [l]ife-time for the love of women. In the second House, it
neither encreaseth riches, nor diminisheth poverty; signifies a theef

---

[93] Travel, not work.

not to be departed from the City, and a thing stollen to be alienated and made away: if a Question be of treasure in a place, it is
resolved there is none. In the third House *Puella* signifies more
sisters then brethren, and encreaseth and continueth good friendship and amity amongst them; denoteth journies to be pleasant
and joyous, and men of good conversations. In the fourth House
Puella signifies a very small patrimony, and a Father not to live
long, but maketh the fields fertile with good fruits. In the fifth
House a woman with child is signified to bring forth a woman-
child; denotes no Embassage, causeth much commerce with women,
and some office to be obtained from them.

   Puella in the sixth House signifies much weakness of the sick,
but causeth the sick shortly to recover; and sheweth a Physitian to
be both unlearned and unskilful, but one who is much esteemed
of in the opinion of the vulgar people; giveth good servants, hand-
maids, cattel and animals. In the seventh House *Puella* giveth a wife
fair, beautiful and pleasant, leading a peaceable and quiet conversation with her husband, notwithstanding one that shall burn much
with lust, and be coveted and lusted after of many men; denoteth
no suits or controversies, which shall depend before a Judge, but
some jarres and wranglings with the common people one amongst
another, which shall be easily dissolved and ended. In the eighth
House, if a Question be of one reputed to be dead, *Puella* declareth
him to be alive: giveth a small portion with a wife, but that which
contenteth her husband. In the ninth House *Puella* signifies very
few journeys, sheweth a man of good religion, indifferent skill or
knowledge in sciences, unless happily Musick, as wel[l] vocal as
instrumental. In the tenth House *Puella* signifies Princes not to
be very potent, but notwithstanding they shall govern peaceably
within their Dominions, and shall be beloved of their Neighbours
and Subjects; it ca[u]seth them to be affable, milde and courteous, and that they shall alwayes exercise themselves with continual
mirth, plays, and huntings; maketh Judges to be good, godly and
merciful; giveth Offices about women, or especially from noble
women. In the eleventh House *Puella* giveth many friends, and
encreaseth favour with women. In the twelfth House *Puella* signifies
few enemies, but contention with women; and delivereth Prisoners
out of prison through the intercession of friends.

LOSS.

Amissio in the first House signifies the sick not to live long, and sheweth a short life; signifies a man of disproportioned members of his body, and one of a wicked life and coversation, and who is marked with some notorious and remarkable defect in some part of his body, as either lame, or maimed, or the like. *Amissio* in the second House consumeth all substance, and maketh one to suffer and undergo the burden of miserable poverty, neither theef, nor the thing stollen shall be found; signifies treasure not to be in the place sought after, and to be sought with loss and damage. In the third House *Amissio* signifies death of brethren, or the want of them, and of kindred and friends; signifieth no journeys, and causeth one to be deceived of many. In the fourth House *Amissio* signifies the utter destruction of ones Patrimony, sheweth the Father to be poor, and Son to die. *Amissio* in the fifth House sheweth death of children, and afflicts a man with divers sorrows; signifieth a woman not to be with child, or else to have miscarried; raiseth no fame or honours, and disperseth false rumors.

In the sixth House *Amissio* signifies the sick to be recovered, or that he shall soon recover; but causeth loss and damage by servants and cattels. In the seventh House *Amissio* giveth an adulterous wife, and contrarying her husband with continual contention; nevertheless she shall not live long; and it causeth contentions to be ended. In the eighth House *Amissio* signifies a man to be dead, consumeth the dowry of a wife; bestoweth or sendeth no inheritances or legacies. In the ninth House *Amissio* causeth no journies, but such as shall be compassed with very great loss; signifies men to be inconstant in Religion, and often changing their opinion from one sect to another, and altogether ignorant of learning. In the tenth House *Amissio* rendereth Princes to be most unfortunate, and sheweth that they shall be compelled to end their lives in exile and banishment; Judges to be wicked; and signifies Offices and Magistracy to be damageable, and sheweth the death of a Mother. In the eleventh House *Amissio* signifies few friends, and causeth them to be easily lost, and turned to become enemies; and causeth a man to have no favour with his Prince, unless it be hurtful to him. In the twelfth House *Amissio* destroyeth all enemies, detaineth long in prison, but preserveth from dangers.

CONJUNCTION.

Conjunctio in the first House maketh a prosperous life, and signifies a man of a middle stature, not lean nor fat, long face, plain hair, a little beard, long fingers and thighs, liberal, amiable, and a friend to many people. In the second House *Conjunctio* doth not signifie any riches to be gotten, but preserveth a man secure and free from the calamities of poverty; detecteth both the theef and the thing stolen, and acquireth hidden treasure. In the third House he giveth various journeys with various success, and signifieth good faith and constancy. In the fourth House *Conjunctio* sheweth a mean Patrimony; causeth a Father to [be] honest, of good report, and of good understanding. In the fifth House he giveth Children of subtile ingenuity and wit, sheweth a woman pregnant to have a male-child, and raiseth men to honours by their own meer proper wit and ingenuity, and disperseth their fame and credit far abroad; and also signifies news and rumours to be true.

In the sixth House *Conjunctio* signifies sicknesses to be tedious and of long continuance; but foresheweth the Physitian to be learned and well experienced; and sheweth servants to be faithful and blameless, and animals profitable. In the seventh House he giveth a wife very obedient, conformable, and dutiful to her husband, and one of a good wit and ingenuity; [it] causeth difficult suits and controversies, and crafty, subtil and malicious adversaries. In the eighth House, him of whom a Question is propounded, *Conjunctio* signifies him to be dead, & pretendeth some gain to be acquired by his death; sheweth a wife shall not be very rich. In the ninth House he giveth a few journeys, but long and tedious, and sheweth one that is absent shall after a long season return. *Conjunctio* in this House increaseth divers Arts, Sciences, and Mysteries of Religion; and giveth a quick, perspicuous, and efficacious wit. In the tenth House *Conjunctio* maketh Princes liberal, affable and benevolent, and who are much delighted and affected with divers Sciences, and secret Arts, and with men learned therein; causeth Judges to be just, and such who with a piercing and subtil speculation, do easily discern causes in controversie before them; enlargeth Offices which are concerned about Letters, Learning, sound Doctrines and Sciences; and signifies a Mother to be honest, of good ingenuity and wit, and also one of a prosperous life. In the eleventh House *Conjunctio* signifies great increase of friends; and very much procureth the grace and favour of Princes, powerful and noble Men. In the twelfth House *Conjunctio* signifies wary and quick-witted enemies; causeth such as are in prison to remain and continue so very long, and causeth a man to eschew very many dangers in his life.

WHITE.

Albus in the first House signifies a life vexed with continual sickness and greivous diseases; signifies a man of a short stature, broad brest, and gross arms, having curled or crisped hair, one of a broad full mouth, a great talker and babler, given much to use vain and unprofitable discourse, but one that is merry, joyous and jocond,[94] and much pleasing to men. In the second House *Albus* enlargeth and augmenteth substance gained by sports, playes, vile and base arts and exercises, but such as are pleasing and delightful; as by playes, pastimes, dancings and laughters: he discovereth both the theef, and the theft or thing stollen, and hideth and concealeth treasure. In the third House *Albus* signifies very few brethren; giveth not many, but tedious and wearisome journyes, and signifies all deceivers. In the fourth House he sheweth very small or no Patrimony, and the Father to be a man much known; but declareth him to be a man of some base and inferiour Office and Imployment. In the fifth House *Albus* giveth no children, or if any, that they shall soon die; declareth a woman to be servile, and causeth such as are with young to miscarry, or else to bring forth Monsters; denoteth all rumours to be false, and raiseth to no honour.

In the sixth House *Albus* causeth very tedious sicknesses and diseases; discovereth the fraud, deceit and wickedness of servants, and signifies diseases and infirmities of cattel to be mortal, and maketh the Physitian to be suspected of the sick Patient. *Albus* in the seventh House giveth a barren wife, but one that is fair and beautiful; few suits or controversies, but such as shall be of very long continuance. In the eighth House if a question be propounded of any one, *Albus* shews the party to be dead; giveth little portion or dowry with a wife, and causeth that to be much strived and contended for. In the ninth House *Albus* denoteth some journyes to be accomplished, but with mean profit; hindereth him that is absent, and signifies he shall not return; and declareth a man to be superstitious in Religion, and given to false and deceitful Sciences.

---

[94] Humorous and good company.

In the tenth *Albus* causeth Princes and Judges to be malevolent; sheweth vile and base Offices and Magistracies; signifies a Mother to be a whore, or one much suspected for adultery. In the eleventh House *Albus* maketh dissembling and false friends; causeth love and favour to be inconstant. *Albus* in the twelfth House denoteth vile, impotent and rustical enemies; sheweth such as are in prison shall not escape, and signifies a great many and various troubles and discommodities of ones life.

CHILD.

Puer[95] in the first House giveth an indifferent long life, but laborious; raiseth men to great fame through military dignity; signifies a person of a strong body, ruddy complexion, a fair countenance, and black hair. In the second House *Puer* increaseth substance, obtained by other mens goods, by plunderings, rapines, confiscations, military Laws, and such like; he concealeth both the theef and the thing stolen, but discovereth no treasure. In the third House *Puer* raiseth a man to honour above his brethren, and to be feared of them; signifies journies to be dangerous, and denoteth persons of good credit. In the fourth House *Puer* signifies dubious inheritances and possessions, and signifies a Father to attain to his substance and estate through violence. In the fifth House *Puer* sheweth good children, and such as shall attain to honors and dignities; he signifies a woman to have a male-child, and sheweth honors to be acquired by military discipline, and great and full fame.

In the sixth House *Puer* causeth violent diseases and infirmities, as wounds, falls, contusions, bruises, but easily delivereth the sick, and sheweth the Physitian and Chirurgion to be good; denoteth servants and animals to be good, strong and profitable. In the seventh House *Puer* causeth a wife to be a virago, of a stout Spirit, of good fidelity, and one that loveth to bear the Rule and Government of a house; maketh cruel strifes and contentions, and such adversaries, as shall scarcely be restrained by Justice. *Puer* in the eighth House sheweth him that is supposed to be dead to live, signifieth the kinde of death not to be painful, or laborious, but to proceed from some hot humour, or by iron, or the sword, or from some other cause of the like kinde; sheweth a man to have no legacies or other inheritance. In the ninth House *Puer*

---

[95] Usually translated as "boy" rather than child.

sheweth journeys not to be undergone without peril and danger
of life, yet nevertheless declareth them to be accomplished pros-
perously and safely; sheweth persons of little Religion, and using
little conscience, notwithstanding giveth the knowledge of natural
philosophy and physick, and many other liberal and excellent Arts.
Puer in the tenth House signifies Princes to be powerful, glorious,
and famous in warlike archievements, but they shall be unconstant
and unchangeable, by reason of the mutable and various success
of victory. *Puer* in this House causeth Judges to [be] cruel and
unmerciful; increaseth offices in warlike affairs; signifies Magistracy
to be exercised by fire and sword; hurteth a Mother, and endan-
gereth her life. In the eleventh House *Puer* sheweth Noble friends,
and Noble men, and such as shall much frequent the Courts of
Princes, and follow after warfare; and causeth many to adhere to
cruel men: nevertheless he causeth much esteem with Princes; but
their favour is to be suspected. *Puer* in the twelfth House causeth
Enemies to be cruel and pernicious; those that are in Prison shall
escape, and maketh them to eschew many dangers.

RED.

Rubeus in the first House, signifies a short life, and an evil end;
signifies a man to be filthy, unprofitable, and of an evil, cruel and
malicious countenance, having some remarkable and notable signe
or scar in some part of his body. In the second House *Rubeus* signifies poverty, and maketh theeves and robbers, and such persons
as shall acquire and seek after their maintenance and livelihoods
by using false, wicked, and evil, and unlawful Arts; preserveth
theeves, and concealeth theft; and signifies no treasure to be hid
nor found. In the third House *Rubeus* renders brethren and kinsmen to be full of hatred, and odious one to another, and sheweth
them to be of evil manners, & ill disposition; causeth journeys
to be very dangerous, and foresheweth false faith and treachery.
In the fourth House he destroyeth and consumeth Patrimonies,
and disperseth and wasteth inheritances, causeth them to come to
nothing; destroyeth the fruits of the field by tempestuous seasons,
and malignancy of the earth; and bringeth the Father to a quick
and sudden death. *Rubeus* in the fifth House giveth many children,
but either they shall be wicked and disobedient, or else shall afflict
their Parents with grief, disgrace and infamy.

In the sixth House *Rubeus* causeth mortal wounds, sicknesses
and diseases; him that is sick shall die; the Physitian shall erre,

servants prove false and treacherous, cattel and beasts shall produce hurt and danger. In the seventh House *Rubeus* signifies a wife to be infamous, publickly adulterate, and contentious; deceitful and treacherous adversaries, who shall endeavour to overcome you, by crafty and subtil wiles and circumventions of the Law. In the eighth House *Rubeus* signifies a violent death to be inflicted, by the execution of publike Justice; and signifies, if any one be enquired after, that he is certainly dead; and wife to have no portion or dowry. *Rubeus* in the ninth House sheweth journeys to be evil and dangerous, and that a man shall be in danger either to spoiled by theeves and robbers, or to be taken by plunderers and robbers; declareth men to be of most wicked opinion in Religion, and of evil faith, and such as will often easily be induced to deny and go from their faith for every small occasion; denoteth Sciences to be false and deceitful, and the professors thereof to be ignorant. In the tenth House *Rubeus* signifies Princes to be cruel and tyrannical, and that their power shall come to an evil end, as that either they shall be cruelly murdered and destroyed by their own Subjects, or that they shall be taken captive by their conquerers, and put to an ignominious and cruel death, or shall miserably end their lives in hard imprisonment; signifies Judges and Officers to be false, theevish, and such as shall be addicted to usury; sheweth that a mother shall soon die, and denoteth her to be blemisht with an evil fame and report. In the eleventh House *Rubeus* giveth no true, nor any faithful friends; sheweth men to be of wicked lives and conversations, and causeth a man to be rejected and cast out from all society and conversation with good and noble persons. *Rubeus* in the twelfth House maketh enemies to be cruel and traiterous, of whom we ought circumspectly to beware; signifies such as are in prison shall come to an evil end; and sheweth a great many inconveniences and mischiefs to happen in a mans life.

PRISON.

Carcer in the first House being posited, giveth a short life; signifies men to be most wicked, of a filthy and cruel unclean figure and shape, and such as are hated and despised of all men. *Carcer* in the second House causeth most cruel and miserable poverty; signifies both the theef and thing stollen to be taken and regained; and sheweth no treasure to be hid. In the third House *Carcer* signifieth hatred and dissention amongst brethren; evil journeys, most wicked faith and conversation. *Carcer* in the fourth House

signifieth a man to have no possessions or inheritances, a Father
to be most wicked, and to die a sudden and evil death. In the fifth
House *Carcer* giveth many children; sheweth a woman not to be
with child, and provoketh those that are with child to miscarry of
their own consent, or slayeth the child; signifieth no honours, and
disperseth most false rumours.

In the sixth House *Carcer* causeth the diseased to undergoe
long sickness; signifieth servants to be wicked, rather unprofitable; Physitians ignorant. In the seventh House *Carcer* sheweth
the wife shall be hated of her husband, and signifies suits and
contentions to be ill ended and determined. In the eighth House
Carcer declareth the kinde of death to be by some fall, mischance,
or false accusation, or that men shall be condemned in prison, or
in publike judgement, and sheweth them to be put to death, or
that they shall often lay violent and deadly hands upon themselves;
denieth a wife to have any portion and legacies. *Carcer* in the ninth
House, sheweth he that is absent shall not return, and signifieth
some evil shall happen to him in his journey; it denotes persons
of no Religion, a wicked conscience, and ignorant of learning. In
the tenth House *Carcer* causeth Princes to be very wicked, and
wretchedly to perish, because when they are established in their
power, they will wholly addict themselves to every voluptuous
lust, pleasure, and tyranny; causeth Judges to be unjust and false;
declareth the Mother to be cruel, and infamous, and noted with
the badge of adultery; giveth no Offices nor Magistracies, but such
as are gotten and obtained either by lying, or through theft, and
base and cruel robbery. In the eleventh House *Carcer* causeth no
friends, nor love, nor favour amongst men. In the twelfth House it
raiseth enemies, detaineth in prison, and inflicteth many evils.

SORROW.

Tristitia in the first House doth not abbreviate life, but afflicteth it
with many molestations; signifieth a person of good manners and
carriage, but one that is solitary, and slow in all his business and
occasions; one that is solitary, melancholly, seldom laughing, but
most covetous after all things. In the second House it giveth much
substance and riches, but they that have them, shall not enjoy them,
but shall rather hide them, and shall scarce afford to themselves
food or sustenance therefrom; treasure shall not be found, neither
shall the theef nor the theft. *Tristitia* in the third House signifieth
a man to have few brethren, but sheweth that he shall outlive them

all; causeth unhappy journeys, but giveth good faith. In the fourth House *Tristitia* consumeth and destroyeth fields, possessions and inheritances; causeth a Father to be old and of long life, and a very covetous hoorder up of money. In the fifth House it signifies no children, or that they shall soon die; sheweth a woman with child to bring forth a woman-child, giveth no fame nor honors.

In the sixth House *Tristitia* sheweth that the sick shall die; servants shall be good, but slothful; and signifies cattel shall be of a small price or value. In the seventh House *Tristitia* sheweth that the wife shall soon die; and declareth suits and contentions to be very hurtful, and determining against you. In the eighth House it signifies the kinde of death to be with long and grievous sickness, and much dolour and pain; giveth legacies and an inheritance, and indoweth a wife with a portion.[96] Tristitia in the ninth House, sheweth that he that is absent shall perish in his journey; or signifies that some evil mischance shall happen unto him; causeth journeys to be very unfortunate, but declareth men to be of good Religion, devout, and profound Scholars. In the tenth House *Tristitia* signifies Princes to be severe, but very good lovers of justice; it causeth just Judges, but such as are tedious and slow in determining of causes; bringeth a Mother to a good old age, with integrity and honesty of life, but mixt with divers discommodities and mis-fortunes; it raiseth to great Offices, but they shall not be long enjoyed nor persevered in; it signifies such Offices as do appertain to the water, or tillage, and manuring of the Earth, or such as are to be imployed about matters of Religion and wisdom. In the eleventh House *Tristitia* signifies scarcity of friends, and the death of friends; and also signifies little love or favour. In the twelfth House it sheweth no enemies; wretchedly condemneth the imprisoned; and causeth many discommodities and disprofits to happen in ones life.

Dragons head.

Caput Draconis in the first House augmenteth life and fortune. In the second House he increaseth riches and substance; saveth and concealeth a theef; and signifies treasure to be hid. In the third House *Caput Draconis* giveth many brethren; causeth journeys, kinsmen, and good faith and credit. In the fourth House he giveth wealthy inheritances; causeth the Father to attain to old age. In the

---

[96] Dowry.

fifth House *Caput Draconis* giveth many children; signifies women
with child to bring forth women-children; and oftentimes to have
twins; it sheweth great honours and fame; and signifies news and
rumours to be true.

Caput Draconis is the sixth House increaseth sicknesses and diseases; signifieth the Physitian to be learned; and giveth very many
servants and chattel. In the seventh House he signifieth a man
shall have many wives; multiplies and stirreth up many adversaries
and suits. In the eight House he sheweth the death to be certain,
increaseth Legacies and inheritances, and giveth a good portion
with a wife. In the ninth House *Caput Draconis* signifies many
journeys, many Sciences, and good Religion; and sheweth that those
that are absent shall soon return. In the tenth House he signifies
glorious Princes, great and magnificent Judges, great Offices, and
gainful Magistracy. In the eleventh House he causeth many friends,
and to be beloved of all men. In the twelfth House *Caput Draconis*
signifieth men to have many enemies, and many women; detaineth
the imprisoned, and evilly punisheth them.

Dragons tail

Cauda Draconis, in all and singular the respective Houses aforesaid,
giveth the contrary judgement to *Caput*. And these are the natures
of the figures of Geomancy, and their judgements, in all and singular their Houses, upon all maner of Questions to be propounded,
of or concerning any matter or thing whatsoever.

[Judgement.]

But now in the maner of proceeding to judgement, this you are
especially to observe; That whensoever any Question shall be proposed to you, which is contained in any of the Houses, that you
shall not onely answer thereunto by the figure contained in such
a House; but beholding and diligently respecting all the figures,
and the Index it self in two Houses, you shall ground the face of
judgement.[97] You shall therefore consider the figure of the thing
quesited or enquired after, if he shall multiply himself by the
other places of the figures, that you may cause them also to be
partakers in your judgement: as for example, if a Question shall

---

[97] You should carefully weigh and polish the answer.

be propounded of the second House concerning a theef, and the figure of the second House shall be found in the sixth, it declareth the theef to be some of ones own houshold or servants: and after this maner shall you judge and consider of the rest; for this whole Art consisteth in the Commixtures of the figures, and the natures thereof; which whosoever doth rightly practice, he shall alwaies declare most true and certain judgements upon every particular thing whatsoever.

GERARD CREMONENSIS

OF

ASTRONOMICAL GEOMANCY

 ECAUSE ASTRONOMY is so transcendent and subtil an Art in it self, that therein a man ought to have respect unto so many things before he can attaine to true judgement thereby, because the eye of the understanding will not pierce unto the half thereof, and few Doctors of our later time have been found so experienced therein that they know sufficiently how to judge thereby.[1] Therefore I have composed this work, which I will have to be named, *Astronomical Geomancy*; wherein, I will sufficiently teach how to judge [geomantic figures] with less labour and study. For in this present science it is not requisite to be hold[2] neither the Ascendant, nor the hour in a Table, as it is in Astrology.

It is expedient therefore, to make four unequal lines, by the points casually set down; and to joyne together those points.[3] And out of the points which are not joyned together, which do remain in the heads of the lines, (as it is done in Geomancie) extract one figure; and the sign of the *Zodiacke* that answereth to that figure, put for the Ascendent, for the words sake.

If *Acquisitio*[4] arise from the heads of those four Lines,[5] let *Aries* be placed in the Ascendent;

---

[1] SB. A semicolon occurs here in the original text.

[2] To examine.

[3] SB. Originally a semicolon here. In other words, while thinking of the question you wished answered, mark four rows of points. Then examine each of these four lines of points. By connecting pairs of points, you will be left with either one or two points. This procedure will make one geomantic figure made up of four levels of either one or two points.

[4] Margin note: *Acquisition*.

[5] Is generated from those points.

if Letitia, or the lesser Fortune[6] [then] put *Taurus* in the Ascendent;
if *Puer* or *Rubeus*, place *Gemini* [in the Ascendant];
if *Albus*, [then put] *Cancer*;
if *Via*, [then put] *Leo*;
if *Conjunctio* or the Dragons Head,[7] [put] *Virgo*;
if *Puella*, [put] *Libra*;
if *Amissio* or *Tristitia*, [put] *Scorpio*;
if [t]he *Dragons Tail*,[8] [put] *Sagittary*;[9]
if *Populus*, [put] *Capricorn*,
if *Fortuna major*, [put] *Aquary*;[10]
if *Carcer*, then put *Pisces* for the Ascendent.

Afterwards in the second House, let that signe be placed which immediately succeeds the other [sign]. In the third House [put] the third
Signe, and so place the rest in order until you come unto the end
of the Signs.[11] And make one square figure divided into twelve equal
parts,[12] and therein place the Signs in order, as it is in Astrology, and
as you may finde them in this figure [see page 211].[13] Neither are we
here to regard the *witnesses, or *Judge,[14] or any other thing which
[usually] belongs to Geomancie; but onely the sixteen Figures, that by
them we may have the twelve Signs, to which they agree; and observe
the manner of the Figure as it is here placed.

Afterwards it is requisite to make four Lines by course for
every Planet, by points casually pricked down; and likewise for
the *Dragons Head*, as you have done for the Ascendent, and divide
those points by twelve.[15] And that which remaineth above twelve,

---

[6] Fortuna Minor.

[7] Caput Draconis.

[8] Cauda Draconis.

[9] Sagittarius.

[10] Aquarius.

[11] SB. Originally a semicolon here.

[12] A horoscope drawn in the old square manner.

[13] SB. Originally a colon here.

[14] The figures of the two Witnesses and the Judge are an integral part of
ordinary geomancy (for which see Agrippa's *On Geomancy* included in this
volume). Gerard of Cremona is making a break with conventional geomancy
by deriving the whole figure solely from the one geomantic figure. This book
is called *Astronomical* Geomancy because he relies much more on an astrological format and interpretation than on conventional geomancy.

[15] SB. Originally a semicolon here.

Look how the twelve Signes are placed in the figure, and so may any other Signe be ascending in his turn, as Aries is here..

[*The astrological figure divided in twelve Houses with planets and zodiac signs*]

or the twelfth it self, if a greater number doth not remain, retaine [it].[16] And the Planet for which the projection was made, place in that House of which the super-abounding number shall be.[17]

That is, if there remain twelve, let the Planet be placed in the twelfth House; if ten, in the tenth House; if one, in the first House; if two, in the second House; and so of the rest. And you ought alwayes to begin from the *Sun*, and afterwards from the *Moon*, then from *Venus* and *Mercury*, and from *Saturn*, *Jupiter* and *Mars*, and the *Dragons Head* and *Dragons Tail*; but you must always take heed, that you do not make a question in a rainy, cloudy, or a very windy season, or when thou art angry, or thy minde busied with many affairs; nor for tempters or deriders,[18] neither that you may renew and reiterate the same Question again under the same figure or forme;[19] for that is error.

---

[16] SB. Originally a comma here.

[17] SB; originally a semicolon here. That is, the remainder, after 12 has been subtracted as many times as necessary.

[18] Clients who request you divine simply to ridicule the art.

[19] Don't continue asking the same question in the hope of getting a different answer.

QUESTIONS OF THE FIRST HOUSE.

If you are desirous to know concerning the life of any man whether it shall be long or short, behold the Lord of the Ascendent, who if he be in strong Angles,[20] it signifies long life; in succedents,[21] a middle age; and in cadent Houses,[22] a short life.[23] And if he be [located] in strong Angles, he signifies greater years; if in Succedents, meaner years;[24] if in Cadents, lesser years.

The lesser years of *Saturn* are thirty, the meaner are forty four years, and the greater fifty eight [years].[25] The lesser years of *Jupiter* are twelve, the meaner years forty, and the greater accordingly are forty seven. The lesser years of *Mars* are fifteen, his meane years forty, and the greater years forty seven. The lesser years of the *Sun* are nineteen, his meane years forty five, and his greater years eighty two. The lesser years of *Venus* are eight, her mean years forty five, and her greater years eighty two. *Mercury's* lesser years are twenty, his mean years forty nine, and his greater years eighty. The lesser years or the *Moon* are fifteen, her mean years thirty nine, and her greater years a hundred and seven.

And also look if *Mars* or *Saturn* shall be in the first House, and the Lord of the eighth with them; and if the *Sun* shall be in the eight, the Querent shall not live.[26] Likewise if the Lord of the Ascendent shall happen to be void of course[27], and Mars be in the eighth, the Querent shall not live; but if the *Sun* and the *Moon* shall be in conjunction in the seventh House, and Venus in the second, he shall live well.

The accidents of the nativity are likewise to be considered. If yo[u] finde *Saturn* or *Mercury* in the first,* he is foolish and talkative; if it be *Mars* and *Mercury*, he will not be servile, but a wrangler[28] and scoffer; if the *Sun* and *Mercury*, he will be a speaker of truth; and if the *Sun* be in *Aries*, he will apply himself to learn whatsoever he shall hear; if *Venus* be in the seventh, he will be luxurious; and if *Saturn*,

---

[20] The 1st, 4th, 7th, 10th Houses.

[21] The 2nd, 5th, 8th, 11th Houses.

[22] The 3rd, 6th, 9th, 12th Houses.

[23] SB. Originally a semicolon.

[24] Middle length.

[25] These years refer to typical life spans.

[26] SB. Originally a colon.

[27] A void-of-course Moon occurs when the Moon finishes its last major aspect in a particular sign before it moves to the next sign. It may run for anything up to 2.5 days.

[28] Argumentative person.

Mercury and *Venus* be in their fall, he will be a Sodomite; if the *Sun* and *Venus* be in the tenth, and the *Moon* in the first, he will be very liberal; if *Venus*, *Mercury* and the *Dragons Head* be in the first, he will be covetous; if the *Moon* and *Mars* be in the first, he will be subject to great bondage; and if *Mars* be Lord of the nativity, he will be rich, and an evil speaker, and litigious; and if the *Sun* be in the first, he will be envious, having a fair body, not very lean, nor very fat; and if *Venus* be in the first, be will be white and fair; if *Mercury* be in the first, he will not be stable, but always in motion; but if the *Moon* be found there [in the first House], it denotes him to have a graceful face, brest and arms; if *Saturn* be there, the man will be black and filthy; if *Jupiter*, he will have a round face, a fair forehead, a ruddy complexion mixt with a little white.

If you would know his office[29] or art: if the *Moon* be in the seventh with *Saturn*, or in the fourth, or in the tenth, or in the first, it is not good for him to build any house in a City, nor to build a ship, neither is it good for him to be a tiller of land, or to dress vines, or plant trees; but to be imployed about some office[30] belonging to the water, or concerning mar[r]iages, or to be a Post or a Messenger; neither let him apply himself much to his master, because he shall gain no repute from him.[31] If the *Moon* be in the fifth or third, it will be good to him; [but if] in the second, eighth, sixth and twelfth, neither good nor evil.

Jupiter signifies [professions such as] Bishops, Prelates, Nobles, Potentates, Judges, Wise men, Merchants and Usurers.[32]

Mars signifies Warriors, Incendiaries, Homicides, Physitians, Barbers, Hangmen, Gold-smiths, Cooks, [jobs associated with] furnaces, and all fireworks. And if *Mars* be in strong Signs, he will be poor and die in captivity, unless he put himself in arms[33] with some souldier of vassal.

The *Sun* signifieth Emperors, Kings, Princes, Nobles, Lords and Judges.

Venus signifies Queens and Ladies, Mariages, Communications, Friendship, Apothecaries, Taylors, and such as make Ornaments for playes, sellers of Cloth, Jesters, Vintners, Players at dice, Whores and Robbers.

---

[29] Profession.

[30] Job.

[31] SB. Originally a colon.

[32] Moneylenders.

[33] Arm himself.

Mercury signifies Clerks,[34] Philosophers, Astrologers, Geo-
metricians, Arithmeticians, Latine writers, and Painters, and all
subtil Artists, as well men as women, and their Arts.

Concerning the intention of the Querent,[35] look unto the Signe
ascending, and his Lord; and where you finde the Lord of the
Ascendent, he comes to inquire about something pertaining to that
House.[36] And if the *Sun* be Lord of the Ascendent, his Question is
concerning fear which he is in of some man; if *Venus*, he enquireth of
Arts, that he may know some proper Arts, or he enquireth concerning things belonging to women. If *Mercury* be Lord of the Ascendent,
he seek after something that is lost, or enquireth concerning some
infirmity. If the *Moon*, he seeketh also for something lost, or inquireth
about sickness, or some disease in his eyes. If *Saturn* be Lord of the
Ascendent, he enquireth about some sickness, or concerning a Prince;
and keepeth silence, but hath some great grief or anguish in his heart.
If *Jupiter* be Lord of the Ascendent, his Question is concerning some
infirmity, or restitution, or for some office which he desireth to have.
If *Mars*, he enquireth for some fear, or of an enemy, death, sickness,
riches, or substance.

QUESTIONS OF THE SECOND HOUSE.

If you would he informed concerning the substance of any man
whether he shall be rich or not, behold the Lord of the second, which
if he shall be with a good Planet, & a good Planet likewise in the second, he shall be rich; but if the Lord of the second be joined with evil
Planets, and an evil Planet shall be in the second, he shall be poor.

If you would know whether you shall have again a thing lent, or
not, look if there be an evil Planet in the second, and disagreeing
with his Lord; then he that detaineth the thing lent, will not willingly render back the same.[37] But if there be a good Planet in the
second, and agreeing with his Lord, it shall easily be recovered; and
if the Lord of the second be exalted and be evil, or if an evil Planet
be with him in the second, or if the Lord of the second be exalted,
he which keepeth the thing deposited, will not willingly restore the
same, but he shall do [retain] it whether he will or not.

---

[34] Clerics, religious persons.

[35] The question being asked.

[36] SB; originally a semicolon. Using this formula you should be able to predict
the type of question being asked, even if the querent has not articulated it.

[37] SB. Orignally a colon.

And if an evil Planet be in the second, it's to be recovered.[38] But if *Mercury* be in the second so that he be his Lord, and bringeth contrariety, then it shall be recovered; and if a good Planet be in the second House, he signifies recovery, although he be the Lord thereof.

Mark therefore the concord and discord of the Planets: the *Moon* and *Jupiter* are friends, the *Moon* and *Mars* enemies; *Mercury* and the *Sun* are friends, *Mercury* and *Venus* enemies; *Venus* and *Jupiter* are friends, *Jupiter* and the *Moon* are enemies.

The Planets are said to be friends, when they agree in one nature and quality, as *Mars* and the *Sun*, because both their natures is hot and dry; *Venus* and the *Moon* do agree in cold and moisture: or when Planets do agree in substance and nature, as *Jupiter* and *Venus* are friends: or when the House of one is the exaltation of another, or on the contrary.

QUESTION OF THE THIRD HOUSE.

If that you desire to know, how many brethren a man hath, see the Lord of the third, and it is to be held, that to so many Planets as he is joyned, so many brethren the Querent hath; and the Masculine Planets signifie brethren, and the female Planets sisters.[39] And note, That *Saturn* and *Mars*, the *Sun*, *Jupiter*, & the *Dragons Head*, are masculine; but the *Moon*, *Venus* and the *Dragons Tail* are foeminine.[40] But *Mercury* is promiscuous, sometimes masculine, and sometimes foeminine; he is masculine when he is joyned to masculine Planets, or when he is in a masculine quarter of the *Zodiacke*; and he is foeminine, when he is joyned to foeminine Planets, or when he is in a foeminine quarter of the *Zodiacke*.

QUESTIONS OF THE FOURTH HOUSE.

If thou wouldst know whether it be good for thee to stay in any Land, City, Village, Territory, or House, or not, behold the Lord of the Ascendent of the fourth, and of the seventh; and if the Lord of the fourth be in the seventh, and be good, and the Lords of the first and the tenth House be good, and with good Planets, then it is good for thee to continue in that place wherein thou art. And if the Lord of the seventh be with a good Planet, and the Lord of

---

[38] SB. Originally a colon.

[39] SB. Originally a semicolon.

[40] Feminine. SB; orignally a colon.

the fourth with an evil Planet, then it is not good for thee to abide there, because if thou dost continue there, thou shalt suffer many losses, & have evil reports raised on thee in that Country.

But if thou wouldst know when any one that is absent will return, behold the Lord of the Ascendent; and if you finde him in any one of the four Angles, he will return in that year; and if he be not in an Angle, then see how far he is distant from the first Angle; for so long he will stay, and so many years as there be Houses.

If you would be informed of the dearth or plenty of things, behold the strong Houses, the Succedents and the Cadents; for the Strong Houses signifie dearth and scarcity, the Succedents a moderate season, neither too dear, nor too cheap, the Cadents signifie plenty and profitableness of things. Consider also the Planet, and their places, which if they be in strong Houses, the things which are signified by those Planets will be rare.[41]

And note, That *Saturn* doth signifie fields, vines, and instruments to work in fields, and leather, and of fruits, corn, acorns, oak-apples, and pomegranates. *Jupiter* hath oil, honey, silk-wormes, cloth, wine, and grass, and things that are odoriferous. *Mars* signifies wine, and flesh, and especially hogs, wars, and armour, and such things as belong thereunto, and red garments. The *Sun* hath signification of wheat, and wine, purple colours, and cloth, and all things that are assimilated unto gold, horses and birds, such as hawks and falcons. *Venus* doth signifie fatness and grapes, figs and dates, fish and pastimes. *Mercury* hath barley, millet, grain, money, and quicksilver. The *Moon* signifies oats, milk, cheese, fire and salt, cows, rams, hens, and silver, and accordingly plenty and scarcity of them.

QUESTIONS OF FIFTH HOUSE.

If you would know whether a woman be with Child, or whether she will have any children, or not, look if the Lord of the Ascendent be in the seventh, or the Lord of the fifth [be] in the first, or the Lord of the first [be] in the fifth, or if the Lord of the fifth be in the seventh, or if the Lord of the seventh be in the fifth, or the *Moon* with them; or if good Planets be in the first, or the fifth, or with the Lord of the fifth, or *R* in the Angles, [then] she is with child, or may have children.[42] But if you finde none of them,[43] but evil Planets in the

---

[41] SB. Originally a colon.

[42] SB. Originally a semicolon.

[43] The above listed indications of child bearing.

same places, [then] she neither is with childe, neither will she have any children.[44] And if there be both good and evil Planets in the said places, then happily she may have children, but they will not live; but if *Cancer*, *Scorpio* or *Pisces* shall be in the first or fifth House, [then] she may have children; but if *Leo* and *Virgo* be there, she is not with child, neither shall she ever have any children; [n]or if the Lord of the fifth shall be in them Houses.

And if, you would know, within how many years she shall have children, look where you finde the Lord of the fifth; for in that year she shall have issue; if he be in the first, [then] in the first year; if in the second, [then] in the second year; and so you may number unto the twelfth House. And if mean Signes be in the Ascendent, she that is with child hath twins in her wombe, which will live, if a good Planet be in the first; and if an evil Planet [be in the first House], they will die.[45] And if there be one good [Planet] and another evil, one shall live, and another die; and if a mean Signe shall be ascending, and *Mars* in that Signe, the mother shall die, and not the childe; if *Saturn*, both the mother and child shall die, and if the *Dragons Tail* be there, its possible they will both die; but the infant shall not escape; and if the *Dragons Tail* be so in the first, and the tenth House fallen: the mother shall die; likewise if *Mars* and the *Moon*, or *Mars* and *Saturn* be in the first, seventh or tenth, the mother shall die.

Whether the party with child shall miscarry, or not. Consider if a moveable Signe be ascending, because if it be so, she will miscarry.

If you would know whether a woman shall bring forth a man-child, or a woman-child; behold the Ascendent and his Lord, which if he be masculine, and in a masculine Signe, or in a masculine quarter of the Figure, it is a male-childe; but if the Lord of the Ascendent be feminine, and in a feminine Signe, or in a feminine quarter of the Circle, it will be a woman-child; and so you shall consider also of the *Moon*. Consider also if more of the Planets be in masculine Signes, then it will be a male-child; and if many Planets be in feminine Signes, then it is a female-childe.

And if you would know whether the child be legitimate or adulterate;[46] see if *Saturn*, *Mars* or the *Dragons Tail* be in the fifth, or with the Lord of the fifth; because if it be so, it is adulterate, but if a good Planet shall be there, it is legitimate: and if the Lord of the first, be in

---

[44] SB. Originally a colon.

[45] SB. Originally a semicolon.

[46] The product of adultery.

the fifth, or with his Lord, it is legitimate; and so likewise if the Lord of the fifth be found in the first, or with the Lord of the first.

If you desire to know whether rumours be true or false, see if you finde *Saturn, Mars* or the *Dragons Tail*, in the Ascendent; because if they be so, then the rumours are false; but if you finde the *Sun, Jupiter* or the *Dragons Head* there, then they are true; and if there be masculine Planets in masculine Signes, & feminine Planets in feminine Signes, then they are true; and if both good and evil Planets be there, then they are partly true and partly false; and if there be a good Signe with the Planet, it testifies the truth; and if the Planet fall with an evil Signe, then it is false; likewise if *Mercury* be in the first, the news is false: but if the *Moon* be in the first in a feminine Signe, or joyned with the Lord of the Ascendent in a feminine Signe, then the rumours are true; also if good Planets be in the first, fifth or ninth, and feminine Signes, they are true; but if otherwise, they are not.

If you would know whether any one that is absent will return, and when; see the Lord of the Ascendent and the first, which if you finde them together, for certain he will come, and is now beginning his journey. Likewise if the Lord of the fifth be in the first, or with the Lord of the first, and if he be in his fall, the messenger is sick in his way; but if the Lord of the fifth be exalted, then he cometh joyfully. And if he be in a cadent Signe, he shall be grievously afflicted with sickness, or shall die.

If you would know if he bringeth that with him for which he went, or not, behold the Lord of the seventh; which if he be good, he bringeth that which he sought for; and if he be in his fall, or an evil Planet be there, be bringeth nothing with him.

QUESTIONS OF THE SIXTH HOUSE.

Whether the sick shall recover his health, or die. If the Question be concerning his sickness, see if *Saturn*, or *Mars*, or the *Dragons Tail* be in the first, and whether his Lord he joyned with an evil Planet, then he shall die soon. And if the Lord of the first be good, and evil Planets be in the first with his Lord, or likewise in the first or the eighth, for certain he will die.[47] But if the Lord of the first be in the eighth, or with the Lord of the eighth; or the Lord of the eighth in the first, or with the Lord of the first, there is doubt of his death. And if evil Planets do possess the Angles, evil

---

[47] SB. Originally a colon.

and destruction is threatned to the sick. But if good Planets shall be in the first, sixth and eighth, and likewise in the Angles, and the Lord of the first be from the eighth & his Lord, then the sick person shall live and recover his health.

If you desire to know whether he will be cured by medicines, give the first House to the Physitian, the tenth to the sick, the seventh to his diseases, and the fourth to the medicines.[48] If evill Planets be in the first, the Physitian shall profit him nothing; but they testifie that this will be worse for the diseased: but the Fortunes[49] do signifie, that he shall be profitable to him.[50] And if evil Planets do occupy the tenth House, the sick person is the cause; for they testifie, that he himself is the cause of his own disease: but the Fortunes being there, signifie the contrary. But if evil Planets be in the tenth House, they change the condition of the sick out of one disease into another; but the Fortunes being there, do deliver him without the help of Physitians or medicines. Also evil Planets being in the fourth, do testifie, that the medicines do augment his grief;[51] & the Fortunes being there, do mitigate and heal him.

If thou wouldst know if thou shalt go unto the person and heal him; consider the place then: for if he shall be with *Saturn, Mars,* or the *Dragons Tail,* or *R* with the *Sun,* go not unto him; but if *Jupiter, Venus* or the *Dragons Head* be in the first or in the seventh, go, for it will be good.[52] And if there be the *Moon* with a good Planet, go, and give him physick;[53] but if she shall be with an evil Planet, and especially in the seventh House, then thou shalt not go; because thou shalt profit him nothing.[54]

And if there be good Planets there, go and look diligently to him, where or in what members he suffers; because *Aries* hath[55] the head, *Taurus* the neck, *Cancer* the breast and lungs, *Leo* the heart and stomack, *Virgo* the belly and intestines, *Libra* the reins[56] and loyns,

---

[48] By allocating each of the elements involved in the illness you can see which will be beneficial, and which will be weak.

[49] Fortuna Major and Fortuna Minor.

[50] In other words, improve his health.

[51] Make his sickness worse.

[52] SB. Originally a colon.

[53] Medicine.

[54] SB. Originally a colon.

[55] Corresponds to.

[56] Kidneys.

Scorpio the secret members,[57] *Sagitary* the thighs, *Capricorn* the knees, *Aquary*[58] the legs, and *Pisces* the feet.

QUESTIONS OF THE SEVENTH HOUSE.

For theft, look unto the Lord of the seventh: which if he be in the first, the theft shall be restored again; but if the Lord of the first be in the seventh, it shall be a long time sought after, and at length shall be found: but if the *Moon* be in the first, or with his Lord, it shall be found; if the *Moon* be in the fifth, or with the Lord of the first, or *R* in the first, it may be found; but if the *Sun* and the *Moon* be in the fifth, and if the Lord of the eighth be with the Lord of the first in the first, it shall be found; but if the Lord of the second be in the eighth, it shall not be found.

And if *Saturn*, or *Mars*, or the *Dragons Tail* be in the second, it shall not be found, nor be altogether lost. And if the Lord of the second be in the first, the thing that is lost shall be found; but it shall not be known from whence it came. If the Lord of the first be in the second, it may be found after much labour. And if the Lord of the second be in his fall, it will never be found; but if he be exalted, it shall be found very well: but the seventh House sheweth the thief.

But if you would know what it is that is stollen, behold the Lord of the second; which if he be *Saturn*, it is lead, iron, a kettle, a trivet, a garment, or some black thing, or leather. If he be *Jupiter*, then it is some white thing, as tin, silver, or mixt with white & yellow veins. The *Sun* signifies gold and precious pearles. *Mars* signifies things belonging to the fire. *Venus* signifies things belonging to women, as gloves, rings, and fair ornaments. The *Moon*, [signifies] beasts, such as horses, mules, &c. perfumes and wars. *Mercury* signifies money, books, writings, pictures, or garments of divers colours.

If you would know how many thieves there were, see the Lord of the sixth; which if he be in the second, or with the Lord of the second, there were many thieves; and if they be in the third, the brethren or kinsmen of the Querent have committed the theft.

If you would know whether the thief do yet remain in the Town: if they be in succedent Houses, he is not gone far off; but if they be in cadent Houses, he is far remote.

If you desire to know towards what Country the thief is fled, see in what Signe the Lord of the seventh is, for if he be in *Aries*, he is in

----

[57] Genitals.

[58] Aquarius.

the middle of the East part. If in *Taurus* [he is] in the South towards the East. If in *Gemini*, in the West towards the South. If in *Cancer*, full North. If in *Leo*, in the East towards the North. If in *Virgo*, in the South towards the West. If in *Libra*, full West. If in *Scorpio*, in the North neer the West. If in *Sagittary*, in the East nigh the North. If in *Capricorn*, full South. If in *Aquary*, in the West towards the North. And if in *Pisces*, in the North towards the West.

If you would know whether the thief hath carried all the things stollen away with him, see the Lord of the seventh and the eighth, and if the Lord of the seventh be in an Angle, he had a desire to carry away the same with him, but could not. If the Lord of the eighth be in a mean House, or in a cadent House, and the Lord of the second in a strong House, he hath carryed the theft wholly with him. And if the Lord of the seventh and the eighth be both in cadent Houses, he neither carryed it away, nor hath it. See by the seventh who is his companion, and what is his gain.

If you would know the descent or nobility of a man or woman, look unto the Lord of the seventh; which if you finde him in Angles, and the Lord of the first in Succedents or cadents, the woman is more noble then the man. But if the Lord of the Ascendent be in an Angle, & the Lord of the seventh in a succedent or cadent House, the man is more noble then the woman. And after the fame manner thou maist judge of two companions, or of any other persons whatsoever. And if the Lord of the seventh be in the ninth House, he will take a wife out of a forreigne Country.

If you desire to know whether an intended marriage shall take effect, or not, look to the Ascendent and his Lord, and the *Moon*, for the Querent; and the seventh House, and his Lord, for the woman. And if the Lord of the Ascendent of the *Moon* be joyned to the Lord of the seventh, or be in the seventh, the marriage will be effected; or if the Lord of the seventh be in the first, or with the Lord of the first, it will easily be brought to pass, and the woman is more desirous thereof, then the man.

If you would know whether thy wife or friend hath any other lover or not, look if *Mars* be in the seventh, so that he be not in his own House, for then she hath not any other lover. And if *Saturn* be there, she loveth another; but he lieth not with her. And if the *Dragons Tail* be in the seventh, he lieth with her. And if *Jupiter* be there, she hardly containeth her self chaste. If *Venus*, she is merry, and much given to play and laughter, by reason whereof, she may be accounted a whore, and is not so.

If *Mercury* be in the seventh, she had a lover, but now hath none. But if the *Moon* be in the seventh, she hath had no lover as yet, but will have one, and will be common. But if the *Sun* or the *Dragons Head* be there, she is chaste. And after the same manner may you judge in the *ninth*[59] concerning friends or lovers.

If you would know which of them shall live longest, see the Lord of the first and of the seventh, which of them shall be in the stronger and better place, or joyned to the strongest Planets; and that person who is most free and remote from the Lord of the eighth and his participation, to whom the Lord of his House answereth, shall live longest.

If you desire to make a society or alliance, and would know whether it shall be brought to pass or not, or what shall happen thereupon, see if there be good Planets in the seventh and the first: and if so, the fellowship will be made, and good will come thereof; and you may judge it to continue so many years, months or dayes, as the Lord of the seventh hath signification of.

If you would know when such society shall be, look what Planet is in the seventh; for if he be good, it shall come to pass that same year: or wedlock, *R* if the Question be thereof.

If you would know whether they will well agree, see the first and his Lord, which is the signifier of the Querent;[60] and the seventh House and his Lord, which is the House of companions, wives and concubines; which if they be concordant amongst themselves, there will be peace and union between them, and they shall profit; but if the Planets be in discord, there will be strife between them, and the society will not profit.

If you would know which of them shall gain most, see the first and his Lord, and the seventh and his Lord, and which of them standeth best; or if they be evil, which of them falleth: and he that falleth shall lose, and he that is exalted shall gain. Or otherwise, and which is better, see the second and his Lord, and the eighth and his Lord; and in which House is the better Planet, or his Lord that shall be found in the better place, or joyned with the better Planets he shall be the greater gainer. The second House and his Lord signifies the gain of the Querent: and the eighth House and his Lord signifies the gain of his fellow, or his part: and if they be both good, they shall both gain; and if both evil, they shall both lose: and if one be good and the other evil, he whose significator is good, shall gain; and he whose is evil, shall lose.

---

[59] Margin note: *Ibidem sorte.*
[60] Represents the questioner in the chart.

And if you would know if two fellows shall love one another, look if the Lords of the first and the seventh be friends and agreeing, then they will love one to another, but if they be enemies and disagree, then they will not.

If you desire to know who shall overcome in any cause, matter or controversie, behold the Lords of the first and the seventh, which if they be in Angles, neither of them shall overcome; and see which of them is joyned with an evil Planet, because he shall overcome; and if the Planet be evil from them both, the victor shall kill the conquered; if one of them be strong, and the other weak, and the Planet which is in the strong House do not fall, nor hath not an evil Planet with him.[61] And if he which is weak be not in his own House, nor in his exaltation, nor with a good Planet, he whose Planet is in the strong House, shall overcome; likewise he whose significator is in a mean House, shall have great fear and doubt in his heart, because sometimes he shall hope to conquer, and otherwhiles fear to be overcome. And note, that in a Question concerning war and kingdom, it is said that there is more power and efficacie, or fortitude in the exaltation of a Planet, then in his House; but in all other Questions the contrary.

If you would be informed concerning any one being that is gone to any fight, whether he shall return safe, see the Lord of the Ascendent; if he be good, that is, with good Planets, and a good Planet in the first, he will return safe; but if the *Sun* be with the Lord of the first, in any part of the Question, let him not go, because the *Sun* burneth him. And if the Lord of the seventh be with a good Planet, and the Lord of the first with a good Planet likewise, he shall have some impediment in the way; but he will not die.

And if an evil Planet be with the Lord of the first, and a good Planet in the first, if he goeth he shall suffer great damage, but not death; nevertheless he may be grievously wounded. And if *Saturn* be in the first, or with the Lord of the first, let him not go; because some impediment will happen unto him by some man that he will meet. And if there be an evil Planet with the Lord of the first, or *Saturn* be in the first, or with the Lord of the first, he will be wounded with wood or with a stone. If *Mars* and the *Dragons Tail* be in the first, or with the Lord of the first; or if there be evil Planets in the first, or with the Lord of the first, he will suffer wounds or death. See likewise if there be an evil Planet in the eighth, because then death is to be feared. And if the *Sun* be

---

[61] SB. Originally a semicolon.

with the Lord of the seventh, or in the eighth, it signifies that it is ill to go. The like judgement, is of the seventh and the tenth.

And if a Question be proposed concerning the event of War, see the seventh and the first, and their Lords: for the first House and his Lord signifies the Querent; and the seventh House and his Lord the adversary. So that if there be good Planets in the first, and evil in the seventh; and if the Lord of the first and seventh be evil, the Querent shall overcome: but if there be an evil Planet with the Lord of the first, and an evil Planet in the first, and the Lord of the seventh good, or *R* in the seventh, the Querent shall be overcome, or taken, or slain.

And if the Lords of them both be in the first, and there be good Planets from the part of the first House, unto the end of the House which is the middle of the Question; and if evil Planets do possess the other half of the Question, that is to say, from the seventh unto the end of the twelfth house, the adversary shall overcome. But if both the Lords shall be in the Ascendent, and if they be good from the part of the first, and evil from the part of the seventh, they shall both suffer great loss; but the Querent shall have the better in the end. But if the Lord of the Ascendent be in the seventh, or in [the House of] his Question, it signifies fortitude of the adversary: and if the Lord of the seventh be in the first, or in his Question, it signifies fortitude of the actor. And if the Lord of the Ascendent be in the eighth, or with the Lord of the eighth; or the Lord of the eighth in the first, or with the Lord of the first, it signifies the death of the Querent. And if the Lord of the seventh be in the second, or with his Lord; or the Lord of the second in the seventh, or with the Lord of the seventh, it signifies the death of the enemy.

If you would know whether War shall continue long or not, if mean or meanly, if the Lords of the first and the seventh do agree, the parties shall be pacified after the War.

If thou wouldest depart from the place wherein thou are, and remove thy self to some other place; and if thou wouldest know whether it be better for thee to stay or go; or concerning two businesses, if thou desirest to know which of them is most expedient for thee to undertake, consider the Lords of the first and the second, for those places to which thou wouldest go, the place wherein thou art, and the gain which thou gettest there; and the seventh and the eighth, and their Lords, for the place to which thou wouldest go, and the gain which thou mayst get there: and those places chuse, whose Lords are the better, or joyned to the better Planets.

Or otherwise: behold the Lord of the Ascendent, and the Moon; which if they be separated from evil Planets, and joyned to good and fortunate Planets, it is better for thee to go from the place where thou art, then to stay there, and to do what business soever thou hast in thy minde. And if the Lord of the Ascendent and the Moon be separated from the Fortunes, and joyned to evil Planets, then it is not good for thee to remove thy self, nor to do thy business. Or thus; See the *Moon*; and if the Planet from which she is separated be better then that to whom she is joyned, do not remove: and if the Planet which she is joyned to, be better then that from which she is separated, then go.

Questions of the eighth House.

Concerning any man or woman, if you would know what kinde of death they shall die, see if *Leo*, *Scorpio*, or †R.† *Mars*, be in the eighth, the party shall die by a beast. And if *Saturn* be in the eighth, or with the Lord of the eighth in *Scorpio*, *Cancer*, or *Pisces*, he shall die in water. And if an evil Planet be in the eighth, or with the Lord of the eighth; or if *Mars* or the *Dragons Tayl* be there, he shall die by fire, iron, or of a fever. And if there be a good Planet in the eighth, or with the Lord of the eighth, he shall die a good death.[62]

Questions of the ninth House.

Concerning long Journeys, see if the Lord of the eighth have good Planets with him: and if *Saturn* be in the ninth, and exalted in the tenth, so that he be not in his own House, do not go: for thou wilt meet with many obstacles, and War. And if an evil Planet be in the ninth, or with the Lord of the ninth, and the Lord of the ninth in his fall, he shall suffer great damage in the way: for if he goeth by water, he shall suffer shipwrack; and if by Land, he shall have misfortunes, be taken, or die. If *Saturn* be in the ninth, or with his Lord, go securely. And if a good Planet be in the ninth, or with the Lord of the ninth, the way is good and secure. And if *Mars* be in the ninth, thou mayest not go: for thou wilt meet with mortal enemies in the way. And if the Lord of the ninth be with an evil† Planet, or the *Sun*, it signifies ill: but he shall not be

---

[62] The treatment of this house is very abbreviated in the original, possibly because it relates to death.

taken. And if the Lord of the ninth have a good Planet neer him, he shall escape: but if evil, he shall be taken.

If *Venus* be in the ninth, or with the Lord of the ninth, the way will be good, because he shall have comfort from women. And if *Mercury* be in the ninth, and the Lord of the ninth with good Planets, the way will be very good: and if he be with evil Planets, it will be evil. And the same is said of the *Moon*, as of *Mercury*. If the *Dragons Tayl* be in the ninth, he will meet with theeves, or some evil people. And if the *Dragons Head* be in the ninth, the way will be good, because he shall be accompanied with Noble-men. And in this maner may you judge in the third House concerning short journeys.

If you would know when the journey shall be accomplished, see the Lord of the ninth, and according to his fortitude or debility judge,[63] because according to the place wherein he is, is signified yeers, months, or days: and so you shall judge concerning his stay, about what time he will come, by turning the years of the Lord of the ninth into days; because so many days he shall tarry,[64] as the Planet signifies in the place where he is. Or otherwise: weak Angles signifie a speedy journey, mean[65] Angles a mean journey; and the Lord of the ninth likewise, according to the place wherein he is found.

And this I say concerning his return. If you would know whether he shall return from his journey with an imperfect voyage or not, see if the Moon be joyned with the Lord of the first, the third, or the ninth, and the Planet thereof be in his fall; because if it be so, he shall return with an imperfect voyage. And if the Moon be in her exaltation, the journey shall speedily be effected. And if there be two strong Planets, and one cadent, the journey shall be made; and if one be strong, and another in his fall, he shall retire back.

QUESTIONS OF THE TENTH HOUSE.

If thou wouldest know whether thou shalt have any honour or benefit from a King, Bishop, or Lord, or not, look unto the first House, and the ninth, and their Lords: and if the Lord of the first be in the ninth, or with the Lord of the ninth, or with any other good Planet; or if the Lord of the ninth be in the first, or with the Lord of the first, or with any other good Planet, as *Venus, Jupiter,*

---

[63] Judge according to his strength or weakness.

[64] Wait or delay.

[65] Average.

or the *Dragons Head*; or if any of them be the Lord of the ninth, or
R. of the first, he shall receive honour and benefits from them.

And if you would know whether he shall have it in his own
Country, or in a forraign Country, look if the Lord of the ninth be
in angles, then it shall be in his own Country: and if in succedents,
it shall be neer; but if in cadent Houses, very far off.

QUESTIONS OF THE ELEVENTH HOUSE.

If you would know when it is good to set forth a Ship to Sea, see
the Ascendent; which if it be stable, the Ship will be ponderous;
but if the Lord thereof be with a good Planet, she will sustain a
great weight. And if the Ascendent be instable, and with a good
Planet, the Ship will be swift, and carry a good burden. And meanly,
if the Ascendent be mean. And after this maner may you judge
concerning an Horse, if a Question be thereof.

And if any unstable Signe be ascending, and his Lord be in his
exaltation, or otherwise fortunate, and the Moon behold him with
a lowring Aspect, or Sextile; let the Ship be applied to the water,
because she will be very swift. And if any evil be imposed upon
her, or that she be like to be drawn into it; then set her out when
a stable Signe is ascending, or when the Moon is in the third, fifth,
eighth, ninth, or tenth house or mansion.

If you would know what winde she shall have, behold the
Ascendent and his Lord, whether he be with good or evil Planets,
and in what place, and accordingly judge.

And if you would have a strong winde, spread forth your Sayls
at the rising of *Aquary*:[66] if a small winde, spread your Canvas
when *Libra* is ascending: If a moderate winde, then direct your
Sayls under *Gemini*.

QUESTIONS OF THE TWELFTH HOUSE.

For Imprisonment, consider the twelfth and the first; and if the
Lord of the twelfth be in the first, or with the Lord of the first, &c.

---

[66] Aquarius.

BIBLIOGRAPHY

Agrippa, Henry Cornelius. *Fourth Book of Occult Philosophy.* First facsimile edition. London: Askin Publishers, 1978.

———. *Three Books of Occult Philosophy.* Donald Tyson, ed. St, Paul, MN: Llewellyn, 1993.

King, Francis and Stephen Skinner. *Techniques of High Magic.* Rochester, VT: Destiny Books, 2000.

Morley, Henry. *The Life of Henry Cornelius Agrippa von Nettesheim.* London, 1856.

Paracelsus. *The Archidoxes of Magic.* Introduction by Stephen Skinner. Berwick, ME: Ibis Press, 2004.

Peterson, Joseph. *The Lesser Key of Solomon.* York Beach, ME: Weiser Books, 2001.

Skinner, Stephen. *The Oracle of Geomancy: Divination by Earth.* New York: Warner, 1977.

———. *Terrestrial Astrology: Divination by Geomancy.* London: Routledge and Kegan Paul, 1980. The most complete book on Western Geomancy.

Skinner, Stephen and David Rankine. *The Keys to the Gateway of Magic: Summoning the Solomonic Archangels and Demon Princes.* London: Golden Hoard Press, 2005.

———. *The Practical Angel Magic of Dr. John Dee's Enochian Tables.* London: Golden Hoard Press, 2004.

ABOUT THE AUTHOR &
THE EDITOR

HENRY CORNELIUS AGRIPPA VON NETTESHEIM (1486-1535) was a German soldier, diplomat, physician, writer and lecturer on magic, the Kabbalah, Greek philosophy, Hermes Trismegistus, and astrology. He was born at Cologne on September 14, 1486. In 1499 he enrolled in the faculty of Arts at the University of Cologne, and graduated in 1502, at the age of 16. He later also obtained formal degrees in canon (church) law, civil law, and medicine. While still young he served Maximilian I of Germany first as a secretary, then as a soldier specializing in political intelligence and intrigue. By 1506 he was the University of Paris, studying magic and forming a brotherhood of students involved in such experiments. By 1508 he was engaging in military strategies on Maximilian's behalf in the Spanish city of Tarragona where he aided in the capture of a previously impregnable fort. From there he traveled to Naples and then back to France where he reformed some of his Paris group in Lyon, studying especially the translations of Hebrew kabbalistic works by Reuchlin.

In 1509 he lectured on Reuchlin's Kabbalah at the University of Dole with resounding success. The University made him professor of theology, and he began the writing of his major work, *De Occulta Philosophia*. He submitted the first draft to his mentor in angel magic, Johannes Trithemius, (the Benedictine Abbot of Saint James at Wurtzburg, formerly of Spanheim), a year later in 1510. He also had time to write his pro-feminist classic *On the Nobility and Preeminence of the Female Sex.* . . . A monk, however, brought a charge of heresy against Agrippa, which compelled him to leave Dole rather rapidly, and resume his former occupation of soldier.

In the following year he was sent on a diplomatic mission to Henry VIII of England, where he saw and marveled at Stonehenge or a similar stone circle. On his return he delivered a series of lectures at Cologne University, and then reluctantly in 1511 followed Maximilian to Italy, to escape religious persecution. Here he passed seven years as a soldier of fortune, serving one patron after another, having been knighted in the field of battle. He was excommunicated for his outspoken views, but a year later Pope Leo X revoked the excommunication. In 1515 he was lecturing at the University of Pavia on the *Pymander* of Hermes

Trismegistus, a key Hermetic document, and the university conferred several doctorates upon him in recognition of his brilliance. Changes of allegiance and more wars made him move on to the court of Charles III, Duke of Savoy, where he became court physician.

Thereafter he held a post at Metz in 1518 where he wrote his *Geomancy* included in this volume, but after unwisely defending a woman charged with witchcraft, was forced to leave the town. He returned to his hometown of Cologne, practiced medicine at Geneva, then Fribourg, and was appointed physician to Louise of Savoy, mother of Francis I. He underwent many vicissitudes of fortune, arriving in Antwerp where the intellectual climate allowed him to flourish and once more take pupils, including Johann Weir, who later penned a short biography of Agrippa. Weir was also responsible for passing on the knowledge of the 72 spirits who later appear in that most famous grimoire, the *Goetia*. He also had the leisure to attend to the publication of some of his many works. Agrippa had completed his major work, the *Three Books of Occult Philosophy* by the time he was 25. The first volume was not published until 1531 in Antwerp, and all three in Cologne in 1533, where he moved just two years before his death. One of the essays on the more practical aspects of evocation was left out of the three books, and it later became part of the *Fourth Book of Occult Philosophy* published in 1554 and 1567, and here published as Part I of this volume. Agrippa died at Grenoble, France in 1535.

Agrippa was acquainted with eight languages, and was evidently a physician of considerable ability, as well as being a soldier, diplomat, orator, theologian, and one of the best read men of his time in classical, magical and kabbalistic lore. He was evidently well thought of, as he had many wealthy and noble patrons. Notwithstanding this, he never seemed to be free from misfortune, persecution and financial difficulties, which were compounded by his argumentative nature and the religious authorities who continually harassed this truly Renaissance man.

STEPHEN SKINNER

Stephen Skinner is an Australian who began his career as a geography lecturer and publisher, but whose long term interest has always been Western magic. While at school he avidly bought grimoires and first editions of the works of Aleister Crowley. He entered university, joined his first magical lodge, and had his first book published all by the time he was 16. At university he wrote and published underground newspapers, introducing the 1960s ideals of Haight-Ashbury to a receptive Australian audience.

His second book (with Neville Drury), the *Search for Abraxas* introduced Austin Osman Spare, fantasy art, Jung, Gnosticism, Casteneda, and obscure aspects of the Kabbalah to his readers. Colin Wilson said of the book, "the authors of this book represent a new phenomenon: the serious study of the practice of magic . . . these practicing magicians have decided that there is something in magic, something as objective as radio waves."

Stephen migrated to London in 1972 where he lived for many years with Helene Hodge in the leafy suburb of Chiswick, former home to W. B. Yeats, Florence Farr, and many other Golden Dawn luminaries, and just a short walk from the Blythe Road Golden Dawn temple. While there, he edited several of Aleister Crowley's works including *Astrology* and the *Magical Diaries of Aleister Crowley, Tunis 1923*. An excursion into alchemy produced *In Pursuit of Gold*, a joint book with Lapidus, one of the last surviving practical "bellows and forge" alchemists.

During the 1970s he was the driving force behind Askin Publishers, producing lovely editions of a number of classic magical works such as Agrippa's *Fourth Book of Occult Philosophy* (this present book) and *Archidoxes of Magic* by Paracelsus (re-released by Ibis Press in 2004), several titles by Austin Osman Spare, Aleister Crowley, Dr. Donald Laycock (*The Enochian Dictionary*) and others, all of which are now collector's items. The first of these is however the one of which he is most proud: a huge quarter leather edition of the then primary source book of Enochian magic, the *True & Faithful Relation of what passed for many Yeers between Dr John Dee . . . and some Spirits*.

Also during the 1970s he co-wrote many books with Francis King, including the still-popular *Techniques of High Magic*, which has gone through many editions since it was first released. Also with Francis King he wrote *Nostradamus*. His interest in prophecy stimulated by this book, he went on to write the best-selling *Millennium Prophecies*.

Although not part of the witchcraft movement, he knew almost all of the most significant figures in modern witchcraft from Cecil Williamson, Stuart Farrer, Alex Sanders, to Jim Baker.

An interest in Western geomancy spurred him on to create what has become the most complete and classic work in that field: originally titled *Terrestrial Astrology*, it is soon to be re-published as *Divinatory Geomancy*.

Stephen is also credited with bringing the art of feng shui to the West. His original interest sprung from his researches into the totally unrelated (but similarly labeled) Western geomancy. Having discovered that sigils used in Western magic are also used in some of the more esoteric parts of feng shui and in Taoist sorcery got him hooked, and in 1976 he wrote the *Living Earth Manual of Feng Shui*, which was the first English book on feng shui in the 20th century.

He went on to produce the magazine *Feng Shui for Modern Living* worldwide in 41 countries, the biggest selling feng shui magazine in the world, selling more copies in the UK initially even than *Elle Deco*. He even launched 34 issues of the magazine in Taiwan printed in traditional Chinese, where the magazine became the biggest-selling feng shui magazine in Chinese. He was told by all his colleagues that he was mad to even think of launching such a magazine, but in 1999 was nominated Publisher of the Year in London for so doing.

He followed the magazine with a spate of books about feng shui, including *Feng Shui the Traditional Oriental Way* (which sold hundreds of thousands of copies in many editions worldwide), *Feng Shui for Modern Living, Feng Shui Before & After, The K.I.S.S. Guide to Feng Shui*, the more technical *Flying Star Feng Shui*, and the glossy coffee table *Feng Shui Style*. In early 2005 an amazing feng shui related *Tibetan Oracle* card pack, which he developed from an original 17th-century Tibetan manuscript, is scheduled to appear.

Over the years there have been many rumors of an unpublished work by Stephen on Enochian magic, written in the 1970s. He did in fact complete a book on Dee that encompassed the whole working system, with a practice guide and results, plus a full life chronology which would have run to about 700 printed pages, but in those days few publishers wanted to print such a large volume. Sadly, the original manuscript was lost some years later.

He again took up the thread of John Dee's work when he published *Practical Angel Magic of Dr. John Dee's Enochian Tables* in 2004 with co-author David Rankine, opening the doors on real 17th-century angel magic in a way never done before. They plan to follow this with more source works that concentrate on the actual mechanics of evocation and invocation of spirits, angels, and other creatures of the netherworlds.

Stephen has lived in some wonderful old buildings, including a 17th-century chateau with 36 rooms in France, a haunted Victorian mansion built over one of the largest Saxon burial grounds in England, and in an old teak palace located on one of the *klongs* in Bangkok. These days he lives near Singapore, where he pursues practical researches into Western magic and feng shui.

Stephen has written more than 20 books, which have been published worldwide in 16 different languages.